Charles Dickens, Adelaide Anne Procter

The Poems of Adelaide A. Procter

Charles Dickens, Adelaide Anne Procter

The Poems of Adelaide A. Procter

ISBN/EAN: 9783744713573

Printed in Europe, USA, Canada, Australia, Japan

Cover: Foto ©Thomas Meinert / pixelio.de

More available books at **www.hansebooks.com**

THE POEMS

OF

ADELAIDE A. PROCTER.

COMPLETE EDITION.

WITH AN INTRODUCTION BY CHARLES DICKENS.

BOSTON:
JAMES R. OSGOOD AND COMPANY,
LATE TICKNOR & FIELDS, AND FIELDS, OSGOOD, & CO.
1873.

AUTHOR'S EDITION.

UNIVERSITY PRESS: WELCH, BIGELOW, & CO.,
CAMBRIDGE.

AN INTRODUCTION.

BY CHARLES DICKENS.

In the spring of the year 1853, I observed, as conductor of the weekly journal, HOUSEHOLD WORDS, a short poem among the proffered contributions, very different, as I thought, from the shoal of verses perpetually setting through the office of such a periodical, and possessing much more merit. Its authoress was quite unknown to me. She was one MISS MARY BERWICK, whom I had never heard of; and she was to be addressed by letter, if addressed at all, at a circulating library in the western district of London. Through this channel, Miss Berwick was informed that her poem was accepted, and was invited to send another. She complied, and became a regular and frequent contributor. Many letters passed between the journal and Miss Berwick, but Miss Berwick herself was never seen.

How we came gradually to establish, at the office of Household Words, that we knew all about Miss Berwick, I have never discovered. But, we settled somehow, to our complete satisfaction, that she was governess in a family; that she went to Italy in that capacity, and returned; and that she had long been in the same family. We really knew nothing whatever of her, except that she was remarkably business-like, punctual, self-reliant, and reliable: so I suppose we insensibly invented the rest. For myself, my mother was not a more real personage to me, than Miss Berwick the governess became.

This went on until December, 1854, when the Christmas number, entitled The Seven Poor Travellers, was sent to press. Happening to be going to dine that day with an old and dear friend, distinguished in literature as BARRY CORNWALL, I took with me an early proof of that number, and remarked, as I laid it on the drawing-room table, that it contained a very pretty poem, written by a certain Miss Berwick. Next day brought me the disclosure that I had so spoken of the poem to the mother of its writer, in its writer's presence; that I had no such correspondent in existence as Miss Berwick; and that the name had been assumed by Barry Cornwall's eldest daughter, MISS ADELAIDE ANNE PROCTER.

The anecdote I have here noted down, besides serving to explain why the parents of the late Miss Procter have looked to me for these poor words of remembrance of their lamented child, strikingly illustrates the honesty, independence, and quiet dignity of the lady's character. I had known her when she was very young; I had been honored with her father's friendship when I was myself a young aspirant; and she had said at home, "If I send him, in my own name, verses that he does not honestly like, either it will be very painful to him to return them, or he will print them for papa's sake, and not for their own. So I have made up my mind to take my chance fairly with the unknown volunteers."

Perhaps it requires an editor's experience of the profoundly unreasonable grounds on which he is often urged to accept unsuitable articles — such as having been to school with the writer's husband's brother-in-law, or having lent an alpenstock in Switzerland to the writer's wife's nephew, when that interesting stranger had broken his own — fully to appreciate the delicacy and the self-respect of this resolution.

Some verses by Miss Procter had been published in the BOOK OF BEAUTY, ten years before she became Miss Berwick. With the exception of two poems in the CORNHILL MAGAZINE, two in GOOD WORDS, and others in a little book called A CHAPLET OF VERSES (issued in 1862 for the benefit of a Night Refuge), her published writings first appeared in HOUSEHOLD WORDS, or ALL THE YEAR ROUND. The present edition contains the whole of her Legends and Lyrics, and originates in the great favor with which they have been received by the public.

Miss Procter was born in Bedford Square, London, on the 30th of October, 1825. Her love of poetry was conspicuous at so early an age, that I have before me a tiny album made of small note-paper, into which her favorite passages were copied for her by her mother's hand before she herself could write.

It looks as if she had carried it about as another little girl might have carried a doll. She soon displayed a remarkable memory, and great quickness of apprehension. When she was quite a young child, she learnt with facility several of the problems of Euclid. As she grew older, she acquired the French, Italian, and German languages, became a clever piano-forte player, and showed a true taste and sentiment in drawing. But, as soon as she had completely vanquished the difficulties of any one branch of study, it was her way to lose interest in it, and pass to another. While her mental resources were being trained, it was not at all suspected in her family that she had any gift of authorship, or any ambition to become a writer. Her father had no idea of her having ever attempted to turn a rhyme, until her first little poem saw the light in print.

When she attained to womanhood, she had read an extraordinary number of books, and throughout her life she was always largely adding to the number. In 1853 she went to Turin and its neighborhood, on a visit to her aunt, a Roman Catholic lady. As Miss Procter had herself professed the Roman Catholic faith two years before, she entered with the greater ardor on the study of the Piedmontese dialect, and the observation of the habits and manners of the peasantry. In the former, she soon became a proficient. On the latter head, I extract from her familiar letters, written home to England at the time, two pleasant pieces of description.

A BETROTHAL.

"We have been to a ball, of which I must give you a description. Last Tuesday we had just done dinner at about seven, and stepped out into the balcony to look at the remains of the sunset behind the mountains, when we heard very distinctly a band of music, which rather excited my astonishment, as a solitary organ is the utmost that toils up here. I went out of the room for a few minutes, and, on my returning, Emily said, 'Oh! that band is playing at the farmer's near here. The daughter is *fiancée* to-day, and they have a ball.' I said, 'I wish I was going!' 'Well,' replied she, 'the farmer's wife did call to invite us.' 'Then I shall certainly go,' I exclaimed. I applied to Madame B., who said she would like it very much, and we had better go, children and all. Some of the servants were already gone. We rushed away to put on some shawls, and put off any shred of black we might have about us (as the people would have been quite annoyed if we had appeared on such an occasion with any black), and we started. When we reached the farmer's, which is a stone's throw above our house, we were received with great enthusiasm; the only drawback being that no one spoke French, and we did not yet speak Piedmontese. We were placed on a bench against the wall, and the people went on dancing. The room was a large white-washed kitchen (I suppose), with several large pictures in black frames, and very smoky. I distinguished the Martyrdom of Saint Sebastian, and the others appeared equally lively and appropriate subjects. Whether they were Old Masters or not, and if so, by whom, I could not ascertain. The band were seated opposite us. Five men, with wind-instruments, part of the band of the National Guard, to which the farmer's sons belong. They played really admirably, and I began to be afraid that some idea of our dignity would prevent my getting a partner; so, by Madame B.'s advice, I went up to the bride, and offered to dance with her. Such a handsome young woman! Like one of Uwins's pictures. Very dark, with a quantity of black hair, and on an immense scale. The children were already dancing, as well as the maids. After we came to an end of our dance, which was what they call a Polka-Mazourka, I saw the bride trying to screw up the courage of her *fiancé* to ask me to dance, which after a little hesitation he did. And admirably he danced, as indeed they all did, — in excellent time, and with a little more spirit than one sees in a ball-room. In fact, they were very like one's ordinary partners, except that they wore ear-rings and were in their shirt-sleeves, and truth compels me to state that they decidedly smelt of garlic. Some of them had been smoking, but threw away their cigars when we came in. The only thing that did not look cheerful was, that the room was only lighted by two or three oil-lamps, and that there seemed to be no preparation for refreshments. Madame B., seeing this, whispered to her maid, who disengaged herself from her partner, and ran off to the house; she and the kitchen-maid presently returning with a large tray covered with all kinds of cakes (of which we are great consumers and always have a stock), and a large hamper full of bottles of wine, with coffee and sugar. This seemed all very acceptable. The *fiancée* was requested to distribute the eatables, and a bucket of water being produced to wash the glasses in, the wine disappeared very quickly, — as fast as they could open the bottles. But, elated I suppose by this, the floor was sprinkled with water, and the musicians played a Monferrino, which is a Piedmontese dance. Madame B. danced with the farmer's son, and Emily with another distinguished member of the company. It was very fatiguing, — something like a Scotch reel. My partner was a little man, like Perrot, and very proud of his dancing. He cut in the air and twisted about, until I was out of breath, though my attempts to imitate him were feeble in the extreme. At last, after seven or eight dances, I was obliged to sit down. We stayed till nine, and I was so dead beat with the heat that I could hardly crawl about the house, and in an agony with the cramp, it is so long since I have danced."

A Marriage.

"The wedding of the farmer's daughter has taken place. We had hoped it would have been in the little chapel of our house, but it seems some special permission was necessary, and they applied for it too late. They all said, 'This is the Constitution. There would have been no difficulty before!' the lower classes making the poor Constitution the scape-goat for everything they don't like. So, as it was impossible for us to climb up to the church where the wedding was to be, we contented ourselves with seeing the procession pass. It was not a very large one, for, it requiring some activity to go up, all the old people remained at home. It is not the etiquette for the bride's mother to go, and no unmarried woman can go to a wedding, — I suppose for fear of its making her discontented with her own position. The procession stopped at our door, for the bride to receive our congratulations. She was dressed in a shot silk, with a yellow handkerchief, and rows of a large gold chain. In the afternoon they sent to request us to go there. On our arrival we found them dancing out of doors, and a most melancholy affair it was. All the bride's sisters were not to be recognized, they had cried so. The mother sat in the house, and could not appear. And the bride was sobbing so she could hardly stand! The most melancholy spectacle of all to my mind was, that the bridegroom was decidedly tipsy. He seemed rather affronted at all the distress. We danced a Monferrino; I with the bridegroom, and the bride crying the whole time. The company did their utmost to enliven her by firing pistols, but without success, and at last they began a series of yells which reminded me of a set of savages. But even this delicate method of consolation failed, and the wishing good-by began. It was altogether so melancholy an affair that Madame B. dropped a few tears, and I was very near it, particularly when the poor mother came out to see the last of her daughter, who was finally dragged off between her brother and uncle, with a last explosion of pistols. As she lives quite near, makes an excellent match, and is one of nine children, it really was a most desirable marriage, in spite of all the show of distress. Albert was so discomfited by it, that he forgot to kiss the bride as he had intended to do, and therefore went to call upon her yesterday, and found her very smiling in her new house, and supplied the omission. The cook came home from the wedding, declaring she was cured of any wish to marry; but I would not recommend any man to act upon that threat and make her an offer. In a couple of days we had some rolls of the bride's first baking, which they call Madonna's. The musicians, it seems, were in the same state as the bridegroom, for, in escorting her home, they all fell down in the mud. My wrath against the bridegroom is somewhat calmed by finding that it is considered bad luck if he does not get tipsy at his wedding."

Those readers of Miss Procter's poems who should suppose from their tone that her mind was of a gloomy or despondent cast would be curiously mistaken. She was exceedingly humorous, and had a great delight in humor. Cheerfulness was habitual with her, she was very ready at a sally or a reply, and in her laugh (as I remember well) there was an unusual vivacity, enjoyment, and sense of drollery. She was perfectly unconstrained and unaffected: as modestly silent about her productions as she was generous with their pecuniary results. She was a friend who inspired the strongest attachments; she was a finely sympathetic woman, with a great accordant heart and a sterling noble nature. No claim can be set up for her, thank God, to the possession of any of the conventional poetical qualities. She never by any means held the opinion that she was among the greatest of human beings; she never suspected the existence of a conspiracy on the part of mankind against her; she never recognized in her best friends her worst enemies; she never cultivated the luxury of being misunderstood and unappreciated; she would far rather have died without seeing a line of her composition in print, than that I should have maundered about her, here, as "the Poet," or "the Poetess."

With the recollection of Miss Procter as a mere child and as a woman fresh upon me, it is natural that I should linger on my way to the close of this brief record, avoiding its end. But, even as the close came upon her, so must it come here.

Always impelled by an intense conviction that her life must not be dreamed away, and that her indulgence in her favorite pursuits must be balanced by action in the real world around her, she was indefatigable in her endeavors to do some good. Naturally enthusiastic, and conscientiously impressed with a deep sense of her Christian duty to her neighbor, she devoted herself to a variety of benevolent objects. Now, it was the visitation of the sick that had possession of her; now, it was the sheltering of the houseless; now, it was the elementary teaching of the densely ignorant; now, it was the raising up of those who had wandered and got trodden under foot; now, it was the wider employment of her own sex in the general business of life; now, it was all these things at once. Perfectly unselfish, swift to sympathize and eager to relieve, she wrought at such designs with a flushed earnestness that disregarded season, weather, time of day or night, food, rest. Under such a hurry of the spirits, and such incessant occupation, the strongest constitution will commonly go down. Hers, neither of the strongest nor the weakest, yielded to the burden, and began to sink.

To have saved her life, then, by taking action on the warning that shone in her eyes and sounded in her voice, would have been impossible without changing her nature. As long as the power of moving about in the old way was left to her, she must exercise it, or be killed by the restraint. And so the time came when she could move about no longer, and took to her bed.

All the restlessness gone then, and all the sweet patience of her natural disposition purified by the resignation of her soul, she lay upon her bed through the whole round of changes of the seasons. She lay upon her bed through fifteen months. In all that time, her old cheerfulness never quitted her. In all that time, not an impatient or a querulous minute can be remembered.

At length, at midnight on the 2d of February, 1864, she turned down a leaf of a little book she was reading, and shut it up.

The ministering hand that had copied the verses into the tiny album was soon around her neck, and she quietly asked, as the clock was on the stroke of one: "Do you think I am dying, mamma?"

"I think you are very, very ill to-night, my dear."

"Send for my sister. My feet are so cold. Lift me up!"

Her sister entering as they raised her, she said: "It has come at last!" And with a bright and happy smile looked upward, and departed.

Well had she written:—

Why shouldst thou fear the beautiful angel, Death,
Who waits thee at the portals of the skies,
Ready to kiss away thy struggling breath,
Ready with gentle hand to close thine eyes?

Oh, what were life, if life were all?
Thine eyes
Are blinded by their tears, or thou wouldst see
Thy treasures wait thee in the far-off skies,
And Death, thy friend, will give them all to thee.

CONTENTS.

	Page
INTRODUCTION	iii

LEGENDS AND LYRICS. A BOOK OF VERSES.
First Series.

The Angel's Story	1
Echoes	5
A False Genius	6
My Picture	6
Judge not	7
Friend Sorrow	8
One by One	8
True Honors	9
A Woman's Question	14
The Three Rulers	15
A Dead Past	16
A Doubting Heart	16
A Student	17
A Knight-Errant	18
Linger, O Gentle Time	19
Homeward Bound	19
Life and Death	24
Now	25
Cleansing Fires	25
The Voice of the Wind	26
Treasures	27
Shining Stars	28
Waiting	28
The Cradle-Song of the Poor	29

CONTENTS.

Be Strong	30
God's Gifts	31
A Tomb in Ghent	32
The Angel of Death	39
A Dream	40
The Present	41
Changes	41
Strive, Wait, and Pray	41
A Lament for the Summer	42
The Unknown Grave	42
Give me thy Heart	43
The Wayside Inn	45
Voices of the Past	48
The Dark Side	48
A First Sorrow	49
Murmurs	49
Give	50
My Journal	50
A Chain	52
The Pilgrims	53
Incompleteness	53
A Legend of Bregenz	54
A Farewell	57
Sowing and Reaping	57
The Storm	58
Words	59
A Love Token	60
A Tryst with Death	60
Fidelis	61
A Shadow	62
The Sailor Boy	63
A Crown of Sorrow	71
The Lesson of the War	71
The Two Spirits	72
A Little Longer	74
Grief	75
The Triumph of Time	77
A Parting	78
The Golden Gate	79
Phantoms	80
Thankfulness	80

CONTENTS.

Home-Sickness	81
Wishes	82
The Peace of God	83
Life in Death and Death in Life	83
Recollections	86
Illusion	87
A Vision	88
Pictures in the Fire	89
The Settlers	90
Hush!	91
Hours	92
The Two Interpreters	93
Comfort	94
Home at Last	95
Unexpressed	96
Because	97
Rest at Evening	97
A Retrospect	98
True or False	99
Golden Words	101

LEGENDS AND LYRICS. A BOOK OF VERSES.
Second Series.

A Legend of Provence	105
Envy	114
Over the Mountain	114
Beyond	115
A Warning	116
Maximus	117
Optimus	118
A Lost Chord	119
Too Late	119
The Requital	120
Returned — "Missing"	121
In the Wood	122
Two Worlds	123
A New Mother	124
Give Place	131
My Will	132
King and Slave	133

CONTENTS.

A Chant	133
Dream-Life	135
Rest	135
The Tyrant and the Captive	137
The Carver's Lesson	138
Three Roses	139
My Picture Gallery	140
Sent to Heaven	142
Never Again	143
Listening Angels	144
Golden Days	145
Philip and Mildred	146
Borrowed Thoughts.	
I. From "Lavater"	153
II. From "Phantastes"	153
III. From "Lost Alice"	154
IV. From * * *	154
Light and Shade	155
A Changeling	157
Discouraged	158
If thou couldst know	159
The Warrior to his Dead Bride	159
A Letter	160
A Comforter	162
Unseen	164
A Remembrance of Autumn	165
Three Evenings in a Life	165
The Wind	172
Expectation	173
An Ideal	174
Our Dead	175
A Woman's Answer	176
The Story of the Faithful Soul	178
A Contrast	179
The Bride's Dream	181
The Angel's Bidding	182
Spring	183
Evening Hymn	184
The Inner Chamber	185
Hearts	185
Two Loves	187
A Woman's Last Word	187

Past and Present	188
For the Future	189

A CHAPLET OF VERSES.

Introduction	195
The Army of the Lord	199
The Star of the Sea	202
The Sacred Heart	202
The Names of Our Lady	204
A Chaplet of Flowers	205
Kyrie Eleison	207
The Annunciation	208
An Appeal	208
The Jubilee of 1850	210
Christmas Flowers	211
A Desire	212
Our Daily Bread	214
Threefold	214
Confido et Conquiesco	215
Ora pro Me	215
The Church in 1849	216
Fishers of Men	216
The Old Year's Blessing	217
Evening Chant	218
A Christmas Carol	219
Our Titles	220
Ministering Angels	221
The Shrines of Mary	222
The Homeless Poor	226
Milly's Expiation	231
A Castle in the Air	239
Per Pacem ad Lucem	240
A Legend	240
Birthday Gifts	241
A Beggar	244
Links with Heaven	245
Homeless	246

Dedicated

TO

MATILDA M. HAYS.

"Our tokens of love are for the most part barbarous. Cold and lifeless, because they do not represent our life. The only gift is a portion of thyself. Therefore let the farmer give his corn; the miner, a gem; the sailor, coral and shells; the painter, his picture; and the poet, his poem."
— EMERSON's *Essays*.

A. A. P.

May, 1858.

LEGENDS AND LYRICS.

A BOOK OF VERSES.

FIRST SERIES.

LEGENDS AND LYRICS.

THE ANGEL'S STORY.

Through the blue and frosty heavens
Christmas stars were shining bright;
Glistening lamps throughout the City
Almost matched their gleaming light;
While the winter snow was lying,
And the winter winds were sighing,
Long ago, one Christmas night.

While, from every tower and steeple,
Pealing bells were sounding clear,
(Never with such tones of gladness,
Save when Christmas time is near,)
Many a one that night was merry
Who had toiled through all the year.

That night saw old wrongs forgiven,
Friends, long parted, reconciled;
Voices all unused to laughter,
Mournful eyes that rarely smiled,
Trembling hearts that feared the morrow,
From their anxious thoughts beguiled.

Rich and poor felt love and blessing
From the gracious season fall;
Joy and plenty in the cottage,
Peace and feasting in the hall;
And the voices of the children
Ringing clear above it all!

Yet one house was dim and darkened;
Gloom, and sickness, and despair,
Dwelling in the gilded chambers,
Creeping up the marble stair,
Even stilled the voice of mourning,—
For a child lay dying there.

Silken curtains fell around him,
  Velvet carpets hushed the
    tread;
Many costly toys were lying,
  All unheeded, by his bed;
And his tangled golden ringlets
  Were on downy pillows spread.

The skill of that mighty City
  To save one little life was
    vain,—
One little thread from being
  broken,
One fatal word from being spo-
  ken;
Nay, his very mother's pain,
  And the mighty love within her,
Could not give him health
    again.

So she knelt there still beside
    him,
  She alone with strength to
    smile,
Promising that he should suffer
  No more in a little while,
Murmuring tender song and
    story
  Weary hours to beguile.

Suddenly an unseen Presence
  Checked those constant moan-
    ing cries,
Stilled the little heart's quick
  fluttering,
Raised those blue and won-
    dering eyes,
Fixed on some mysterious vision,
  With a startled sweet sur-
    prise.

For a radiant angel hovered,
  Smiling, o'er the little bed;
White his raiment, from his
    shoulders
  Snowy dove-like pinions
    spread,
And a starlike light was shining
  In a Glory round his head.

While, with tender love, the an-
    gel,
  Leaning o'er the little nest,
In his arms the sick child fold-
    ing,
  Laid him gently on his breast,
Sobs and wailings told the moth-
    er
  That her darling was at rest.

So the angel, slowly rising,
  Spread his wings, and through
    the air
Bore the child, and, while he
    held him
  To his heart with loving care,
Placed a branch of crimson
    roses
  Tenderly beside him there.

While the child, thus clinging,
    floated
  Towards the mansions of the
    Blest,
Gazing from his shining guar-
    dian
  To the flowers upon his breast,
Thus the angel spake, still smil-
    ing
  On the little heavenly guest:

"Know, dear little one, that Heaven
  Does no earthly thing disdain,
Man's poor joys find there an echo
  Just as surely as his pain;
Love, on earth so feebly striving,
  Lives divine in Heaven again!

"Once in that great town below us,
  In a poor and narrow street,
Dwelt a little sickly orphan;
  Gentle aid, or pity sweet,
Never in life's rugged pathway
  Guided his poor tottering feet.

"All the striving anxious forethought
  That should only come with age
Weighed upon his baby spirit,
  Showed him soon life's sternest page;
Grim Want was his nurse, and Sorrow
  Was his only heritage.

"All too weak for childish pastimes,
  Drearily the hours sped;
On his hands so small and trembling
  Leaning his poor aching head,
Or, through dark and painful hours,
  Lying sleepless on his bed.

"Dreaming strange and longing fancies
  Of cool forests far away;
And of rosy, happy children,
  Laughing merrily at play,
Coming home through green lanes, bearing
  Trailing boughs of blooming May.

"Scarce a glimpse of azure heaven
  Gleamed above that narrow street,
And the sultry air of summer
  (That you call so warm and sweet)
Fevered the poor orphan, dwelling
  In the crowded alley's heat.

"One bright day, with feeble footsteps
  Slowly forth he tried to crawl,
Through the crowded city's pathways,
  Till he reached a garden-wall,
Where 'mid princely halls and mansions
  Stood the lordliest of all.

"There were trees with giant branches,
  Velvet glades where shadows hide;
There were sparkling fountains glancing,
  Flowers, which in luxuriant pride

Even wafted breaths of perfume
  To the child who stood outside.

"He against the gate of iron
  Pressed his wan and wistful face,
Gazing with an awe-struck pleasure
  At the glories of the place;
Never had his brightest day-dream
  Shone with half such wondrous grace.

"You were playing in that garden,
  Throwing blossoms in the air,
Laughing when the petals floated
  Downwards on your golden hair;
And the fond eyes watching o'er you,
And the splendor spread before you,
  Told a House's Hope was there.

"When your servants, tired of seeing
  Such a face of want and woe,
Turning to the ragged orphan,
  Gave him coin, and bade him go,
Down his cheeks so thin and wasted
  Bitter tears began to flow.

"But that look of childish sorrow
  On your tender child-heart fell,
And you plucked the reddest roses
  From the tree you loved so well
Passed them through the stern cold grating,
  Gently bidding him 'Farewell!'

"Dazzled by the fragrant treasure
  And the gentle voice he heard,
In the poor forlorn boy's spirit,
  Joy, the sleeping Seraph, stirred;
In his hand he took the flowers,
In his heart the loving word.

"So he crept to his poor garret;
  Poor no more, but rich and bright,
For the holy dreams of childhood—
  Love, and Rest, and Hope, and Light—
Floated round the orphan's pillow
  Through the starry summer night.

"Day dawned, yet the visions lasted;
  All too weak to rise he lay;
Did he dream that none spake harshly,—

All were strangely kind that
  day?
Surely then his treasured roses
  Must have charmed all ills
  away.

"And he smiled, though they
  were fading;
  One by one their leaves were
  shed;
'Such bright things could never
  perish,
  They would bloom again,' he
  said.
When the next day's sun had
  risen
  Child and flowers both were
  dead.

"Know, dear little one! our
  Father
Will no gentle deed disdain:
Love on the cold earth begin-
  ning
  Lives divine in Heaven again,
While the angel hearts that beat
  there
  Still all tender thoughts re-
  tain."

So the angel ceased, and gently
  O'er his little burden leant;
While the child gazed from the
  shining,
  Loving eyes that o'er him
  bent,
To the blooming roses by him,
  Wondering what that mystery
  meant.

Thus the radiant angel answered,
  And with tender meaning
  smiled:
"Ere your childlike, loving
  spirit,
  Sin and the hard world defiled,
God has given me leave to seek
  you, —
  I was once that little child!"

* * * *

In the churchyard of that city
  Rose a tomb of marble rare,
Decked, as soon as Spring awak-
  ened,
  With her buds and blossoms
  fair, —
And a humble grave beside it, —
  No one knew who rested there.

ECHOES.

STILL the angel stars are shining,
  Still the rippling waters flow,
But the angel-voice is silent
  That I heard so long ago.
Hark! the echoes murmur
  low,
    Long ago!

Still the wood is dim and lonely,
  Still the plashing fountains
  play,
But the past and all its beauty,
  Whither has it fled away?
Hark! the mournful echoes
  say,
    Fled away!

Still the bird of night complaineth,
  (Now, indeed, her song is pain,)
Visions of my happy hours,
  Do I call and call in vain?
Hark! the echoes cry again,
        All in vain!

Cease, O echoes, mournful echoes!
  Once I loved your voices well;
Now my heart is sick and weary—
  Days of old, a long farewell!
Hark! the echoes sad and dreary
        Cry farewell, farewell!

A FALSE GENIUS.

I SEE a Spirit by thy side,
Purple-winged and eagle-eyed,
Looking like a heavenly guide.

Though he seem so bright and fair,
Ere thou trust his proffered care,
Pause a little, and beware!

If he bid thee dwell apart,
Tending some ideal smart
In a sick and coward heart;

In self-worship wrapped alone,
Dreaming thy poor griefs are grown
More than other men have known;

Dwelling in some cloudy sphere,
Though God's work is waiting here,
And God deigneth to be near;

If his torch's crimson glare
Show the evil everywhere,
Tainting all the wholesome air;

While with strange distorted choice,
Still disdaining to rejoice,
Thou *wilt* hear a wailing voice;

If a simple, humble heart
Seem to thee a meaner part
Than thy noblest aim and art;

If he bid thee bow before
Crownéd Mind and nothing more,
The great idol men adore;

And with starry veil enfold
Sin, the trailing serpent old,
Till his scales shine out like gold;

Though his words seem true and wise,
Soul, I say to thee, Arise,
He is a Demon in disguise!

MY PICTURE.

STAND this way — more near the window —
  By my desk — you see the light
Falling on my picture better —
  Thus I see it while I write!

Who the head may be I know
  not,
But it has a student air;
With a look half sad, half stately,
  Grave sweet eyes and flowing
  hair.

Little care I who the painter,
  How obscure a name he bore;
Nor, when some have named
  Velasquez,
  Did I value it the more.

As it is, I would not give it
  For the rarest piece of art;
It has dwelt with me, and listened
  To the secrets of my heart.

Many a time, when to my garret,
  Weary, I returned at night,
It has seemed to look a welcome
  That has made my poor room
  bright.

Many a time, when ill and sleepless,
  I have watched the quivering
  gleam
Of my lamp upon that picture,
  Till it faded in my dream.

When dark days have come, and
  friendship
  Worthless seemed, and life in
  vain,
That bright friendly smile has
  sent me
  Boldly to my task again.

Sometimes when hard need has
  pressed me
To bow down where I despise,
I have read stern words of counsel
  In those sad, reproachful eyes.

Nothing that my brain imagined,
  Or my weary hand has
  wrought,
But it watched the dim Idea
  Spring forth into arméd
  Thought.

It has smiled on my successes,
  Raised me when my hopes
  were low,
And by turns has looked upon
  me
  With all the loving eyes I
  know.

Do you wonder that my picture
  Has become so like a friend?—
It has seen my life's beginnings,
  It shall stay and cheer the
  end!

JUDGE NOT.

JUDGE not; the workings of his
  brain
  And of his heart thou canst
  not see;
What looks to thy dim eyes a
  stain,
  In God's pure light may only
  be

A scar, brought from some well-
    won field,
Where thou wouldst only faint
    and yield.

The look, the air, that frets thy
    sight,
May be a token, that below
The soul has closed in deadly
    fight
With some infernal fiery foe,
Whose glance would scorch thy
    smiling grace,
And cast thee shuddering on thy
    face !

The fall thou darest to despise —
    Maybe the angel's slackened
    hand
Has suffered it, that he may rise
    And take a firmer, surer stand ;
Or, trusting less to earthly things,
May henceforth learn to use his
    wings.

And judge none lost ; but wait
    and see,
    With hopeful pity, not disdain ;
The depth of the abyss may be
    The measure of the height of
    pain
And love and glory that may
    raise
This soul to God in after days !

FRIEND SORROW.

Do not cheat thy Heart and tell
    her,
    " Grief will pass away,
Hope for fairer times in future,
    And forget to-day." —
Tell her, if you will, that sorrow
    Need not come in vain ;
Tell her that the lesson taught
    her
Far outweighs the pain.

Cheat her not with the old com-
    fort,
    " Soon she will forget," —
Bitter truth, alas ! but matter
    Rather for regret ;
Bid her not " Seek other pleas-
    ures,
    Turn to other things " ; —
Rather nurse her caged sorrow
    Till the captive sings.

Rather bid her go forth bravely,
    And the stranger greet ;
Not as foe, with spear and buckler,
    But as dear friends meet :
Bid her with a strong clasp hold
    her,
    By her dusky wings,
Listening for the murmured
    blessing
Sorrow always brings.

ONE BY ONE.

One by one the sands are flow-
    ing,
    One by one the moments fall ;
Some are coming, some are go-
    ing ;
    Do not strive to grasp them
    all.

One by one thy duties wait
  thee,
Let thy whole strength go to
  each,
Let no future dreams elate thee,
Learn thou first what these
  can teach.

One by one (bright gifts from
  Heaven)
Joys are sent thee here be-
  low;
Take them readily when given,
Ready too to let them go.

One by one thy griefs shall meet
  thee,
Do not fear an arméd band;
One will fade as others greet
  thee;
Shadows passing through the
  land.

Do not look at life's long sorrow;
See how small each moment's
  pain,
God will help thee for to-morrow,
So each day begin again.

Every hour that fleets so slowly
  Has its task to do or bear;
Luminous the crown, and holy,
  When each gem is set with
  care.

Do not linger with regretting,
  Or for passing hours despond;
Nor, the daily toil forgetting,
  Look too eagerly beyond.

Hours are golden links, God's
  token,
Reaching heaven; but one by
  one
Take them, lest the chain be
  broken
Ere the pilgrimage be done.

TRUE HONORS.

Is my darling tired already,
  Tired of her day of play?
Draw your little stool beside me,
  Smooth this tangled hair away.
Can she put the logs together,
  Till they make a cheerful
  blaze?
Shall her blind old Uncle tell
  her
  Something of his youthful
  days?

Hark! The wind among the
  cedars
  Waves their white arms to and
  fro;
I remember how I watched them
  Sixty Christmas Days ago:
Then I dreamt a glorious vision
  Of great deeds to crown each
  year;
Sixty Christmas Days have found
  me
  Useless, helpless, blind — and
  here!

Yes, I feel my darling stealing
　Warm soft fingers into mine:
Shall I tell her what I fancied
　In that strange old dream of
　　mine?
I was kneeling by the window,
　Reading how a noble band,
With the red cross on their
　　breastplates,
　Went to gain the Holy Land.

While with eager eyes of wonder
　Over the dark page I bent,
Slowly twilight shadows gath-
　　ered
　Till the letters came and went;
Slowly, till the night was round
　　me;
　Then my heart beat loud and
　　fast,
For I felt before I saw it
　That a spirit near me passed.

Then I raised my eyes, and,
　　shining
　Where the moon's first ray
　　was bright,
Stood a wingéd Angel-warrior
　Clothed and panoplied in
　　light:
So, with Heaven's love upon him,
　Stern in calm and resolute will,
Looked St. Michael, — does the
　　picture
　Hang in the old cloister still?

Threefold were the dreams of
　　honor
　That absorbed my heart and
　　brain;

Threefold crowns the Angel
　　promised,
　Each one to be bought by pain:
While he spoke, a threefold bless-
　　ing
　Fell upon my soul like rain.
HELPER OF THE POOR AND SUF-
　　FERING;
VICTOR IN A GLORIOUS
　　STRIFE;
SINGER OF A NOBLE POEM:
　Such the honors of my life.

Ah, that dream! Long years
　　that gave me
　Joy and grief as real things
Never touched the tender memory
　Sweet and solemn that it
　　brings, —
Never quite effaced the feeling
　Of those white and shadowing
　　wings.

Do those blue eyes open wider?
　Does my faith too foolish
　　seem?
Yes, my darling, years have
　　taught me
　It was nothing but a dream.
Soon, too soon, the bitter knowl-
　　edge
　Of a fearful trial rose,
Rose to crush my heart, and
　　sternly
　Bade my young ambition close.

More and more my eyes were
　　clouded,
　Till at last God's glorious
　　light

Passed away from me forever,
　And I lived and live in night.
Dear, I will not dim your pleasure,
　Christmas should be only
　　gay: —
In my night the stars have risen,
　And I wait the dawn of day.

Spite of all I could be happy;
　For my brothers' tender care
In their boyish pastimes ever
　Made me take, or feel a share.
Philip, even then so thoughtful,
　Max so noble, brave, and tall,
And your father, little Godfrey,
　The most loving of them all.

Philip reasoned down my sorrow,
　Max would laugh my gloom
　　away,
Godfrey's little arms put round
　　me
　Helped me through my drea-
　　riest day;
While the promise of my Angel,
　Like a star, now bright, now
　　pale,
Hung in blackest night above me,
　And I felt it could not fail.

Years passed on, my brothers
　　left me,
　Each went out to take his
　　share
In the struggle of life; my por-
　　tion
　Was a humble one — to bear.
Here I dwelt, and learnt to wan-
　　der
　Through the woods and fields
　　alone,

Every cottage in the village
　Had a corner called my own.

Old and young, all brought their
　　troubles,
　Great or small, for me to
　　hear;
I have often blessed my sorrow
　That drew others' grief so
　　near.
Ah, the people needed helping —
　Needed love — (for Love and
　　Heaven
Are the only gifts not bartered,
　They alone are freely given) —

And I gave it. Philip's bounty
　(We were orphans, dear) made
　　toil
Prosper, and want never fastened
　On the tenants of the soil.
Philip's name (O, how I gloried,
　He so young, to see it rise!)
Soon grew noted among states-
　　men
　As a patriot true and wise.

And his people all felt honored
　To be ruled by such a name;
I was proud too that they loved
　　me;
　Through their pride in him it
　　came.
He had gained what I had longed
　　for,
　I meanwhile grew glad and
　　gay,
'Mid his people, to be serving
　Him and them, in some poor
　　way.

How his noble earnest speeches
  With untiring fervor came!
HELPER OF THE POOR AND
    SUFFERING;
  Truly he deserved the name!
Had my Angel's promise failed
    me?
  Had that word of hope grown
    dim?
Why, my Philip had fulfilled it,
  And I loved it best in him!

Max meanwhile — ah, you, my
    darling,
  Can his loving words recall —
'Mid the bravest and the noblest,
  Braver, nobler, than them all.
How I loved him! how my heart
    thrilled
  When his sword clanked by
    his side,
When I touched his gold em-
    broidery,
  Almost *saw* him in his pride!

So we parted; he all eager
  To uphold the name he bore,
Leaving in my charge — he
    loved me —
  Some one whom he loved still
    more:
I must tend this gentle flower,
  I must speak to her of him,
For he feared — Love still is
    fearful —
  That his memory might grow
    dim.

I must guard her from all sorrow,
  I must play a brother's part,
Shield all grief and trial from
    her,
  If it need be, with my heart.
Years passed, and his name grew
    famous;
  We were proud, both she and I;
And we lived upon his letters,
  While the slow days fleeted by.

Then at last — you know the
    story,
  How a fearful rumor spread,
Till all hope had slowly faded,
  And we heard that he was
    dead.
Dead!   O, those were bitter
    hours;
  Yet within my soul there
    dwelt
A warning, and while others
    mourned him,
  Something like a hope I felt.

His was no weak life as mine
    was,
  But a life, so full and strong —
No, I could not think he per-
    ished
  Nameless, 'mid a conquered
    throng.
How she drooped! Years passed;
    no tidings
  Came, and yet that little flame
Of strange hope within my spirit
  Still burnt on, and lived the
    same.

Ah! my child, our hearts will
    fail us,
  When to us they strongest
    seem:

I can look back on those hours
As a fearful, evil dream.
She had long despaired; what wonder
That her heart had turned to mine?
Earthly loves are deep and tender,
Not eternal and divine!

Can I say how bright a future
Rose before my soul that day?
O, so strange, so sweet, so tender!
And I had to turn away.
Hard and terrible the struggle,
For the pain not mine alone ;
I called back my Brother's spirit,
And I bade him claim his own.

Told her — now I dared to do it —
That I felt the day would rise
When he would return to gladden
My weak heart and her bright eyes.
And I pleaded — pleaded sternly —
In his name, and for his sake:
Now, I can speak calmly of it,
Then, I thought my heart would break.

Soon — ah, Love had not deceived me,
(Love's true instincts never err,)
Wounded, weak, escaped from prison,
He returned to me, — to her.

I could thank God that bright morning,
When I felt my Brother's gaze,
That my heart was true and loyal,
As in our old boyish days.

Bought by wounds and deeds of daring,
Honors he had brought away ;
Glory crowned his name — my Brother's ;
Mine too! — we were one that day.
Since the crown on him had fallen,
"VICTOR IN A NOBLE STRIFE,"
I could live and die contented
With my poor ignoble life.

Well, my darling, almost weary
Of my story? Wait awhile;
For the rest is only joyful ;
I can tell it with a smile.
One bright promise still was left me,
Wound so close about my soul,
That, as one by one had failed me,
This dream now absorbed the whole.

"SINGER OF A NOBLE POEM,"—
Ah, my darling, few and rare
Burn the glorious names of Poets,
Like stars in the purple air.
That too, and I glory in it,
That great gift my Godfrey won ;

I have my dear share of honor,
  Gained by that belovéd one.

One day shall my darling read
    it;
  Now she cannot understand
All the noble thoughts that
    lighten
  Through the genius of the
    land.
I am proud to be his brother,
  Proud to think that hope was
    true;
Though I longed and strove so
    vainly,
  What I failed in, he could do.

I was long before I knew it,
  Longer ere I felt it so;
Then I strung my rhymes to-
    gether
  Only for the poor and low.
And, it pleases me to know it,
  (For I love them well indeed,)
They care for my humble verses,
  Fitted for their humble need.

And, it cheers my heart to hear
    it,
  Where the far-off settlers roam,
My poor words are sung and
    cherished,
  Just because they speak of
    Home.
And the little children sing them,
  (That, I think, has pleased me
    best,)
Often, too, the dying love them,
  For they tell of Heaven and
    rest.

So my last vain dream has faded;
  (Such as I to think of fame!)
Yet I will not say it failed me,
  For it crowned my Godfrey's
    name.
No; my Angel did not cheat me,
  For my long life *has* been
    blest;
He did give me Love and Sor-
    row,
  He will bring me Light and
    Rest.

A WOMAN'S QUESTION.

Before I trust my Fate to thee,
  Or place my hand in thine,
Before I let thy Future give
  Color and form to mine,
Before I peril all for thee, question
  thy soul to-night for me.

I break all slighter bonds, nor
    feel
  A shadow of regret:
Is there one link within the Past
  That holds thy spirit yet?
Or is thy Faith as clear and free
  as that which I can pledge to
    thee?

Does there within thy dimmest
    dreams
  A possible future shine,
Wherein thy life could hence-
    forth breathe,
  Untouched, unshared by mine?
If so, at any pain or cost, O, tell
  me before all is lost.

Look deeper still. If thou canst feel
Within my inmost soul,
That thou hast kept a portion back,
While I have staked the whole;
Let no false pity spare the blow,
but in true mercy tell me so.

Is there within thy heart a need
That mine cannot fulfil?
One chord that any other hand
Could better wake or still?
Speak now — lest at some future day my whole life wither and decay.

Lives there within thy nature hid
The demon-spirit Change,
Shedding a passing glory still
On all things new and strange? —
It may not be thy fault alone —
but shield my heart against thy own.

Couldst thou withdraw thy hand one day
And answer to my claim,
That Fate, and that to-day's mistake —
Not thou — had been to blame?
Some soothe their conscience thus; but thou wilt surely warn and save me now.

Nay, answer *not*, — I dare not hear,
The words would come too late;
Yet I would spare thee all remorse,
So, comfort thee, my Fate —
Whatever on my heart may fall
— remember, I *would* risk it all!

THE THREE RULERS.

I SAW a Ruler take his stand,
And trample on a mighty land;
The People crouched before his beck,
His iron heel was on their neck,
His name shone bright through blood and pain,
His sword flashed back their praise again.

I saw another Ruler rise:
His words were noble, good, and wise;
With the calm sceptre of his pen
He ruled the minds and thoughts of men:
Some scoffed, some praised, — while many heard,
Only a few obeyed his word.

Another Ruler then I saw:
Love and sweet Pity were his law;
The greatest and the least had part

(Yet most the unhappy) in his
   heart:
The People, in a mighty band,
Rose up, and drove him from
   the land!

A DEAD PAST.

Spare her at least: look, you
   have taken from me
The Present, and I murmur not,
   nor moan;
The Future too, with all her
   glorious promise;
But do not leave me utterly
   alone.

Spare me the Past: for, see, she
   cannot harm you,
She lies so white and cold,
   wrapped in her shroud;
All, all my own! and, trust me,
   I will hide her
Within my soul, nor speak to
   her aloud.

I folded her soft hands upon her
   bosom,
And strewed my flowers upon
   her, — *they* still live:
Sometimes I like to kiss her
   closed white eyelids,
And think of all the joy she
   used to give.

Cruel indeed it were to take her
   from me;
She sleeps, she will not wake —
   no fear — again:

And so I laid her, such a gentle
   burden,
Quietly on my heart to still its
   pain.

I do not think that any smiling
   Present,
Any vague Future, spite of all
   her charms,
Could ever rival her. You know
   you laid her,
Long years ago, then living, in
   my arms.

Leave her at least: while my
   tears fall upon her,
I dream she smiles, just as she
   did of yore;
As dear as ever to me, — nay, it
   may be,
Even dearer still, — since I have
   nothing more.

A DOUBTING HEART.

Where are the swallows fled?
   Frozen and dead,
Perchance upon some bleak and
   stormy shore.
O doubting heart!
   Far over purple seas,
   They wait, in sunny ease,
The balmy southern breeze,
To bring them to their northern
   homes once more.

Why must the flowers die?
   Prisoned they lie

In the cold tomb, heedless of
    tears or rain.
      O doubting heart!
  They only sleep below
  The soft white ermine snow,
    While winter winds shall blow,
To breathe and smile upon you
    soon again.

The sun has hid its rays
    These many days;
Will dreary hours never leave
    the earth?
      O doubting heart!
  The stormy clouds on high
  Veil the same sunny sky,
    That soon (for spring is nigh)
Shall wake the summer into
    golden mirth.

Fair hope is dead, and light
    Is quenched in night.
What sound can break the silence of despair?
      O doubting heart!
  Thy sky is overcast,
  Yet stars shall rise at last,
  Brighter for darkness past,
And angels' silver voices stir the
    air.

A STUDENT.

Over an ancient scroll I bent,
  Steeping my soul in wise content,
Nor paused a moment, save to chide
A low voice whispering at my side.

I wove beneath the stars' pale shine
A dream, half human, half divine;
And shook off (not to break the charm)
A little hand laid on my arm.

I read; until my heart would glow
With the great deeds of long ago;
Nor heard, while with those mighty dead,
Pass to and fro a faltering tread.

On the old theme I pondered long, —
The struggle between right and wrong;
I could not check such visions high,
To soothe a little quivering sigh.

I tried to solve the problem — Life;
Dreaming of that mysterious strife,
How could I leave such reasonings wise,
To answer two blue pleading eyes?

I strove how best to give, and when,
My blood to save my fellow-men, —

How could I turn aside, to look
At snowdrops laid upon my
    book?

Now Time has fled — the world
    is strange,
Something there is of pain and
    change;
My books lie closed upon the
    shelf;
I miss the old heart in myself.

I miss the sunbeams in my
    room, —
It was not always wrapped in
    gloom:
I miss my dreams, — they fade
    so fast,
Or flit into some trivial past.

The great stream of the world
    goes by;
None care, or heed, or question,
    why
I, the lone student, cannot raise
My voice or hand as in old days.

No echo seems to wake again
My heart to anything but pain,
Save when a dream of twilight
    brings
The fluttering of an angel's
    wings!

A KNIGHT-ERRANT.

Though he lived and died among
    us,
  Yet his name may be enrolled
With the knights whose deeds of
    daring
  Ancient chronicles have told.

Still a stripling, he encountered
  Poverty, and struggled long,
Gathering force from every effort,
  Till he knew his arm was
    strong.

Then his heart and life he of-
    fered
  To his radiant mistress, —
    Truth;
Never thought, or dream, or fal-
    tering,
  Marred the promise of his
    youth.

So he rode forth to defend her,
  And her peerless worth pro-
    claim;
Challenging each recreant doubt-
    er
  Who aspersed her spotless
    name.

First upon his path stood Igno-
    rance,
  Hideous in his brutal might;
Hard the blows and long the
    battle
  Ere the monster took to flight.

Then, with light and fearless
    spirit,
  Prejudice he dared to brave;
Hunting back the lying craven
  To her black sulphureous
    cave.

Followed by his servile minions,
　Custom, the old Giant, rose;
Yet he, too, at last was conquered
　By the good Knight's weighty
　　blows.

Then he turned, and, flushed with
　　victory,
　Struck upon the brazen shield
Of the world's great king, Opin-
　　ion,
　And defied him to the field.

Once again he rose a conqueror,
　And, though wounded in the
　　fight,
With a dying smile of triumph
　Saw that Truth had gained
　　her right.

On his failing ear re-echoing
　Came the shouting round her
　　throne;
Little cared he that no future
　With her name would link his
　　own.

Spent with many a hard-fought
　　battle,
　Slowly ebbed his life away,
And the crowd that flocked to
　　greet her
　Trampled on him where he
　　lay.

Gathering all his strength, he
　　saw her
　Crowned and reigning in her
　　pride;
Looked his last upon her beauty,
　Raised his eyes to God, and
　　died.

LINGER, O GENTLE TIME.

LINGER, O gentle Time,
Linger, O radiant grace of bright
　　To-day!
Let not the hours' chime
　　Call thee away,
But linger near me still with
　　fond delay.

Linger, for thou art mine!
What dearer treasures can the
　　future hold?
What sweeter flowers than
　　thine
　　Can she unfold?
What secrets tell my heart thou
　　hast not told?

O, linger in thy flight!
For shadows gather round, and
　　should we part,
A dreary, starless night
　　May fill my heart, —
Then pause and linger yet ere
　　thou depart.

Linger, I ask no more, —
Thou art enough forever — thou
　　alone;
What future can restore,
　　When thou art flown,
All that I hold from thee and call
　　my own?

HOMEWARD BOUND.

I HAVE seen a fiercer tempest,
　Known a louder whirlwind
　　blow;

I was wrecked off red Algiers,
  Six-and-thirty years ago.
Young I was, and yet old seamen
  Were not strong or calm as I ;
While life held such treasures for me,
I felt sure I could not die.

Life I struggled for, — and saved it ;
  Life alone, — and nothing more ;
Bruised, half dead, alone and helpless
I was cast upon the shore.
I feared the pitiless rocks of Ocean ;
  So the great sea rose, — and then
Cast me from her friendly bosom,
On the pitiless hearts of men.

Gaunt and dreary ran the mountains,
  With black gorges, up the land ;
Up to where the lonely Desert
  Spreads her burning, dreary sand :
In the gorges of the mountains,
  On the plain beside the sea,
Dwelt my stern and cruel masters,
  The black Moors of Barbary.

Ten long years I toiled among them,
  Hopeless — as I used to say ;
Now I know Hope burnt within me
  Fiercer, stronger, day by day :
Those dim years of toil and sorrow
  Like one long, dark dream appear ;
One long day of weary waiting, —
  Then each day was like a year.

How I cursed the land, — my prison ;
  How I cursed the serpent sea,
And the Demon Fate that showered
  All her curses upon me;
I was mad, I think — God pardon
  Words so terrible and wild —
This voyage would have been my last one,
  For I left a wife and child.

Never did one tender vision
  Fade away before my sight,
Never once through all my slavery,
  Burning day or dreary night ;
In my soul it lived, and kept me,
  Now I feel, from black despair,
And my heart was not quite broken,
  While they lived and blest me there.

When at night my task was over,
  I would hasten to the shore ;
(All was strange and foreign inland,
  Nothing I had known before ;)

Strange looked the bleak mountain passes,
Strange the red glare and black shade,
And the Oleanders, waving
To the sound the fountains made.

Then I gazed at the great Ocean,
Till she grew a friend again;
And because she knew old England,
I forgave her all my pain:
So the blue still sky above me,
With its white clouds' fleecy fold,
And the glimmering stars (though brighter),
Looked like home and days of old.

And a calm would fall upon me,
Worn perhaps with work and pain,
The wild, hungry longing left me,
And I was myself again:
Looking at the silver waters,
Looking up at the far sky,
Dreams of home and all I left there
Floated sorrowfully by.

A fair face, but pale with sorrow,
With blue eyes, brimful of tears,
And the little red mouth, quivering
With a smile, to hide its fears;

Holding out her baby towards me,
From the sky she looked on me;
So it was that last I saw her,
As the ship put out to sea.

Sometimes (and a pang would seize me
That the years were floating on)
I would strive to paint her, altered,
And the little baby gone:
She no longer young and girlish,
The child standing by her knee,
And her face more pale and saddened
With the weariness for me.

Then I saw, as night grew darker,
How she taught my child to pray,
Holding its small hands together,
For its father, far away;
And I felt her sorrow, weighing
Heavier on me than my own,
Pitying her blighted spring-time,
And her joy so early flown.

Till upon my hands (now hardened
With the rough, harsh toil of years)
Bitter drops of anguish falling,
Woke me from my dream, to tears;
Woke me as a slave, an outcast,
Leagues from home, across the deep;

So — though you may call it childish —
So I sobbed myself to sleep.

Well, the years sped on, — my Sorrow,
Calmer, and yet stronger grown,
Was my shield against all suffering,
Poorer, meaner than her own.
Thus my cruel master's harshness
Fell upon me all in vain,
Yet the tale of what we suffered
Echoed back from main to main.

You have heard in a far country
Of a self-devoted band,
Vowed to rescue Christian captives
Pining in a foreign land.
And these gentle-hearted strangers
Year by year go forth from Rome,
In their hands the hard-earned ransom,
To restore some exiles home.

I was freed: they broke the tidings
Gently to me: but indeed
Hour by hour sped on, I knew not
What the words meant — I was freed!
Better so, perhaps; while sorrow
(More akin to earthly things)
Only strains the sad heart's fibres,
Joy, bright stranger, breaks the strings.

Yet at last it rushed upon me,
And my heart beat full and fast;
What were now my years of waiting,
What was all the dreary past?
Nothing — to the impatient throbbing
I must bear across the sea:
Nothing — to the eternal hours
Still between my home and me!

How the voyage passed, I know not;
Strange it was once more to stand
With my countrymen around me,
And to clasp an English hand.
But, through all, my heart was dreaming
Of the first words I should hear,
In the gentle voice that echoed,
Fresh as ever, on my ear.

Should I see her start of wonder,
And the sudden truth arise,
Flushing all her face and lightening
The dimmed splendor of her eyes?
Oh! to watch the fear and doubting
Stir the silent depths of pain,

And the rush of joy — then melting
  Into perfect peace again.

And the child! — but why remember
  Foolish fancies that I thought?
Every tree and every hedge-row
  From the well-known past I brought;
I would picture my dear cottage,
  See the crackling wood-fire burn,
And the two beside it seated,
  Watching, waiting, my return.

So, at last we reached the harbor.
  I remember nothing more
Till I stood, my sick heart throbbing,
  With my hand upon the door.
There I paused — I heard her speaking;
  Low, soft, murmuring words she said;
Then I first knew the dumb terror
  I had had lest she were dead.

It was evening in late autumn,
  And the gusty wind blew chill;
Autumn leaves were falling round me,
  And the red sun lit the hill.
Six-and-twenty years are vanished
  Since then, — I am old and gray, —
But I never told to mortal
  What I saw, until this day.

She was seated by the fire,
  In her arms she held a child,
Whispering baby-words caressing,
  And then, looking up, she smiled;
Smiled on him who stood beside her —
  Oh! the bitter truth was told,
In her look of trusting fondness —
  I had seen the look of old!

But she rose and turned towards me
  (Cold and dumb I waited there)
With a shriek of fear and terror,
  And a white face of despair.
He had been an ancient comrade, —
  Not a single word we said,
While we gazed upon each other,
  He the living: I the dead!

I drew nearer, nearer to her,
  And I took her trembling hand,
Looking on her white face, looking
  That her heart might understand
All the love and all the pity
  That my lips refused to say, —
I thank God no thought save sorrow
  Rose in our crushed hearts that day.

Bitter tears that desolate moment,
  Bitter, bitter tears we wept,

We three broken hearts together,
  While the baby smiled and
    slept.
Tears alone — no words were
    spoken,
Till he — till her husband said
That my boy, (I had forgotten
  The poor child,) that he was
    dead.

Then at last I rose, and, turning,
  Wrung his hand, but made no
    sign ;
And I stooped and kissed her
    forehead
Once more, as if she were mine.
Nothing of farewell I uttered,
  Save in broken words to pray
That God would ever guard and
    bless her, —
Then in silence passed away.

Over the great restless ocean
  Six-and-twenty years I roam ;
All my comrades, old and weary,
  Have gone back to die at home.
Home ! yes, I shall reach a
    haven,
  I, too, shall reach home and
    rest ;
I shall find her waiting for me
  With our baby on her breast.

LIFE AND DEATH.

"What is Life, father ? "
      "A Battle, my child,
Where the strongest lance may
    fail,
Where the wariest eyes may be
    beguiled,
And the stoutest heart may
    quail.
Where the foes are gathered on
    every hand,
And rest not day or night,
And the feeble little ones must
    stand
In the thickest of the fight."

"What is Death, father ? "
      " The rest, my child,
When the strife and the toil are
    o'er ;
The angel of God, who, calm
    and mild,
Says we need fight no more ;
Who, driving away the demon
    band,
Bids the din of the battle
    cease ;
Takes banner and spear from
    our failing hand,
And proclaims an eternal
    peace."

"Let me die, father ! I tremble,
    and fear
  To yield in that terrible
    strife ! "

" The crown must be won for
    Heaven, dear,
  In the battle-field of life:
My child, though thy foes are
    strong and tried,
He loveth the weak and small ;
The angels of heaven are on thy
    side,
  And God is over all ! "

NOW.

Rise! for the day is passing,
   And you lie dreaming on;
The others have buckled their
    armor,
   And forth to the fight are
    gone:
A place in the ranks awaits
    you,
   Each man has some part to
    play;
The Past and the Future are
    nothing,
   In the face of the stern To-
    day.

Rise from your dreams of the
    Future, —
   Of gaining some hard-fought
    field;
Of storming some airy fortress,
   Or bidding some giant yield;
Your Future has deeds of glory,
   Of honor (God grant it may!)
But your arm will never be
    stronger,
   Or the need so great as To-day.

Rise! if the Past detains you,
   Her sunshine and storms
    forget;
No chains so unworthy to hold
    you
   As those of a vain regret:
Sad or bright, she is lifeless ever;
   Cast her phantom arms away,
Nor look back, save to learn the
    lesson
   Of a nobler strife To-day.

Rise! for the day is passing;
   The sound that you scarcely
    hear
Is the enemy marching to bat-
    tle: —
   Arise! for the foe is here!
Stay not to sharpen your weap-
    ons,
   Or the hour will strike at last,
When, from dreams of a coming
    battle,
   You may wake to find it past!

CLEANSING FIRES.

Let thy gold be cast in the fur-
    nace,
   Thy red gold, precious and
    bright;
Do not fear the hungry fire,
   With its caverns of burning
    light;
And thy gold shall return more
    precious,
   Free from every spot and
    stain;
For gold must be tried by fire,
   As a heart must be tried by
    pain!

In the cruel fire of Sorrow
   Cast thy heart, do not faint or
    wail;
Let thy hand be firm and steady,
   Do not let thy spirit quail:
But wait till the trial is over,
   And take thy heart again;

For as gold is tried by fire,
  So a heart must be tried by pain!
I shall know by the gleam and glitter
  Of the golden chain you wear,
By your heart's calm strength in loving,
  Of the fire they have had to bear.
Beat on, true heart, forever;
  Shine bright, strong golden chain;
And bless the cleansing fire,
  And the furnace of living pain!

THE VOICE OF THE WIND.

LET us throw more logs on the fire!
  We have need of a cheerful light,
And close round the hearth to gather,
  For the wind has risen to-night.
With the mournful sound of its wailing
  It has checked the children's glee,
And it calls with a louder clamor
  Than the clamor of the sea.
    Hark to the voice of the wind!

Let us listen to what it is saying,
  Let us hearken to where it has been;
For it tells, in its terrible crying,
  The fearful sights it has seen.
It clatters loud at the casements,
  Round the house it hurries on,
And shrieks with redoubled fury
  When we say, "The blast is gone!"
    Hark to the voice of the wind!

It has been on the field of battle,
  Where the dying and wounded lie;
And it brings the last groan they uttered,
  And the ravenous vulture's cry.
It has been where the icebergs were meeting,
  And closed with a fearful crash:
On shores where no foot has wandered
  It has heard the waters dash.
    Hark to the voice of the wind!

It has been on the desolate ocean
  When the lightning struck the mast;
It has heard the cry of the drowning,
  Who sank as it hurried past;
The words of despair and anguish,
  That were heard by no living ear,
The gun that no signal answered,
  It brings them all to us here.
    Hark to the voice of the wind!

has been on the lonely moorland,
Where the treacherous snow-
 drift lies,
here the traveller, spent and
 weary,
Gasped fainter and fainter
 cries;
has heard the bay of the blood-
 hounds
On the track of the hunted
 slave,
he lash and the curse of the
 master,
And the groan that the captive gave.
    Hark to the voice of
      the wind!

has swept through the gloomy
 forest,
Where the sledge was urged
 to its speed,
here the howling wolves were
 rushing
On the track of the panting
 steed.
here the pool was black and
 lonely,
It caught up a splash and a
 cry,—
nly the bleak sky heard it,
And the wind as it hurried by.
    Hark to the voice of
      the wind!

hen throw more logs on the
 fire,
Since the air is bleak and
 cold,

And the children are drawing
 nigher,
For the tales that the wind
 has told.
So closer and closer gather
Round the red and crackling
 light;
And rejoice (while the wind is
 blowing)
We are safe and warm to-
 night.
    Hark to the voice of
      the wind!

TREASURES.

LET me count my treasures,
  All my soul holds dear,
Given me by dark spirits
  Whom I used to fear.

Through long days of anguish,
  And sad nights, did Pain
Forge my shield, Endurance,
  Bright and free from stain!

Doubt, in misty caverns,
  'Mid dark horrors sought,
Till my peerless jewel,
  Faith, to me she brought.

Sorrow, that I wearied
  Should remain so long,
Wreathed my starry glory,
  The bright Crown of Song.

Strife, that racked my spirit
  Without hope or rest,

Left the blooming flower,
  Patience, on my breast.

Suffering, that I dreaded,
  Ignorant of her charms,
Laid the fair child, Pity,
  Smiling, in my arms.

So I count my treasures,
  Stored in days long past,—
And I thank the givers,
  Whom I know at last!

SHINING STARS.

SHINE, ye stars of heaven,
  On a world of pain!
See old Time destroying
  All our hoarded gain;
All our sweetest flowers,
  Every stately shrine,
All our hard-earned glory,
  Every dream divine!

Shine, ye stars of heaven,
  On the rolling years!
See how Time, consoling,
  Dries the saddest tears,
Bids the darkest storm-clouds
  Pass in gentle rain,
While upspring in glory
  Flowers and dreams again!

Shine, ye stars of heaven,
  On a world of fear!
See how Time, avenging,
  Bringeth judgment here:
Weaving ill-won honors
  To a fiery crown;
Bidding hard hearts perish;
  Casting proud hearts down.

Shine, ye stars of heaven,
  On the hours' slow flight!
See how Time, rewarding,
  Gilds good deeds with light;
Pays with kingly measure;
  Brings earth's dearest prize;
Or, crowned with rays diviner,
  Bids the end arise!

WAITING.

"WHEREFORE dwell so sad and lonely
  By the desolate sea-shore,
With the melancholy surges
  Beating at your cottage door?

"You shall dwell beside the castle
  Shadowed by our ancient trees;
And your life shall pass on gently,
  Cared for, and in rest and ease."

"Lady, one who loved me dearly
  Sailed for distant lands away;
And I wait here his returning
  Hopefully from day to day.

"To my door I bring my spinning,
  Watching every ship I see;
Waiting, hoping, till the sunset
  Fades into the western sea.

After sunset, at my casement,
  Still I place a signal light;
He will see its well-known shining
  Should his ship return at night.

Lady, see your infant smiling,
  With its flaxen curling hair, —
remember when your mother
  Was a baby just as fair.

I was watching then, and hoping:
  Years have brought great change to all;
To my neighbors in their cottage,
  To you nobles at the hall.

Not to me, — for I am waiting,
  And the years have fled so fast,
I must look at you to tell me
  That a weary time has past!

When I hear a footstep coming
  On the shingle — years have fled —
Yet amid a thousand others,
  I shall know his quick, light tread.

When I hear (to-night it may be)
  Some one pausing at my door,
I shall know the gay, soft accents,
  Heard and welcomed oft before!

"So each day I am more hopeful,
  He may come before the night;
Every sunset I feel surer
  He must come ere morning light.

"Then I thank you, noble lady,
  But I cannot do your will:
Where he left me he must find me,
  Waiting, watching, hoping, still!"

―――

THE CRADLE-SONG OF THE POOR.

Hush! I cannot bear to see thee
  Stretch thy tiny hands in vain;
Dear, I have no bread to give thee,
  Nothing, child, to ease thy pain!
When God sent thee first to bless me,
  Proud, and thankful too, was I;
Now, my darling, I, thy mother,
  Almost long to see thee die.
    Sleep, my darling, thou art weary;
    God is good, but life is dreary.

I have watched thy beauty fading
  And thy strength sink day by day,
Soon, I know, will Want and Fever
  Take thy little life away.

Famine makes thy father reckless,
  Hope has left both him and
  me;
We could suffer all, my baby,
  Had we but a crust for thee.
    Sleep, my darling, thou
      art weary;
    God is good, but life is
      dreary.

Better thou shouldst perish early,
  Starve so soon, my darling
  one,
Than in helpless sin and sorrow
  Vainly live, as I have done.
Better that thy angel spirit
  With my joy, my peace, were
  flown,
Than thy heart grew cold and
  careless,
Reckless, hopeless, like my
  own.
    Sleep, my darling, thou
      art weary;
    God is good, but life is
      dreary.

I am wasted, dear, with hunger,
  And my brain is all opprest,
I have scarcely strength to press
  thee,
  Wan and feeble, to my breast.
Patience, baby, God will help us,
  Death will come to thee and
  me,
He will take us to his heaven,
  Where no want or pain can be.
    Sleep, my darling, thou
      art weary;
    God is good, but life is
      dreary.

Such the plaint that, late and
  early,
Did we listen, we might hear
Close beside us, — but the thun-
  der
Of a city dulls our ear.
Every heart, as God's bright
  Angel,
Can bid one such sorrow cease;
God has glory when his children
  Bring his poor ones joy and
  peace!
    Listen, nearer while she
      sings
    Sounds the fluttering of
      wings!

BE STRONG.

BE strong to *hope*, O Heart!
  Though day is bright,
The stars can only shine
  In the dark night.
Be strong, O Heart of mine,
  Look towards the light!

Be strong to *bear*, O Heart!
  Nothing is vain:
Strive not, for life is care,
  And God sends pain;
Heaven is above, and there
  Rest will remain!

Be strong to *love*, O Heart!
  Love knows not wrong;
Didst thou love — creatures
  even,
  Life were not long;
Didst thou love God in heaven,
  Thou wouldst be strong!

GOD'S GIFTS.

God gave a gift to Earth: a child,
Weak, innocent, and undefiled,
Opened its ignorant eyes and smiled.

It lay so helpless, so forlorn,
Earth took it coldly and in scorn,
Cursing the day when it was born.

She gave it first a tarnished name,
For heritage, a tainted fame,
Then cradled it in want and shame.

All influence of Good or Right,
All ray of God's most holy light,
She curtained closely from its sight.

Then turned her heart, her eyes away,
Ready to look again, the day
Its little feet began to stray.

In dens of guilt the baby played,
Where sin, and sin alone, was made
The law that all around obeyed.

With ready and obedient care,
He learnt the tasks they taught him there;
Black sin for lesson, — oaths for prayer.

Then Earth arose, and, in her might,
To vindicate her injured right,
Thrust him in deeper depths of night;

Branding him with a deeper brand
Of shame, he could not understand,
The felon outcast of the land.

God gave a gift to Earth: a child,
Weak, innocent, and undefiled,
Opened its ignorant eyes and smiled.

And Earth received the gift, and cried
Her joy and triumph far and wide,
Till echo answered to her pride.

She blessed the hour when first he came
To take the crown of pride and fame,
Wreathed through long ages for his name.

Then bent her utmost art and skill
To train the supple mind and will,
And guard it from a breath of ill.

She strewed his morning path with flowers,
And Love, in tender dropping showers,
Nourished the blue and dawning hours.

She shed, in rainbow hues of light,
A halo round the Good and Right,
To tempt and charm the baby's sight.

And every step, of work or play,
Was lit by some such dazzling ray,
Till morning brightened into day.

And then the World arose, and said,
Let added honors now be shed
On such a noble heart and head!

O World, both gifts were pure and bright,
Holy and sacred in God's sight:—
God will judge them and thee aright!

A TOMB IN GHENT.

A SMILING look she had, a figure slight,
With cheerful air, and step both quick and light;
A strange and foreign look the maiden bore,
That suited the quaint Belgian dress she wore;
Yet the blue, fearless eyes in her fair face,
And her soft voice, told her of English race;
And ever, as she flitted to and fro,
She sang, (or murmured, rather,) soft and low,
Snatches of song, as if she did not know
That she was singing, but the happy load
Of dream and thought thus from her heart o'erflowed:
And while on household cares she passed along,
The air would bear me fragments of her song;
Not such as village maidens sing, and few
The framers of her changing music knew;
Chants such as heaven and earth first heard of when
The master Palestrina held the pen.
But I with awe had often turned the page,
Yellow with time, and half defaced by age,
And listened, with an ear not quite unskilled,
While heart and soul to the grand echo thrilled;
And much I marvelled, as her cadence fell
From the Laudate, that I knew so well,
Into Scarlatti's minor fugue, how she
Had learned such deep and solemn harmony.
But what she told I set in rhyme, as meet
To chronicle the influence, dim and sweet,

A TOMB IN GHENT.

'Neath which her young and innocent life had grown :
Would that my words were simple as her own.

Many years since, an English
workman went
Over the seas, to seek a home in
Ghent,
Where English skill was prized ;
nor toiled in vain ;
Small, yet enough, his hard-
earned daily gain.
He dwelt alone, — in sorrow, or
in pride.
He mixed not with the workers
by his side ;
He seemed to care but for one
present joy, —
To tend, to watch, to teach his
sickly boy.
Severe to all beside, yet for the
child
He softened his rough speech to
soothings mild ;
For him he smiled, with him each
day he walked
Through the dark, gloomy
streets ; to him he talked
Of home, of England, and
strange stories told
Of English heroes in the days of
old ;
And (when the sunset gilded
roof and spire)
The marvellous tale which never
seemed to tire :
How the gilt dragon, glaring
fiercely down
From the great belfry, watching
all the town,
Was brought, a trophy of the
wars divine,
By a Crusader from far Palestine,
And given to Bruges ; and how
Ghent arose,
And how they struggled long as
deadly foes,
Till Ghent, one night, by a brave
soldier's skill,
Stole the great dragon ; and she
keeps it still.
One day the dragon — so 't is
said — will rise,
Spread his bright wings, and
glitter in the skies,
And over desert lands and azure
seas
Will seek his home 'mid palm
and cedar trees.
So, as he passed the belfry every
day,
The boy would look if it were
flown away ;
Each day surprised to find it
watching there,
Above him, as he crossed the
ancient square,
To seek the great cathedral, that
had grown
A home for him — mysterious
and his own.

Dim with dark shadows of
the ages past,
St. Bavon stands, solemn and
rich and vast ;
The slender pillars, in long
vistas spread,

Like forest arches meet and close
  o'erhead;
So high that, like a weak and
  doubting prayer,
Ere it can float to the carved
  angels there,
The silver clouded incense faints
  in air:
Only the organ's voice, with peal
  on peal,
Can mount to where those far-off
  angels kneel.
Here the pale boy, beneath a low
  side-arch,
Would listen to its solemn chant
  or march;
Folding his little hands, his simple prayer
Melted in childish dreams, and
  both in air:
While the great organ over all
  would roll,
Speaking strange secrets to his
  innocent soul,
Bearing on eagle-wings the great
  desire
Of all the kneeling throng, and
  piercing higher
Than aught but love and prayer
  can reach, until
Only the silence seemed to listen
  still;
Or gathering like a sea still more
  and more,
Break in melodious waves at
  heaven's door,
And then fall, slow and soft, in
  tender rain,
Upon the pleading, longing
  hearts again.

Then he would watch the rosy
  sunlight glow,
That crept along the marble floor
  below,
Passing, as life does, with the
  passing hours,
Now by a shrine all rich with
  gems and flowers,
Now on the brazen letters of a
  tomb,
Then, leaving it again to shade
  and gloom,
And creeping on, to show, dis-
  tinct and quaint,
The kneeling figure of some
  marble saint:
Or lighting up the carvings
  strange and rare,
That told of patient toil, and
  reverent care;
Ivy that trembled on the spray,
  and ears
Of heavy corn, and slender bul-
  rush spears,
And all the thousand tangled
  weeds that grow
In summer, where the silver rivers flow;
And demon-heads grotesque,
  that seemed to glare
In impotent wrath on all the
  beauty there:
Then the gold rays up pillared
  shaft would climb,
And so be drawn to heaven, at
  evening time.
And deeper silence, darker shadows flowed
On all around, only the windows
  glowed

With blazoned glory, like the
shields of light
Archangels bear, who, armed
with love and might,
Watch upon heaven's battlements at night.
Then all was shade; the silver
lamps that gleamed,
Lost in the daylight, in the darkness seemed
Like sparks of fire in the dim
aisles to shine,
Or trembling stars before each
separate shrine.
Grown half afraid, the child
would leave them there,
And come out, blinded by the
noisy glare
That burst upon him from the
busy square.

The church was thus his home
for rest or play;
And as he came and went again
each day,
The pictured faces that he knew
so well
Seemed to smile on him welcome
and farewell.
But holier, and dearer far than all,
One sacred spot his own he loved
to call;
Save at mid-day, half hidden by
the gloom;
The people call it The White
Maiden's Tomb:
For there she stands; her folded
hands are pressed
Together, and laid softly on her
breast,
As if she waited but a word to
rise
From the dull earth, and pass to
the blue skies;
Her lips expectant part, she holds
her breath,
As listening for the angel voice
of death.
None know how many years have
seen her so,
Or what the name of her who
sleeps below.
And here the child would come,
and strive to trace,
Through the dim twilight, the
pure, gentle face
He loved so well, and here he oft
would bring
Some violet-blossom of the early
spring,
And, climbing softly by the fret-
ted stand,
Not to disturb her, lay it in her
hand;
Or, whispering a soft, loving
message sweet,
Would stoop and kiss the little
marble feet.
So, when the organ's pealing
music rang,
He thought amid the gloom the
Maiden sang;
With reverent, simple faith by
her he knelt,
And fancied what she thought,
and what she felt;
"Glory to God," re-echoed from
her voice,
And then his little spirit would
rejoice;

Or when the Requiem sobbed
upon the air,
His baby tears dropped with her
mournful prayer.

So years fled on, while childish
fancies past,
The childish love and simple faith
could last.
The artist-soul awoke in him, the
flame
Of genius, like the light of Heaven,
came
Upon his brain, and (as it will,
if true)
It touched his heart and lit his
spirit, too.
His father saw, and with a proud
content
Let him forsake the toil where
he had spent
His youth's first years, and on
one happy day
Of pride, before the old man
passed away,
He stood with quivering lips, and
the big tears
Upon his cheek, and heard the
dream of years
Living and speaking to his very
heart, —
The low, hushed murmur at the
wondrous art
Of him who with young, trembling fingers made
The great church-organ answer
as he played;
And, as the uncertain sound grew
full and strong,
Rush with harmonious spirit-wings along,
And thrill with master-power
the breathless throng.

The old man died, and years
passed on, and still
The young musician bent his
heart and will
To his dear toil. St. Bavon now
had grown
More dear to him, and even more
his own;
And as he left it every night he
prayed
A moment by the archway in the
shade,
Kneeling once more within the
sacred gloom
Where the White Maiden
watched upon her tomb.
His hopes of travel and a world-wide fame,
Cold Time had sobered, and his
fragile frame;
Content at last only in dreams
to roam,
Away from the tranquillity of
home;
Content that the poor dwellers
by his side
Saw in him but the gentle friend
and guide,
The patient counsellor in the
poor strife
And petty details of their common life,
Who comforted where woe and
grief might fall,

Nor slighted any pain or want as
    small,
But whose great heart took in
    and felt for all.

Still he grew famous; — many
    came to be
His pupils in the art of harmony.
One day a voice floated so pure
    and free
Above his music, that he turned
    to see
What angel sang, and saw before
    his eyes,
What made his heart leap with
    a strange surprise,
His own White Maiden, calm,
    and pure, and mild,
As in his childish dreams she
    sang and smiled;
Her eyes raised up to Heaven,
    her lips apart,
And music overflowing from her
    heart.
But the faint blush that tinged
    her cheek betrayed
No marble statue, but a living
    maid;
Perplexed and startled at his
    wondering look,
Her rustling score of Mozart's
    Sanctus shook;
The uncertain notes, like birds
    within a snare,
Fluttered and died upon the
    trembling air.

Days passed; each morning
    saw the maiden stand,
Her eyes cast down, her lesson in
    her hand,
Eager to study, never weary,
    while
Repaid by the approving word
    or smile
Of her kind master; days and
    months fled on;
One day the pupil from the choir
    was gone;
Gone to take light, and joy, and
    youth once more
Within the poor musician's hum-
    ble door;
And to repay, with gentle, hap-
    py art,
The debt so many owed his gen-
    erous heart.
And now, indeed, was one who
    knew and felt
That a great gift of God within
    him dwelt;
One who could listen, who could
    understand,
Whose idle work dropped from
    her slackened hand,
While with wet eyes entranced
    she stood, nor knew
How the melodious wingéd hours
    flew;
Who loved his art as none had
    loved before,
Yet prized the noble, tender spirit
    more.
While the great organ brought
    from far and near
Lovers of harmony to praise and
    hear,
Unmarked by aught save what
    filled every day,
Duty, and toil, and rest, years
    passed away:

And now by the low archway in
the shade
Beside her mother knelt a little
maid,
Who through the great cathedral
learned to roam,
Climb to the choir, and bring her
father home;
And stand, demure and solemn
by his side,
Patient till the last echo softly
died;
Then place her little hand in his,
and go
Down the dark winding stair to
where below
The mother knelt, within the
gathering gloom
Waiting and praying by the
Maiden's Tomb.

So their life went, until, one
winter's day,
Father and child came there
alone to pray,—
The mother, gentle soul, had fled
away!
Their life was altered now, and
yet the child
Forgot her passionate grief in
time, and smiled,
Half wondering why, when
spring's fresh breezes came,
To see her father was no more
the same.
Half guessing at the shadow of
his pain,
And then contented if he smiled
again,

A sad, cold smile, that passed in
tears away,
As reassured she ran once more
to play.
And now each year that added
grace to grace,
Fresh bloom and sunshine to the
young girl's face,
Brought a strange light in the
musician's eyes,
As if he saw some starry hope
arise,
Breaking upon the midnight of
sad skies.
It might be so: more feeble
year by year,
The wanderer to his resting-place
drew near.
One day the Gloria he could
play no more,
Echoed its grand rejoicing as of
yore;
His hands were clasped, his weary
head was laid,
Upon the tomb where the White
Maiden prayed;
Where the child's love first
dawned, his soul first spoke,
The old man's heart there
throbbed its last and broke.
The grave cathedral that had
nursed his youth,
Had helped his dreaming, and
had taught him truth,
Had seen his boyish grief and
baby tears,
And watched the sorrows and
the joys of years,
Had lit his fame and hope with
sacred rays,

And consecrated sad and happy days,
Had blessed his happiness, and soothed his pain,
Now took her faithful servant home again.

He rests in peace: some travellers mention yet
An organist whose name they all forget.
He has a holier and a nobler fame
By poor men's hearths, who love and bless the name
Of a kind friend; and in low tones to-day
Speak tenderly of him who passed away.
Too poor to help the daughter of their friend,
They grieved to see the little pittance end;
To see her toil and strive with cheerful heart,
To bear the lonely orphan's struggling part;
They grieved to see her go at last alone
To English kinsmen she had never known:
And here she came; the foreign girl soon found
Welcome, and love, and plenty all around,
And here she pays it back with earnest will,
By well-taught housewife watchfulness and skill;
Deep in her heart she holds her father's name,

And tenderly and proudly keeps his fame;
And while she works with thrifty Belgian care,
Past dreams of childhood float upon the air;
Some strange old chant, or solemn Latin hymn,
That echoed through the old cathedral dim,
When as a little child each day she went
To kneel and pray by an old tomb in Ghent.

THE ANGEL OF DEATH.

Why shouldst thou fear the beautiful angel, Death,
 Who waits thee at the portals of the skies,
Ready to kiss away thy struggling breath,
 Ready with gentle hand to close thine eyes?

How many a tranquil soul has passed away,
 Fled gladly from fierce pain and pleasures dim,
To the eternal splendor of the day;
 And many a troubled heart still calls for him.

Spirits too tender for the battle here
 Have turned from life, its hopes, its fears, its charms;

And children, shuddering at a
    world so drear,
  Have smiling passed away
    into his arms.

He whom thou fearest will, to
    ease its pain,
  Lay his cold hand upon thy
    aching heart:
Will soothe the terrors of thy
    troubled brain,
  And bid the shadow of earth's
    grief depart.

He will give back what neither
    time, nor might,
  Nor passionate prayer, nor
    longing hope restore,
(Dear as to long-blind eyes re-
    covered sight,)
  He will give back those who
    are gone before.

O, what were life, if life were
    all? Thine eyes
  Are blinded by their tears, or
    thou wouldst see
Thy treasures wait thee in the
    far-off skies,
  And Death, thy friend, will
    give them all to thee.

A DREAM.

ALL yesterday I was spinning,
  Sitting alone in the sun;
And the dream that I spun was
    so lengthy,
  It lasted till day was done.

I heeded not cloud or shadow
    That flitted over the hill,
  Or the humming-bees, or the
    swallows,
    Or the trickling of the rill.

I took the threads for my spin-
    ning,
  All of blue summer air,
And a flickering ray of sunlight
  Was woven in here and there.

The shadows grew longer and
    longer,
  The evening wind passed by,
And the purple splendor of
    sunset
  Was flooding the western sky.

But I could not leave my spin-
    ning,
  For so fair my dream had
    grown,
I heeded not, hour by hour,
  How the silent day had flown.

At last the gray shadows fell
    round me,
  And the night came dark and
    chill,
And I rose and ran down the
    valley,
  And left it all on the hill.

I went up the hill this morning
  To the place where my spin-
    ning lay,—
There was nothing but glistening
    dew-drops
  Remained of my dream to-day.

THE PRESENT.

Do not crouch to-day, and worship
　The old Past, whose life is fled;
Hush your voice to tender reverence;
　Crowned he lies, but cold and dead:
For the Present reigns our monarch,
　With an added weight of hours;
Honor her, for she is mighty!
Honor her, for she is ours!

See the shadows of his heroes
　Girt around her cloudy throne;
Every day the ranks are strengthened
　By great hearts to him unknown;
Noble things the great Past promised,
　Holy dreams, both strange and new;
But the Present shall fulfil them,
What he promised she shall do.

She inherits all his treasures,
　She is heir to all his fame,
And the light that lightens round her
　Is the lustre of his name;
She is wise with all his wisdom,
　Living on his grave she stands,
On her brow she bears his laurels,
　And his harvest in her hands.

Coward, can she reign and conquer
　If we thus her glory dim?
Let us fight for her as nobly
　As our fathers fought for him.
God, who crowns the dying ages,
　Bids her rule, and us obey,—
Bids us cast our lives before her,
Bids us serve the great To-day.

———

CHANGES.

Mourn, O rejoicing heart!
　The hours are flying;
Each one some treasure takes,
Each one some blossom breaks,
　And leaves it dying;
The chill dark night draws near,
Thy sun will soon depart,
　And leave thee sighing;
Then mourn, rejoicing heart,
　The hours are flying!

Rejoice, O grieving heart!
　The hours fly fast;
With each some sorrow dies,
With each some shadow flies,
　Until at last
The red dawn in the east
　Bids weary night depart,
　And pain is past.
Rejoice then, grieving heart,
　The hours fly fast!

———

STRIVE, WAIT, AND PRAY.

Strive; yet I do not promise
　The prize you dream of to-day

Will not fade when you think
    to grasp it,
And melt in your hand away;
But another and holier treasure,
    You would now perchance disdain,
Will come when your toil is over,
    And pay you for all your pain.

Wait; yet I do not tell you
    The hour you long for now
Will not come with its radiance
    vanished,
And a shadow upon its brow;
Yet far through the misty future,
    With a crown of starry light,
An hour of joy you know not
    Is winging her silent flight.

Pray; though the gift you ask for
    May never comfort your fears,
May never repay your pleading,
    Yet pray, and with hopeful tears;
An answer, not that you long for,
    But diviner, will come one day;
Your eyes are too dim to see it,
    Yet strive, and wait, and pray.

A LAMENT FOR THE SUMMER.

Moan, O ye Autumn Winds!
    Summer has fled,
The flowers have closed their
    tender leaves and die;
The lily's gracious head
All low must lie,
    Because the gentle Summer
    now is dead.

Grieve, O ye Autumn Winds!
    Summer lies low;
The rose's trembling leaves will
    soon be shed,
    For she that loved her so,
Alas! is dead,
    And one by one her loving
    children go.

Wail, O ye Autumn Winds!
    She lives no more,
The gentle Summer, with her
    balmy breath,
    Still sweeter than before
When nearer death,
    And brighter every day the
    smile she wore!

Mourn, mourn, O Autumn Winds,
    Lament and mourn;
How many half-blown buds must
    close and die;
    Hopes with the Summer born
All faded lie,
    And leave us desolate and
    Earth forlorn!

THE UNKNOWN GRAVE.

No name to bid us know
    Who rests below,
No word of death or birth,

GIVE ME THY HEART.

Only the grass's wave,
Over a mound of earth,
Over a nameless grave.

Did this poor wandering heart
In pain depart?
Longing, but all too late,
For the calm home again,
Where patient watchers wait,
And still will wait in vain.

Did mourners come in scorn,
And thus forlorn
Leave him, with grief and shame,
To silence and decay,
And hide the tarnished name
Of the unconscious clay?

It may be from his side
His loved ones died,
And, last of some bright band,
(Together now once more,)
He sought his home, the land
Where they had gone before.

No matter, — limes have made
As cool a shade,
And lingering breezes pass
As tenderly and slow,
As if beneath the grass
A monarch slept below.

No grief, though loud and deep,
Could stir that sleep;
And earth and heaven tell
Of rest that shall not cease,
Where the cold world's farewell
Fades into endless peace.

With echoing steps the worshippers
Departed one by one;
The organ's pealing voice was stilled,
The vesper hymn was done;
The shadows fell from roof and arch,
Dim was the incensed air,
One lamp alone, with trembling ray,
Told of the Presence there!

In the dark church she knelt alone;
Her tears were falling fast;
"Help, Lord," she cried, "the shades of death
Upon my soul are cast!
Have I not shunned the path of sin,
And chosen the better part?"—
What voice came through the sacred air?—
"*My child, give me thy Heart!*"

"Have I not laid before Thy shrine
My wealth, O Lord?" she cried;
"Have I kept aught of gems or gold,
To minister to pride?
Have I not bade youth's joys retire,
And vain delights depart?"—
But sad and tender was the voice,—
"*My child, give me thy Heart!*"

"Have I not, Lord, gone day by day
  Where Thy poor children dwell;
And carried help, and gold, and food?
  O Lord, Thou knowest it well!
From many a house, from many a soul,
  My hand bids care depart":—
More sad, more tender was the voice,—
  "*My child, give me thy Heart!*"

"Have I not worn my strength away
  With fast and penance sore?
Have I not watched and wept?" she cried;
  "Did Thy dear Saints do more?
Have I not gained Thy grace, O Lord,
  And won in Heaven my part?"—
It echoed louder in her soul,—
  "*My child, give me thy Heart!*

"For I have loved thee with a love
  No mortal heart can show;
A love so deep, my Saints in heaven
  Its depths can never know:
When pierced and wounded on the Cross,
  Man's sin and doom were mine,
I loved thee with undying love,
  Immortal and divine!

"I loved thee ere the skies were spread;
  My soul bears all thy pains;
To gain thy love my sacred Heart
  In earthly shrines remains:
Vain are thy offerings, vain thy sighs,
  Without one gift divine;
Give it, my child, thy Heart to me,
  And it shall rest in mine!"

In awe she listened, and the shade
  Passed from her soul away;
In low and trembling voice she cried,—
  "Lord, help me to obey!
Break Thou the chains of earth, O Lord,
  That bind and hold my heart;
Let it be Thine, and Thine alone,
  Let none with Thee have part.

"Send down, O Lord, Thy sacred fire!
  Consume and cleanse the sin
That lingers still within its depths:
  Let heavenly love begin.
That sacred flame Thy Saints have known,
  Kindle, O Lord, in me,
Thou above all the rest forever,
  And all the rest in Thee."

The blessing fell upon her soul;
  Her angel by her side

Knew that the hour of peace was
 come;
Her soul was purified:
The shadows fell from roof and
 arch,
Dim was the incensed air, —
But Peace went with her as she
 left
The sacred Presence there!

THE WAYSIDE INN.

A LITTLE past the village
 The Inn stood, low and white;
Green shady trees behind it,
 And an orchard on the right;
Where over the green paling
 The red-cheeked apples hung,
As if to watch how wearily
 The sign-board creaked and
  swung.

The heavy-laden branches,
 Over the road hung low,
Reflected fruit or blossom
 From the wayside well below;
Where children, drawing water,
 Looked up and paused to see,
Amid the apple-branches,
 A purple Judas-Tree.

The road stretched winding on-
  ward
 For many a weary mile, —
So dusty, foot-sore wanderers
 Would pause and rest awhile;
And panting horses halted,
 And travellers loved to tell

The quiet of the wayside inn,
 The orchard, and the well.

Here Maurice dwelt; and often
 The sunburnt boy would stand
Gazing upon the distance,
 And shading with his hand
His eyes, while watching vainly
 For travellers, who might need
His aid to loose the bridle,
 And tend the weary steed.

And once (the boy remembered
 That morning many a day, —
The dew lay on the hawthorn,
 The bird sang on the spray)
A train of horsemen, nobler
 Than he had seen before,
Up from the distance galloped,
 And halted at the door.

Upon a milk-white pony,
 Fit for a faery queen,
Was the loveliest little damsel
 His eyes had ever seen:
A serving-man was holding
 The leading rein, to guide
The pony and its mistress,
 Who cantered by his side.

Her sunny ringlets round her
 A golden cloud had made,
While her large hat was keeping
 Her calm blue eyes in shade;
One hand held fast the silke
  reins
 To keep her steed in check,
The other pulled his tangled
  mane,
 Or stroked his glossy neck.

And as the boy brought water,
  And loosed the rein, he heard
The sweetest voice that thanked
    him
In one low gentle word;
She turned her blue eyes from
    him,
  Looked up, and smiled to see
The hanging purple blossoms
  Upon the Judas-Tree;

And showed it with a gesture,
  Half pleading, half command,
Till he broke the fairest blossom,
  And laid it in her hand;
And she tied it to her saddle
  With a ribbon from her hair,
While her happy laugh rang
    gayly,
  Like silver on the air.

But the champing steeds were
    rested, —
The horsemen now spurred on,
And down the dusty highway
  They vanished and were gone.
Years passed, and many a traveller
  Paused at the old inn-door,
But the little milk-white pony
  And the child returned no
    more.

Years passed, the apple-branches
  A deeper shadow shed;
And many a time the Judas-Tree,
  Blossom and leaf, lay dead;
When on the loitering western
    breeze
  Came the bells' merry sound,

And flowery arches rose, and
    flags
  And banners waved around.

Maurice stood there expectant:
  The bridal train would stay
Some moments at the inn-door,
  The eager watchers say;
They come, — the cloud of dust
    draws near, —
'Mid all the state and pride,
He only sees the golden hair
  And blue eyes of the bride.

The same, yet, ah, still fairer;
  He knew the face once more
That bent above the pony's neck
  Years past at that inn-door:
Her shy and smiling eyes looked
    round,
  Unconscious of the place,
Unconscious of the eager gaze
  He fixed upon her face.

He plucked a blossom from the
    tree, —
  The Judas-Tree, — and cast
Its purple fragrance towards the
    Bride,
  A message from the Past.
The signal came, the horses
    plunged, —
Once more she smiled around:
The purple blossom in the dust
  Lay trampled on the ground.

Again the slow years fleeted,
  Their passage only known
By the height the Passion-flower
  Around the porch had grown;

And many a passing traveller
  Paused at the old inn-door,
But the bride, so fair and blooming,
  The bride returned no more.

One winter morning, Maurice,
  Watching the branches bare,
Rustling and waving dimly
  In the gray and misty air,
Saw blazoned on a carriage
  Once more the well-known shield,
The stars and azure fleurs-de-lis
  Upon a silver field.

He looked — was that pale woman,
  So grave, so worn, so sad,
The child, once young and smiling,
  The bride, once fair and glad?
What grief had dimmed that glory,
  And brought that dark eclipse
Upon her blue eyes' radiance,
  And paled those trembling lips?

What memory of past sorrow,
  What stab of present pain,
Brought that deep look of anguish,
  That watched the dismal rain,
That watched (with the absent spirit
  That looks, yet does not see)
The dead and leafless branches
  Upon the Judas-Tree?

The slow dark months crept onward
  Upon their icy way,

Till April broke in showers,
  And Spring smiled forth in May;
Upon the apple-blossoms
  The sun shone bright again,
When slowly up the highway
  Came a long funeral train.

The bells tolled slowly, sadly,
  For a noble spirit fled;
Slowly, in pomp and honor,
  They bore the quiet dead.
Upon a black-plumed charger
  One rode, who held a shield,
Where stars and azure fleurs-de-lis
  Shone on a silver field.

'Mid all that homage given
  To a fluttering heart at rest,
Perhaps an honest sorrow
  Dwelt only in one breast.
One by the inn-door standing
  Watched with fast-dropping tears
The long procession passing,
  And thought of bygone years.

The boyish, silent homage
  To child and bride unknown,
The pitying, tender sorrow
  Kept in his heart alone,
Now laid upon the coffin
  With a purple flower, might be
Told to the cold, dead sleeper; —
  The rest could only see
A fragrant purple blossom,
  Plucked from a Judas-Tree.

VOICES OF THE PAST.

You wonder that my tears should flow
  In listening to that simple strain;
That those unskilful sounds should fill
  My soul with joy and pain:
How can you tell what thoughts it stirs
  Within my heart again?

You wonder why that common phrase,
  So all unmeaning to your ear,
Should stay me in my merriest mood,
  And thrill my soul to hear:
How can you tell what ancient charm
  Has made me hold it dear?

You marvel that I turn away
  From all those flowers so fair and bright,
And gaze at this poor herb, till tears
  Arise and dim my sight:
You cannot tell how every leaf
  Breathes of a past delight.

You smile to see me turn and speak
  With one whose converse you despise;
You do not see the dreams of old
  That with his voice arise:
How can you tell what links have made
  Him sacred in my eyes?

O, these are Voices of the Past,
  Links of a broken chain,
Wings that can bear me back to Times
  Which cannot come again;
Yet God forbid that I should lose
  The echoes that remain!

THE DARK SIDE.

Thou hast done well, perhaps,
  To lift the bright disguise,
And lay the bitter truth
  Before our shrinking eyes;
When evil crawls below
  What seems so pure and fair,
Thine eyes are keen and true
  To find the serpent there:
And yet — I turn away;
  Thy task is not divine, —
The evil angels look
  On earth with eyes like thine.

Thou hast done well, perhaps,
  To show how closely wound
Dark threads of sin and self
  With our best deeds are found,
How great and noble hearts,
  Striving for lofty aims,
Have still some earthly chord
  A meaner spirit claims;
And yet — although thy task
  Is well and fairly done —
Methinks for such as thou
  There is a holier one.

Shadows there are, who dwell
  Among us, yet apart,

Deaf to the claim of God,
  Or kindly human heart;
Voices of earth and heaven
  Call, but they turn away,
And Love, through such black
    night
Can see no hope of day;
And yet — our eyes are dim,
  And thine are keener far:
Then gaze till thou canst see
  The glimmer of some star.

The black stream flows along
  Whose waters we despise, —
Show us reflected there
  Some fragment of the skies;
'Neath tangled thorns and briers,
  (The task is fit for thee,)
Seek for the hidden flowers,
  We are too blind to see;
Then will I thy great gift
  A crown and blessing call;
Angels look thus on men,
  And God sees good in all!

A FIRST SORROW.

Arise! this day shall shine,
  Forevermore,
To thee a star divine,
  On Time's dark shore.

Till now thy soul has been
  All glad and gay:
Bid it awake, and look
  At grief to-day!

No shade has come between
  Thee and the sun;
Like some long childish dream
  Thy life has run:

But now the stream has reached
  A dark, deep sea,
And Sorrow, dim and crowned,
  Is waiting thee.

Each of God's soldiers bears
  A sword divine:
Stretch out thy trembling hands
  To-day for thine!

To each anointed Priest
  God's summons came:
O Soul, he speaks to-day,
  And calls thy name.

Then, with slow reverent step,
  And beating heart,
From out thy joyous days
  Thou must depart.

And, leaving all behind,
  Come forth alone,
To join the chosen band
  Around the throne.

Raise up thine eyes — be strong,
  Nor cast away
The crown that God has given
  Thy soul to-day!

MURMURS.

Why wilt thou make bright music
  Give forth a sound of pain?
Why wilt thou weave fair flowers
  Into a weary chain?

Why turn each cool gray shadow
　　Into a world of fears?
Why say the winds are wailing?
　　Why call the dew-drops tears?

The voices of happy nature,
　　And the Heaven's sunny gleam,
Reprove thy sick heart's fancies,
　　Upbraid thy foolish dream.

Listen, and I will tell thee
　　The song Creation sings,
From the humming of bees in the heather,
　　To the flutter of angels' wings.

An echo rings forever,
　　The sound can never cease;
It speaks to God of glory,
　　It speaks to Earth of peace.

Not alone did angels sing it
　　To the poor shepherds' ear;
But the spheréd Heavens chant it,
　　While listening ages hear.

Above thy peevish wailing
　　Rises that holy song;
Above Earth's foolish clamor,
　　Above the voice of wrong.

No creature of God's too lowly
　　To murmur peace and praise:
When the starry nights grow silent,
　　Then speak the sunny days.

So leave thy sick heart's fancies,
　　And lend thy little voice
To the silver song of glory
　　That bids the world rejoice.

GIVE.

See the rivers flowing
　　Downwards to the sea,
Pouring all their treasures
　　Bountiful and free:
Yet to help their giving
　　Hidden springs arise;
Or, if need be, showers
　　Feed them from the skies!

Watch the princely flowers
　　Their rich fragrance spread,
Load the air with perfumes,
　　From their beauty shed:
Yet their lavish spending
　　Leaves them not in dearth,
With fresh life replenished
　　By their mother earth!

Give thy heart's best treasures,—
　　From fair Nature learn;
Give thy love—and ask not,
　　Wait not a return!
And the more thou spendest
　　From thy little store,
With a double bounty,
　　God will give thee more.

MY JOURNAL.

It is a dreary evening;
　　The shadows rise and fall:
With strange and ghostly changes,
　　They flicker on the wall.

Make the charred logs burn brighter;
　　I will show you, by their blaze,

The half-forgotten record
　Of bygone things and days.

Bring here the ancient volume;
　The clasp is old and worn,
The gold is dim and tarnished,
　And the faded leaves are torn.

The dust has gathered on it,—
　There are so few who care
To read what Time has written
　Of joy and sorrow there.

Look at the first fair pages;
　Yes, I remember all:
The joys now seem so trivial,
　The griefs so poor and small.

Let us read the dreams of glory
　That childish fancy made;
Turn to the next few pages,
　And see how soon they fade.

Here, where still waiting, dreaming,
　For some ideal Life,
The young heart all unconscious
　Had entered on the strife.

See how this page is blotted:
　What, could those tears be mine?
How coolly I can read you
　Each blurred and trembling line!

Now I can reason calmly,
　And, looking back again,
Can see divinest meaning
　Threading each separate pain.

Here strong resolve—how broken;
　Rash hope, and foolish fear,
And prayers, which God in pity
　Refused to grant or hear.

Nay, I will turn the pages
　To where the tale is told
Of how a dawn diviner
　Flushed the dark clouds with gold.

And see, that light has gilded
　The story,—nor shall set;
And, though in mist and shadow,
　You know I see it yet.

Here—well, it does not matter,
　I promised to read all;
I know not why I falter,
　Or why my tears should fall;

You see each grief is noted;
　Yet it was better so—
I can rejoice to-day—the pain
　Was over, long ago.

I read—my voice is failing,
　But you can understand
How the heart beat that guided
　This weak and trembling hand.

Pass over that long struggle,
　Read where the comfort came,
Where the first time is written
　Within the book your name.

Again it comes, and oftener,
　Linked, as it now must be,
With all the joy or sorrow
　That Life may bring to me.

So all the rest — you know it:
  Now shut the clasp again,
And put aside the record
  Of bygone hours of pain.

The dust shall gather on it,
  I will not read it more:
Give me your hand — what was it
  We were talking of before?

I know not why — but tell me
  Of something gay and bright.
It is strange — my heart is heavy,
  And my eyes are dim to-night.

A CHAIN.

The bond that links our souls together;
Will it last through stormy weather?
Will it moulder and decay
As the long hours pass away?
Will it stretch if Fate divide us,
When dark and weary hours have tried us?
O, if it look too poor and slight,
Let us break the links to-night!

It was not forged by mortal hands,
Or clasped with golden bars and bands;
Save thine and mine, no other eyes
The slender link can recognize:
In the bright light it seems to fade —
And it is hidden in the shade;
While Heaven nor Earth have never heard,
Or solemn vow, or plighted word.

Yet what no mortal hand could make,
No mortal power can ever break;
What words or vows could never do,
No words or vows can make untrue;
And if to other hearts unknown
The dearer and the more our own,
Because too sacred and divine
For other eyes, save thine and mine.

And see, though slender, it is made
Of Love and Trust, and can they fade?
While, if too slight it seem, to bear
The breathings of the summer air,
We know that it could bear the weight
Of a most heavy heart of late,
And as each day and hour flew
The stronger for its burden grew.

And, too, we know and feel again
It has been sanctified by pain,
For what God deigns to try with sorrow
He means not to decay to-morrow;
But through that fiery trial last
When earthly ties and bonds are past;

What slighter things dare not
  endure
Will make our Love more safe
  and pure.

Love shall be purified by Pain,
And Pain be soothed by Love
  again:
So let us now take heart and go
Cheerfully on, through joy and
  woe;
No change the summer sun can
  bring,
Or the inconstant skies of spring,
Or the bleak winter's stormy
  weather,
For we shall meet them, Love,
  together!

THE PILGRIMS.

The way is long and dreary,
The path is bleak and bare;
Our feet are worn and weary,
But we will not despair.
More heavy was Thy burden,
More desolate Thy way; —
O Lamb of God who takest
The sin of the world away,
  Have mercy on us.

The snows lie thick around us
In the dark and gloomy night;
And the tempest wails above us,
And the stars have hid their
  light;
But blacker was the darkness
Round Calvary's Cross that
  day; —

O Lamb of God who takest
The sin of the world away,
  Have mercy on us.

Our hearts are faint with sorrow,
Heavy and hard to bear;
For we dread the bitter morrow,
But we will not despair:
Thou knowest all our anguish,
And Thou wilt bid it cease, —
O Lamb of God who takest
The sin of the world away,
  Give us Thy Peace!

INCOMPLETENESS.

Nothing resting in its own
  completeness
Can have worth or beauty: but
  alone
Because it leads and tends to
  further sweetness,
Fuller, higher, deeper than its
  own.

Spring's real glory dwells not
  in the meaning,
Gracious though it be, of her
  blue hours;
But is hidden in her tender leaning
To the Summer's richer wealth
  of flowers.

Dawn is fair, because the mists
  fade slowly
Into Day, which floods the world
  with light;

Twilight's mystery is so sweet
   and holy
Just because it ends in starry
   Night.

Childhood's smiles unconscious
   graces borrow
From Strife, that in a far-off future lies;
And angel glances (veiled now
   by Life's sorrow)
Draw our hearts to some belovéd
   eyes.

Life is only bright when it pro-
   ceedeth
Towards a truer, deeper Life
   above;
Human Love is sweetest when it
   leadeth
To a more divine and perfect
   Love.

Learn the mystery of Progression
   duly:
Do not call each glorious change,
   Decay;
But know we only hold our
   treasures truly,
When it seems as if they passed
   away.

Nor dare to blame God's gifts
   for incompleteness;
In that want their beauty lies:
   they roll
Towards some infinite depth of
   love and sweetness,
Bearing onward man's reluctant
   soul.

A LEGEND OF BREGENZ.

Girt round with rugged mountains
   The fair Lake Constance lies;
In her blue heart reflected
   Shine back the starry skies;
And, watching each white cloudlet
   Float silently and slow,
You think a piece of Heaven
   Lies on our earth below!

Midnight is there: and Silence,
   Enthroned in Heaven, looks down
Upon her own calm mirror,
   Upon a sleeping town:
For Bregenz, that quaint city
   Upon the Tyrol shore,
Has stood above Lake Constance
   A thousand years and more.

Her battlements and towers,
   From off their rocky steep,
Have cast their trembling shadow
   For ages on the deep:
Mountain, and lake, and valley,
   A sacred legend know,
Of how the town was saved, one night,
   Three hundred years ago.

Far from her home and kindred,
   A Tyrol maid had fled,
To serve in the Swiss valleys,
   And toil for daily bread;
And every year that fleeted
   So silently and fast,
Seemed to bear farther from her
   The memory of the Past.

She served kind, gentle masters,
　Nor asked for rest or change;
Her friends seemed no more new
　　ones,
　Their speech seemed no more
　　strange;
And when she led her cattle
　To pasture every day,
She ceased to look and wonder
　On which side Bregenz lay.

She spoke no more of Bregenz,
　With longing and with tears;
Her Tyrol home seemed faded
　In a deep mist of years;
She heeded not the rumors
　Of Austrian war and strife;
Each day she rose, contented,
　To the calm toils of life.

Yet, when her master's children
　Would clustering round her
　　stand,
She sang them ancient ballads
　Of her own native land;
And when at morn and evening
　She knelt before God's throne,
The accents of her childhood
　Rose to her lips alone.

And so she dwelt: the valley
　More peaceful year by year;
When suddenly strange portents
　Of some great deed seemed
　　near.
The golden corn was bending
　Upon its fragile stock,
While farmers, heedless of their
　　fields,
　Paced up and down in talk.

The men seemed stern and al-
　　tered,
　With looks cast on the ground;
With anxious faces, one by one,
　The women gathered round;
All talk of flax, or spinning,
　Or work, was put away;
The very children seemed afraid
　To go alone to play.

One day, out in the meadow
　With strangers from the town,
Some secret plan discussing,
　The men walked up and down.
Yet now and then seemed watch-
　　ing
　A strange uncertain gleam,
That looked like lances 'mid the
　　trees,
　That stood below the stream.

At eve they all assembled,
　Then care and doubt were fled;
With jovial laugh they feasted;
　The board was nobly spread.
The elder of the village
　Rose up, his glass in hand,
And cried, "We drink the down-
　　fall
　Of an accursed land!

"The night is growing darker,
　Ere one more day is flown,
Bregenz, our foemen's strong-
　　hold,
　Bregenz shall be our own!"
The women shrank in terror,
　(Yet Pride, too, had her part,)
But one poor Tyrol maiden
　Felt death within her heart.

Before her stood fair Bregenz;
  Once more her towers arose;
What were the friends beside her?
  Only her country's foes!
The faces of her kinsfolk,
  The days of childhood flown,
The echoes of her mountains,
  Reclaimed her as their own!

Nothing she heard around her,
  (Though shouts rang forth again,)
Gone were the green Swiss valleys,
  The pasture, and the plain;
Before her eyes one vision,
  And in her heart one cry,
That said, "Go forth, save Bregenz,
  And then, if need be, die!"

With trembling haste and breathless,
  With noiseless step, she sped;
Horses and weary cattle
  Were standing in the shed;
She loosed the strong, white charger,
  That fed from out her hand,
She mounted, and she turned his head
  Towards her native land.

Out — out into the darkness —
  Faster, and still more fast;
The smooth grass flies behind her,
  The chestnut wood is past;
She looks up; clouds are heavy:
  Why is her steed so slow? —
Scarcely the wind beside them
  Can pass them as they go.

"Faster!" she cries, "O faster!"
  Eleven the church-bells chime:
"O God," she cries, "help Bregenz,
  And bring me there in time!"
But louder than bells' ringing,
  Or lowing of the kine,
Grows nearer in the midnight
  The rushing of the Rhine.

Shall not the roaring waters
  Their headlong gallop check?
The steed draws back in terror,
  She leans upon his neck
To watch the flowing darkness;
  The bank is high and steep;
One pause — he staggers forward,
  And plunges in the deep.

She strives to pierce the blackness,
  And looser throws the rein;
Her steed must breast the waters
  That dash above his mane.
How gallantly, how nobly,
  He struggles through the foam,
And see — in the far distance
  Shine out the lights of home!

Up the steep banks he bears her,
  And now, they rush again
Towards the heights of Bregenz,
  That tower above the plain.
They reach the gate of Bregenz,
  Just as the midnight rings,
And out come serf and soldier
  To meet the news she brings.

Bregenz is saved! Ere daylight
  Her battlements are manned;

Defiance greets the army
  That marches on the land.
And if to deeds heroic
  Should endless fame be paid,
Bregenz does well to honor
  The noble Tyrol maid.

Three hundred years are vanished,
  And yet upon the hill
An old stone gateway rises,
  To do her honor still.
And there, when Bregenz women
  Sit spinning in the shade,
They see in quaint old carving
  The Charger and the Maid.

And when, to guard old Bregenz,
  By gateway, street, and tower,
The warder paces all night long
  And calls each passing hour;
"Nine," "ten," "eleven," he cries aloud,
  And then (O crown of Fame!)
When midnight pauses in the skies,
  He calls the maiden's name!

A FAREWELL.

Farewell, O dream of mine!
  I dare not stay;
The hour is come, and time
  Will not delay:
Pleasant and dear to me
  Wilt thou remain;
No future hour
  Brings thee again.

She stands, the Future dim,
  And draws me on,
And shows me dearer joys, —
  But thou art gone!
Treasures and Hopes more fair
  Bears she for me,
And yet I linger,
  O dream, with thee!

Other and brighter days
  Perhaps she brings;
Deeper and holier songs
  Perchance she sings;
But thou and I, fair time,
  We too must sever: —
O dream of mine,
  Farewell forever!

SOWING AND REAPING.

Sow with a generous hand;
  Pause not for toil or pain;
Weary not through the heat of summer,
  Weary not through the cold spring rain;
But wait till the autumn comes
  For the sheaves of golden grain.

Scatter the seed, and fear not,
  A table will be spread;
What matter if you are too weary
  To eat your hard-earned bread!
Sow, while the earth is broken,
  For the hungry must be fed.

Sow;—while the seeds are lying
  In the warm earth's bosom
    deep,
And your warm tears fall upon
    it,—
  They will stir in their quiet
    sleep;
And the green blades rise the
    quicker,
  Perchance, for the tears you
    weep.

Then sow;—for the hours are
    fleeting,
  And the seed must fall to-day;
And care not what hands shall
    reap it,
  Or if you shall have passed
    away
Before the waving cornfields
  Shall gladden the sunny day.

Sow; and look onward, upward,
  Where the starry light appears,—
Where, in spite of the coward's
    doubting,
  Or your own heart's trembling
    fears,
You shall reap in joy the harvest
  You have sown to-day in tears.

THE STORM.

THE tempest rages wild and
    high,
The waves lift up their voice and
    cry
Fierce answers to the angry
    sky,—
    Miserere Domine.

Through the black night and
    driving rain
A ship is struggling, all in
    vain,
To live upon the stormy main;—
    Miserere Domine.

The thunders roar, the lightnings glare,
Vain is it now to strive or dare;
A cry goes up of great despair,—
    Miserere Domine.

The stormy voices of the main,
The moaning wind and pelting
    rain
Beat on the nursery windowpane:—
    Miserere Domine.

Warm curtained was the little
    bed,
Soft pillowed was the little
    head;
"The storm will wake the child,"
    they said:—
    Miserere Domine.

Cowering among his pillows
    white
He prays, his blue eyes dim with
    fright,
"Father, save those at sea tonight!"—
    Miserere Domine.

The morning shone all clear and gay,
On a ship at anchor in the bay,
And on a little child at play, —
    Gloria tibi Domine!

WORDS.

Words are lighter than the cloud-foam
  Of the restless ocean spray;
Vainer than the trembling shadow
  That the next hour steals away.
By the fall of summer rain-drops
  Is the air as deeply stirred;
And the rose-leaf that we tread on
  Will outlive a word.

Yet, on the dull silence breaking
  With a lightning flash, a Word,
Bearing endless desolation
  On its blighting wings, I heard:
Earth can forge no keener weapon,
  Dealing surer death and pain,
And the cruel echo answered
  Through long years again.

I have known one word hang starlike
  O'er a dreary waste of years,
And it only shone the brighter
  Looked at through a mist of tears;
While a weary wanderer gathered
  Hope and heart on Life's dark way,
By its faithful promise, shining
  Clearer day by day.

I have known a spirit, calmer
  Than the calmest lake, and clear
As the heavens that gazed upon it,
  With no wave of hope or fear;
But a storm had swept across it,
  And its deepest depths were stirred,
(Never, never more to slumber,)
  Only by a word.

I have known a word more gentle
  Than the breath of summer air;
In a listening heart it nestled,
  And it lived forever there.
Not the beating of its prison
  Stirred it ever, night or day;
Only with the heart's last throbbing
  Could it fade away.

Words are mighty, words are living:
  Serpents with their venomous stings,
Or bright angels, crowding round us,
  With heaven's light upon their wings:
Every word has its own spirit,

True or false, that never dies;
Every word man's lips have ut-
    tered
  Echoes in God's skies.

A LOVE TOKEN.

Do you grieve no costly offer-
    ing
  To the Lady you can make?
One there is, and gifts less worthy
  Queens have stooped to take.

Take a Heart of virgin silver,
  Fashion it with heavy blows,
Cast it into Love's hot furnace
  When it fiercest glows.

With Pain's sharpest point trans-
    fix it,
  And then carve, in letters fair,
Tender dreams and quaint de-
    vices,
  Fancies sweet and rare.

Set within it Hope's blue sap-
    phire,
  Many-changing opal fears,
Blood-red ruby-stones of daring,
  Mixed with pearly tears.

And when you have wrought and
    labored
  Till the gift is all complete,
You may humbly lay your offer-
    ing
  At the Lady's feet.

Should her mood perchance be
    gracious,
  With disdainful, smiling pride,
She will place it with the trinkets
  Glittering at her side.

A TRYST WITH DEATH.

I AM footsore and very weary,
  But I travel to meet a Friend:
The way is long and dreary,
  But I know that it soon must
    end.

He is travelling fast like the
    whirlwind,
  And though I creep slowly on,
We are drawing nearer, nearer,
  And the journey is almost done.

Through the heat of many sum-
    mers,
  Through many a springtime
    rain,
Through long autumns and weary
    winters,
  I have hoped to meet him, in
    vain.

I know that he will not fail me,
  So I count every hour chime,
Every throb of my own heart's
    beating,
  That tells of the flight of Time.

On the day of my birth he
    plighted
  His kingly word to me: —

I have seen him in dreams so often,
  That I know what his smile must be.

I have toiled through the sunny woodland,
  Through fields that basked in the light;
And through the lone paths in the forest
  I crept in the dead of night.

I will not fear at his coming,
  Although I must meet him alone;
He will look in my eyes so gently,
  And take my hand in his own.

Like a dream all my toil will vanish,
  When I lay my head on his breast:
But the journey is very weary,
  And he only can give me rest!

FIDELIS.

You have taken back the promise
  That you spoke so long ago;
Taken back the heart you gave me, —
  I must even let it go.
Where Love once has breathed,
    Pride dieth:
  So I struggled, but in vain,
First to keep the links together,
  Then to piece the broken chain.

But it might not be — so freely
  All your friendship I restore,
And the heart that I had taken
  As my own forevermore.
No shade of reproach shall touch you,
  Dread no more a claim from me:
But I will not have you fancy
  That I count myself as free.

I am bound by the old promise;
  What can break that golden chain?
Not even the words that you have spoken,
  Or the sharpness of my pain:
Do you think, because you fail me
  And draw back your hand to-day,
That from out the heart I gave you
  My strong love can fade away?

It will live. No eyes may see it;
  In my soul it will lie deep,
Hidden from all; but I shall feel it
  Often stirring in its sleep.
So remember, that the friendship,
  Which you now think poor and vain,
Will endure in hope and patience,
  Till you ask for it again.

Perhaps in some long twilight hour,
  Like those we have known of old,

When past shadows gather round
  you,
  And your present friends grow
    cold,
You may stretch your hands out
    towards me, —
  Ah! you will — I know not
    when —
I shall nurse my love and keep it
  Faithfully, for you, till then.

A SHADOW.

What lack the valleys and
    mountains
  That once were green and gay?
What lack the babbling foun-
    tains?
  Their voice is sad to-day.
    Only the sound of a voice,
    Tender and sweet and low,
    That made the earth rejoice,
    A year ago!

What lack the tender flowers?
  A shadow is on the sun:
What lack the merry hours,
  That I long that they were
    done?
    Only two smiling eyes,
    That told of joy and mirth;
    They are shining in the skies,
    I mourn on earth!

What lacks my heart, that makes
    it
  So weary and full of pain,
That trembling Hope forsakes it,
  Never to come again?

Only another heart,
  Tender and all mine own,
In the still grave it lies;
  I weep alone!

THE SAILOR BOY.

My Life you ask of? why, you
    know
Full soon my little Life is told;
It has had no great joy or woe,
For I am only twelve years old.
Erelong I hope I shall have been
On my first voyage, and wonders
    seen.
Some princess I may help to free
From pirates on a far-off sea;
Or, on some desert isle be left,
Of friends and shipmates all bereft.

For the first time I venture
    forth
From our blue mountains of the
    north.
My kinsman kept the lodge that
    stood
Guarding the entrance near the
    wood,
By the stone gateway gray and
    old,
With quaint devices carved about,
And broken shields; while drag-
    ons bold
Glared on the common world
    without:
And the long trembling ivy spray
Half hid the centuries' decay.
In solitude and silence grand

The castle towered above the land:
The castle of the Earl, whose name
(Wrapped in old bloody legends)
came
Down through the times when Truth and Right
Bent down to arméd Pride and Might.
He owned the country far and near;
And, for some weeks in every year,
(When the brown leaves were falling fast
And the long, lingering autumn past,)
He would come down to hunt the deer,
With hound and horse in splendid pride.
The story lasts the live-long year,
The peasant's winter evening fills,
When he is gone and they abide
In the lone quiet of their hills.

I longed, too, for the happy night,
When, all with torches flaring bright,
The crowding villagers would stand,
A patient, eager, waiting band,
Until the signal ran like flame,
"They come!" and, slackening speed, they came.
Outriders first, in pomp and state,
Pranced on their horses through the gate;
Then the four steeds as black as night,
All decked with trappings blue and white,
Drew through the crowd that opened wide,
The Earl and Countess side by side.
The stern grave Earl, with formal smile
And glistening eyes and stately pride,
Could ne'er my childish gaze beguile
From the fair presence by his side.
The lady's soft sad glance, her eyes,
(Like stars that shone in summer skies,)
Her pure white face so calmly bent,
With gentle greetings round her sent;
Her look, that always seemed to gaze
Where the blue past had closed again
Over some happy shipwrecked days,
With all their freight of love and pain:
She did not even seem to see
The little lord upon her knee.
And yet he was like angel fair,
With rosy cheeks and golden hair,
That fell on shoulders white as snow:

But the blue eyes that shone below
His clustering rings of auburn
  curls
Were not his mother's, but the
  Earl's.

I feared the Earl, so cold and
  grim,
I never dared be seen by him.
When through our gate he used
  to ride,
My kinsman Walter bade me
  hide;
He said he was so stern.
So, when the hunt came past
  our way,
I always hastened to obey,
Until I heard the bugles play
The notes of their return.
But she, — my very heart-strings
  stir
Whene'er I speak or think of
  her, —
The whole wide world could
  never see
A noble lady such as she,
So full of angel charity.

Strange things of her our
  neighbors told
In the long winter evenings cold,
Around the fire. They would
  draw near
And speak half-whispering, as in
  fear;
As if they thought the Earl
  could hear
Their treason 'gainst his name.
They thought the story that his
  pride
Had stooped to wed a low-born
  bride,
A stain upon his fame.
Some said 't was false; there
  could not be
Such blot on his nobility:
But others vowed that they had
  heard
The actual story word for word,
From one who well my lady
  knew,
And had declared the story true.

In a far village, little known,
She dwelt — so ran the tale —
  alone.
A widowed bride, yet, oh! so
  bright,
Shone through the mist of grief,
  her charms;
They said it was the loveliest
  sight —
She with her baby in her arms.
The Earl, one summer morning,
  rode
By the sea-shore where she
  abode;
Again he came — that vision
  sweet
Drew him reluctant to her feet.
Fierce must the struggle in his
  heart
Have been, between his love and
  pride,
Until he chose that wondrous
  part,
To ask her to become his bride.
Yet, ere his noble name she bore,
He made her vow that nevermore
She would behold her child again,

But hide his name and hers from men.
The trembling promise duly spoken,
All links of the low past were broken;
And she arose to take her stand
Amid the nobles of the land.
Then all would wonder — could it be
That one so lowly born as she,
Raised to such height of bliss, should seem
Still living in some weary dream?
'T is true she bore with calmest grace
The honors of her lofty place,
Yet never smiled, in peace or joy,
Not even to greet her princely boy.
She heard, with face of white despair,
The cannon thunder through the air,
That she had given the Earl an heir.
Nay, even more, (they whispered low,
As if they scarce durst fancy so,)
That, through her lofty wedded life,
No word, no tone, betrayed the wife.
Her look seemed ever in the past;
Never to him it grew more sweet;
The self-same weary glance she cast
Upon the greyhound at her feet,
As upon him, who bade her claim
The crowning honor of his name.

This gossip, if old Walter heard,
He checked it with a scornful word:
I never durst such tales repeat;
He was too serious and discreet
To speak of what his lord might do;
Besides, he loved my lady too.
And many a time, I recollect,
They were together in the wood;
He, with an air of grave respect,
And earnest look, uncovered stood.
And though their speech I never heard,
(Save now and then a louder word,)
I saw he spake as none but one
She loved and trusted durst have done;
For oft I watched them in the shade
That the close forest branches made,
Till slanting golden sunbeams came
And smote the fir-trees into flame,
A radiant glory round her lit,
Then down her white robes seemed to flit,
Gilding the brown leaves on the ground,
And all the waving ferns around.

While by some gloomy pine she leant
And he in earnest talk would stand,
I saw the tear-drops, as she bent,
Fall on the flowers in her hand.—
Strange as it seemed and seems to be,
That one so sad, so cold as she,
Could love a little child like me,
Yet so it was. I never heard
Such tender words as she would say,
And murmurs, sweeter than a word,
Would breathe upon me as I lay.
While I, in smiling joy, would rest,
For hours, my head upon her breast.
Our neighbors said that none could see
In me the common childish charms,
(So grave and still I used to be,)
And yet she held me in her arms,
In a fond clasp, so close, so tight,
I often dream of it at night.
She bade me tell her all,— no other
My childish thoughts e'er cared to know:
For I— I never knew my mother;
I was an orphan long ago.
And I could all my fancies pour,
That gentle, loving face before.
She liked to hear me tell her all;
How that day I had climbed the tree,
To make the largest fir-cones fall;
And how one day I hoped to be
A sailor on the deep blue sea,—
She loved to hear it all!

Then wondrous things she used to tell,
Of the strange dreams that she had known.
I used to love to hear them well,
If only for her sweet low tone,
Sometimes so sad, although I knew -
That such things never could be true.
One day she told me such a tale
It made me grow all cold and pale,
The fearful thing she told!
Of a poor woman mad and wild
Who coined the life-blood of her child,
And, tempted by a fiend, had sold
The heart out of her breast for gold.
But when she saw me frightened seem,
She smiled, and said it was a dream.
When I look back and think of her,
My very heart-strings seem to stir;
How kind, how fair she was, how good,
I cannot tell you. If I could,

You, too, would love her. The
  mere thought
Of her great love for me has
  brought
Tears in my eyes: though far
  away,
It seems as it were yesterday.
And just as when I look on high,
Through the blue silence of the
  sky,
Fresh stars shine out, and more
  and more,
Where I could see so few before;
So, the more steadily I gaze
Upon those far-off misty days,
Fresh words, fresh tones, fresh
  memories start
Before my eyes and in my heart.
I can remember how one day
(Talking in silly childish way)
I said how happy I should be
If I were like her son, — as fair,
With just such bright blue eyes
  as he,
And such long locks of golden
  hair.
A strange smile on her pale face
  broke,
And in strange, solemn words
  she spoke:
  "My own, my darling one, —
    no, no!
I love you, far, far better so.
I would not change the look you
  bear,
Or one wave of your dark brown
  hair.
The mere glance of your sunny
  eyes,
Deep in my deepest soul I prize
Above that baby fair!
Not one of all the Earl's proud
  line
In beauty ever matched with
  thine;
And, 't is by thy dark locks thou
  art
Bound even faster round my
  heart,
And made more wholly mine!"
And then she paused, and weep-
  ing said,
"You are like one who now is
  dead, —
Who sleeps in a far-distant grave.
O, may God grant that you may
  be
As noble and as good as he,
As gentle and as brave!"
Then in my childish way I cried,
"The one you tell me of who died,
Was he as noble as the Earl?"
I see her red lips scornful curl,
I feel her hold my hand again,
So tightly, that I shrink in
  pain, —
I seem to hear her say,
"He whom I tell you of, who
  died,
He was so noble and so gay,
So generous and so brave,
That the proud Earl by his dear
  side
Would look a craven slave."
She paused; then, with a quiv-
  ering sigh,
She laid her hand upon my
  brow:
"Live like him, darling, and so
  die.

Remember that he tells you now,
True peace, real honor, and con-
tent,
In cheerful, pious toil abide;
That gold and splendor are but
sent
To curse our vanity and pride."

One day some childish fever
pain
Burnt in my veins and fired my
brain.
Moaning, I turned from side to
side;
And, sobbing in my bed, I cried,
Till night in calm and darkness
crept
Around me, and at last I slept.
When suddenly I woke to see
The Lady bending over me.
The drops of cold November rain
Were falling from her long, damp
hair;
Her anxious eyes were dim with
pain;
Yet she looked wondrous fair.
Arrayed for some great feast she
came,
With stones that shone and burnt
like flame;
Wound round her neck, like some
bright snake,
And set like stars within her hair,
They sparkled so, they seemed
to make
A glory everywhere.
I felt her tears upon my face,
Her kisses on my eyes;
And a strange thought I could
not trace

I felt within my heart arise;
And, half in feverish pain, I
said:
"O if my mother were not
dead!"
And Walter bade me sleep; but
she
Said, "Is it not the same to thee
That *I* watch by thy bed?"
I answered her, "I love you,
too;
But it can never be the same;
She was no Countess like to you,
Nor wore such sparkling stones
of flame."
O the wild look of fear and
dread!
The cry she gave of bitter woe!
I often wonder what I said
To make her moan and shudder
so.
Through the long night she tend-
ed me
With such sweet care and charity.
But I should weary you to tell
All that I know and love so well:
Yet one night more stands out
alone
With a sad sweetness all its own.

The wind blew loud that drea-
ry night:
Its wailing voice I well remem-
ber;
The stars shone out so large and
bright
Upon the frosty fir-boughs white
That dreary night of cold Decem-
ber.
I saw old Walter silent stand,

Watching the soft, white flakes
of snow
With looks I could not under-
stand,
Of strange perplexity and woe.
At last he turned and took my
hand,
And said the Countess just had
sent
To bid us come; for she would
fain
See me once more, before she
went
Away — never to come again.
We came in silence through the
wood
(Our footfall was the only sound)
To where the great white castle
stood,
With darkness shadowing it
around.
Breathless, we trod with cautious
care
Up the great echoing marble
stair;
Trembling, by Walter's hand I
held,
Scared by the splendors I be-
held:
Now thinking, "Should the Earl
appear!"
Now looking up with giddy fear
To the dim, vaulted roof that
spread
Its gloomy arches overhead.
Long corridors we softly passed,
(My heart was beating loud and
fast,)
And reached the Lady's room at
last:

A strange, faint odor seemed to
weigh
Upon the dim and darkened air;
One shaded lamp, with softened
ray,
Scarce showed the gloomy splen-
dor there.
The dull red brands were burn-
ing low,
And yet a fitful gleam of light
Would now and then, with sud-
den glow,
Start forth, then sink again in
night.
I gazed around, yet half in fear,
Till Walter told me to draw
near:
And in the strange and flicker-
ing light,
Towards the Lady's bed I crept;
All folded round with snowy
white,
She lay; (one would have said
she slept;)
So still the look of that white face,
It seemed as it were carved in
stone,
I paused before I dared to place
Within her cold white hand my
own.
But, with a smile of sweet sur-
prise,
She turned to me her dreamy
eyes;
And slowly, as if life were pain,
She drew me in her arms to lie:
She strove to speak, and strove
in vain;
Each breath was like a long-
drawn sigh.

The throbs that seemed to shake her breast,
The trembling clasp, so loose and weak,
At last grew calmer, and at rest;
And then she strove once more to speak:
"My God, I thank thee, that my pain
Of day by day, and year by year,
Has not been suffered all in vain,
And I may die while he is near.
I will not fear but that Thy grace
Has swept away my sin and woe,
And sent this little angel face,
In my last hour, to tell me so."
(And here her voice grew faint and low,)
"My child, where'er thy life may go,
To know that thou art brave and true,
Will pierce the highest heavens through,
And even there my soul shall be
More joyful for this thought of thee."
She folded her white hands, and stayed;
All cold and silently she lay:
I knelt beside the bed, and prayed
The prayer she used to make me say.
I said it many times, and then
She did not move, but seemed to be
In a deep sleep, nor stirred again.
No sound woke in the silent room,
Or broke the dim and solemn gloom,
Save when the brands that burnt so low,
With noisy, fitful gleam of light,
Would spread around a sudden glow,
Then sink in silence and in night.
How long I stood I do not know:
At last poor Walter came, and said
(So sadly) that we now must go,
And whispered, she we loved was dead.
He bade me kiss her face once more,
Then led me sobbing to the door.
I scarcely knew what dying meant,
Yet a strange grief, before unknown,
Weighed on my spirit as we went
And left her lying all alone.

We went to the far North once more,
To seek the well-remembered home
Where my poor kinsman dwelt before,
Whence now he was too old to roam;
And there six happy years we past,
Happy and peaceful till the last;
When poor old Walter died, and he

Blessed me and said I now might be
A sailor on the deep blue sea.
And so I go; and yet in spite
Of all the joys I long to know,
Though I look onward with delight,
With something of regret I go;
And young or old, on land or sea,
One guiding memory I shall take, —
Of what She prayed that I might be,
And what I will be for her sake!

A CROWN OF SORROW.

A sorrow, wet with early tears
  Yet bitter, had been long with me;
I wearied of this weight of years,
  And would be free.

I tore my Sorrow from my heart,
  I cast it far away in scorn;
Right joyful that we two could part,
  Yet most forlorn.

I sought (to take my Sorrow's place)
  Over the world for flower or gem;
But she had had an ancient grace
  Unknown to them.

I took once more with strange delight
My slighted Sorrow; proudly now
I wear it, set with stars of light,
  Upon my brow.

THE LESSON OF THE WAR.
1855.

The feast is spread through England
  For rich and poor to-day;
Greetings and laughter may be there,
  But thoughts are far away;
Over the stormy ocean,
  Over the dreary track,
Where some are gone, whom England
  Will never welcome back.

Breathless she waits, and listens
  For every eastern breeze
That bears upon its bloody wings
  News from beyond the seas.
The leafless branches stirring
  Make many a watcher start;
The distant tramp of steed may send
  A throb from heart to heart.

The rulers of the nation,
  The poor ones at their gate,
With the same eager wonder
  The same great news await.
The poor man's stay and comfort,
  The rich man's joy and pride,

Upon the bleak Crimean shore
  Are fighting side by side.

The bullet comes — and either
  A desolate hearth may see;
And God alone to-night knows
    where
The vacant place may be!
The dread that stirs the peasant
  Thrills nobles' hearts with
    fear;
Yet above selfish sorrow
  Both hold their country dear.

The rich man who reposes
  In his ancestral shade,
The peasant at his ploughshare,
  The worker at his trade,
Each one his all has perilled,
  Each has the same great stake,
Each soul can but have patience,
  Each heart can only break!

Hushed is all party clamor;
  One thought in every heart,
One dread in every household,
  Has bid such strife depart.
England has called her children;
  Long silent — the word came
That lit the smouldering ashes
  Through all the land to flame.

O you who toil and suffer,
  You gladly heard the call;
But those you sometimes envy,
  Have they not given their all?
O you who rule the nation,
  Take now the toil-worn hand:
Brothers you are in sorrow,
  In duty to your land.

Learn but this noble lesson
  Ere Peace returns again,
And the life-blood of Old England
  Will not be shed in vain.

THE TWO SPIRITS.

1855.

Last night, when weary silence
  fell on all,
  And starless skies arose so dim
    and vast,
I heard the Spirit of the Present
    call
  Upon the sleeping Spirit of
    the Past.
Far off and near, I saw their
    radiance shine,
And listened while they spoke
    of deeds divine.

The Spirit of the Past.

My deeds are writ in iron;
  My glory stands alone;
A veil of shadowy honor
  Upon my tombs is thrown;
The great names of my heroes
  Like gems in history lie;
To live they deemed ignoble,
  Had they the chance to die!

The Spirit of the Present.

My children, too, are honored;
  Dear shall their memory be
To the proud lands that own
    them;
Dearer than thine to thee;

For, though they hold that sa-
cred
  Is God's great gift of life,
At the first call of duty
  They rush into the strife!

The Spirit of the Past!

Then, with all valiant precepts
  Woman's soft heart was fraught;
"Death, not dishonor," echoed
  The war-cry she had taught.
Fearless and glad, those mothers,
  At bloody deaths elate,
Cried out they bore their chil-
dren
  Only for such a fate!

The Spirit of the Present.

Though such stern laws of honor
  Are faded now away,
Yet many a mourning mother,
  With nobler grief than they,
Bows down in sad submission:
  The heroes of the fight
Learnt at her knee the lesson,
  "For God and for the Right!"

The Spirit of the Past.

No voice there spake of sorrow:
  They saw the noblest fall
With no repining murmur;
  Stern Fate was lord of all.
And when the loved ones per-
ished,
  One cry alone arose,
Waking the startled echoes,
  "Vengeance upon our foes!"

The Spirit of the Present.

Grief dwells in France and Eng-
land
  For many a noble son;
Yet louder than the sorrow,
  "Thy will, O God, be done!"
From desolate homes is rising
  One prayer, — "Let carnage cease!
On friends and foes have mercy,
  O Lord, and give us peace!"

The Spirit of the Past.

Then, every hearth was honored
  That sent its children forth,
To spread their country's glory,
  And gain her south or north.
Then, little recked they numbers,
  No band would ever fly,
But stern and resolute they stood
  To conquer or to die.

The Spirit of the Present.

And now from France and Eng-
land
  Their dearest and their best
Go forth to succor freedom,
  To help the much oppressed;
Now, let the far-off Future
  And Past bow down to-day,
Before the few young hearts that
hold
  Whole armaments at bay.

The Spirit of the Past.

Then, each one strove for honor,
  Each for a deathless name;

Love, home, rest, joy, were offered
  As sacrifice to Fame.
They longed that in far ages
  Their deeds might still be told,
And distant times and nations
  Their names in honor hold.

The Spirit of the Present.

Though nursed by such old legends,
  Our heroes of to-day
Go cheerfully to battle
  As children go to play;
They gaze with awe and wonder
  On your great names of pride,
Unconscious that their own will shine
  In glory side by side!

Day dawned; and as the Spirits passed away,
Methought I saw, in the dim morning gray,
The Past's bright diadem had paled before
The starry crown the glorious Present wore.

A LITLLE LONGER.

A LITTLE longer yet — a little longer,
  Shall violets bloom for thee, and sweet birds sing;
And the lime-branches, where soft winds are blowing,
  Shall murmur the sweet promise of the Spring!

A little longer yet — a little longer,
  Thou shalt behold the quiet of the morn;
While tender grasses and awakening flowers
  Send up a golden mist to greet the dawn!

A little longer yet — a little longer,
  The tenderness of twilight shall be thine,
The rosy clouds that float o'er dying daylight,
  Nor fade till trembling stars begin to shine.

A little longer yet — a little longer,
  Shall starry night be beautiful for thee;
And the cold moon shall look through the blue silence,
  Flooding her silver path upon the sea.

A little longer yet — a little longer,
  Life shall be thine; life with its power to will;
Life with its strength to bear, to love, to conquer,
  Bringing its thousand joys thy heart to fill.

A little longer yet — a little longer,
The voices thou hast loved shall charm thine ear;
And thy true heart, that now beats quick to hear them,
A little longer yet shall hold them dear.

A little longer yet — joy while thou mayest;
Love and rejoice! for time has naught in store:
And soon the darkness of the grave shall bid thee
Love and rejoice and feel and know no more.

A little longer still — Patience, Belovéd:
A little longer still, ere Heaven unroll
The Glory, and the Brightness, and the Wonder,
Eternal, and divine, that waits thy Soul!

A little longer ere Life true, immortal,
(Not this our shadowy Life,) will be thine own;
And thou shalt stand where winged Archangels worship,
And trembling bow before the Great White Throne.

A little longer still, and Heaven awaits thee,
And fills thy spirit with a great delight;

Then our pale joys will seem a dream forgotten,
Our Sun a darkness, and our Day a Night.

A little longer, and thy Heart, Belovéd,
Shall beat forever with a Love divine;
And joy so pure, so mighty, so eternal,
No creature knows and lives, will then be thine.

A little longer yet — and angel voices
Shall ring in heavenly chant upon thine ear;
Angels and Saints await thee, and God needs thee:
Belovéd, can we bid thee linger here!

GRIEF.

An ancient enemy have I,
And either he or I must die;
For he never leaveth me,
Never gives my soul relief,
Never lets my sorrow cease,
Never gives my spirit peace, —
For mine enemy is Grief!
Pale he is, and sad and stern;
And whene'er he cometh nigh,
Blue and dim the torches burn,
Pale and shrunk the roses turn;
While my heart that he has pierced
Many a time with fiery lance,
Beats and trembles at his glance:

Clad in burning steel is he,
All my strength he can defy;
For he never leaveth me —
And one of us must die!

I have said, "Let ancient sages
Charm me from my thoughts of
    pain!"
So I read their deepest pages,
And I strove to think — in vain!
Wisdom's cold, calm words I
    tried,
But he was seated by my side; —
Learning I have won in vain;
She cannot rid me of my pain.

When at last soft sleep comes
    o'er me,
A cold hand is on my heart;
Stern sad eyes are there before
    me;
Not in dreams will he depart:
And when the same dreary vision
From my weary brain has fled,
Daylight brings the living phan-
    tom,
He is seated by my bed,
Bending o'er me all the while,
With his cruel, bitter smile,
Ever with me, ever nigh; —
And either he or I must die!

Then I said, long time ago,
"I will flee to other climes,
I will leave mine ancient foe!"
Though I wandered far and
    wide —
Still he followed at my side.

And I fled where the blue waters
Bathe the sunny isles of Greece;
Where Thessalian mountains rise
Up against the purple skies;
Where a haunting memory liv-
    eth
In each wood and cave and rill;
But no dream of gods could help
    me, —
He went with me still!

I have been where Nile's broad
    river
Flows upon the burning sand;
Where the desert monster brood-
    eth,
Where the Eastern palm-trees
    stand;
I have been where pathless forests
Spread a black eternal shade;
Where the lurking panther hiding
Glares from every tangled glade;
But in vain I wandered wide,
He was always by my side!

Then I fled where snows eternal
Cold and dreary ever lie;
Where the rosy lightnings gleam,
Flashing through the northern
    sky;
Where the red sun turns again
Back upon his path of pain; —
But a shadowy form was with
    me, —
I had fled in vain!

I have thought, "If I can gaze
Sternly on him he will fade,
For I know that he is nothing
But a dim ideal shade."
As I gazed at him the more,
He grew stronger than before!

Then I said, "Mine arm is strong,
I will make him turn and flee";
I have struggled with him long —
But that could never be!

Once I battled with him so
That I thought I laid him low;
Then in trembling joy I fled,
While again and still again
Murmuring to myself I said,
"Mine old enemy is dead!"
And I stood beneath the stars,
When a chill came on my frame,
And a fear I could not name,
And a sense of quick despair,
And, lo! — mine enemy was
    there!

Listen, for my soul is weary,
Weary of its endless woe;
I have called on one to aid me
Mightier even than my foe.
Strength and hope fail day by
    day;
I shall cheat him of his prey;
Some day soon, I know not when,
He will stab me through and
    through;
He has wounded me before,
But my heart can bear no
    more;
Pray that hour may come to
    me,
Only then shall I be free;
Death alone has strength to take
    me
Where my foe can never be;
Death, and Death alone, has
    power
To conquer mine old enemy!

THE TRIUMPH OF TIME.

The tender, delicate Flow-
    ers,
I saw them fanned by a warm
    western wind,
Fed by soft summer show-
    ers,
Shielded by care, and yet, (O
    Fate unkind!)
Fade in a few short hours.

The gentle and the gay,
Rich in a glorious Future of
    bright deeds,
Rejoicing in the day,
Are met by Death, who sternly,
    sadly leads
Them far away.

And Hopes, perfumed and
    bright,
So lately shining, wet with dew
    and tears,
Trembling in morning light;
I saw them change to dark and
    anxious fears
Before the night!

I wept that all must die:
"Yet Love," I cried, "doth live,
    and conquer death —"
And time passed by,
And breathed on Love, and
    killed it with his breath
Ere Death was nigh.

More bitter far than all
It was to know that Love could
    change and die! —

Hush! for the ages call,
"The Love of God lives through
  eternity,
  And conquers all!"

A PARTING.

WITHOUT one bitter feeling let
  us part,—
  And for the years in which
  your love has shed
  A radiance like a glory round
  my head,
I thank you, yes, I thank you
  from my heart.

I thank you for the cherished
  hope of years,
  A starry future, dim and yet
  divine,
  Winging its way from Heaven
  to be mine,
Laden with joy, and ignorant of
  tears.

I thank you, yes, I thank you
  even more
  That my heart learnt not without love to live,
  But gave and gave, and still
  had more to give,
From an abundant and exhaustless store.

I thank you, and no grief is in
  these tears;
  I thank you, not in bitterness
  but truth,

For the fair vision that adorned
  my youth
And glorified so many happy
  years.

Yet how much more I thank you
  that you tore
  At length the veil your hand
  had woven away,
  Which hid my idol was a thing
  of clay,
And false the altar I had knelt
  before.

I thank you that you taught me
  the stern truth,
  (None other could have told
  and I believed,)
  That vain had been my life,
  and I deceived,
And wasted all the purpose of
  my youth.

I thank you that your hand
  dashed down the shrine,
  Wherein my idol worship I
  had paid;
  Else had I never known a soul
  was made
To serve and worship only the
  Divine.

I thank you that the heart I cast
  away
  On such as you, though bro
  ken, bruised, and crushed,
  Now that its fiery throbbing is
  all hushed,
Upon a worthier altar I can lay

I thank you for the lesson that
    such love
Is a perverting of God's royal
    right,
That it is made but for the
    Infinite,
And all too great to live except
    above.

I thank you for a terrible awak-
    ing,
And if reproach seemed hidden
    in my pain,
And sorrow seemed to cry on
    your disdain,
Know that my blessing lay in
    your forsaking.

Farewell forever now: in peace
    we part;
And should an idle vision o'
    my tears
Arise before your soul in after
    years,
Remember that I thank you from
    my heart!

THE GOLDEN GATE.

Dim shadows gather thickly round, and up the misty stair they climb,
The cloudy stair that upward leads to where the closéd portals shine,
Round which the kneeling spirits wait the opening of the Golden Gate.

And some with eager longing go, still pressing forward, hand in hand,
And some, with weary step and slow, look back where their Belovéd
    stand :
Yet up the misty stair they climb, led onward by the Angel Time.

As unseen hands roll back the doors, the light that floods the very air
Is but the shadow from within, of the great glory hidden there :
And morn and eve, and soon and late, the shadows pass within the gate.

As one by one they enter in, and the stern portals close once more,
The halo seems to linger round those kneeling closest to the door :
The joy that lightened from that place shines still upon the watcher's
    face.

The faint low echo that we hear of far-off music seems to fill
The silent air with love and fear, and the world's clamors all grow still,
Until the portals close again, and leave us toiling on in pain.

Complain not that the way is long : what road is weary that leads there?
But let the Angel take thy hand, and lead thee up the misty stair,
And then with beating heart await the opening of the Golden Gate.

PHANTOMS.

Back, ye Phantoms of the Past;
 In your dreary caves remain:
What have I to do with memories
 Of a long-forgotten pain?

For my Present is all peaceful,
 And my Future nobly planned:
Long ago Time's mighty billows
 Swept your footsteps from the sand.

Back into your caves; nor haunt me
 With your voices full of woe;
I have buried grief and sorrow
 In the depths of Long-ago.

See the glorious clouds of morning
 Roll away, and clear and bright
Shine the rays of cloudless daylight:—
 Wherefore will ye moan of night?

Never shall my heart be burdened
 With its ancient woe and fears;
I can drive them from my presence,
 I can check these foolish tears.

Back, ye Phantoms; leave, O leave me,
 To a new and happy lot;
Speak no more of things departed;
 Leave me — for I know ye not.

Can it be that 'mid my gladness
 I must ever hear you wail,
Of the grief that wrung my spirit,
 And that made my cheek so pale?

Joy is mine; but your sad voices
 Murmur ever in mine ear:
Vain is all the Future's promise,
 While the dreary Past is here.

Vain, O worse than vain, the Visions
 That my heart, my life, would fill,
If the Past's relentless phantoms
 Call upon me still!

THANKFULNESS.

My God, I thank Thee who hast made
 The Earth so bright;
So full of splendor and of joy,
 Beauty and light;
So many glorious things are here,
 Noble and right!

I thank Thee, too, that Thou hast made
 Joy to abound;

So many gentle thoughts and deeds
    Circling us round,
That in the darkest spot of Earth
    Some love is found.

I thank Thee *more* that all our joy
    Is touched with pain;
That shadows fall on brightest hours;
    That thorns remain;
So that Earth's bliss may be our guide,
    And not our chain.

For Thou who knowest, Lord, how soon
    Our weak heart clings,
Hast given us joys, tender and true,
    Yet all with wings,
So that we see, gleaming on high,
    Diviner things!

I thank Thee, Lord, that Thou hast kept
    The best in store;
We have enough, yet not too much
    To long for more:
A yearning for a deeper peace,
    Not known before.

I thank Thee, Lord, that here our souls,
    Though amply blest,
Can never find, although they seek,
    A perfect rest, —
Nor ever shall, until they lean
    On Jesus' breast!

HOME-SICKNESS.

Where I am, the halls are gilded,
    Stored with pictures bright and rare;
Strains of deep melodious music
    Float upon the perfumed air: —
Nothing stirs the dreary silence
    Save the melancholy sea,
Near the poor and humble cottage,
    Where I fain would be!

Where I am, the sun is shining,
    And the purple windows glow,
Till their rich armorial shadows
    Stain the marble floor below: —
Faded autumn leaves are trembling
    On the withered jasmine-tree,
Creeping round the little casement,
    Where I fain would be!

Where I am, the days are passing
    O'er a pathway strewn with flowers;
Song and joy and starry pleasures
    Crown the happy, smiling hours: —
Slowly, heavily, and sadly,
    Time with weary wings must flee,
Marked by pain, and toil, and sorrow,
    Where I fain would be!

Where I am, the great and noble
　Tell me of renown and fame,
And the red wine sparkles highest,
　To do honor to my name : —
Far away a place is vacant,
　By a humble hearth, for me,
Dying embers dimly show it,
　Where I fain would be !

Where I am are glorious dream-
　　ings,
　Science, genius, art divine;
And the great minds whom all
　　honor
　Interchange their thoughts
　　with mine : —
A few simple hearts are waiting,
　Longing, wearying, for me,
Far away where tears are falling,
　Where I fain would be !

Where I am, all think me happy,
　For so well I play my part,
None can guess, who smile
　　around me,
　How far distant is my heart, —
Far away, in a poor cottage,
　Listening to the dreary sea,
Where the treasures of my life
　　are,
　Where I fain would be !

WISHES.

ALL the fluttering wishes
　Caged within thy heart
Beat their wings against it,
　Longing to depart,
Till they shake their prison
　With their wounded cry;
Open wide thy heart to-day,
　And let the captives fly.

Let them first fly upward
　Through the starry air,
Till you almost lose them,
　For their home is there;
Then, with outspread pinions,
　Circling round and round,
Wing their way wherever
　Want and woe are found.

Where the weary stitcher
　Toils for daily bread;
Where the lonely watcher
　Watches by her dead;
Where, with thin, weak fingers,
　Toiling at the loom,
Stand the little children,
　Blighted ere they bloom ; —

Where, by darkness blinded,
　Groping for the light,
With distorted conscience,
　Men do wrong for right;
Where, in the cold shadow,
　By smooth pleasure thrown,
Human hearts by hundreds
　Harden into stone ; —

Where on dusty highways,
　With faint heart and slow,
Cursing the glad sunlight,
　Hungry outcasts go ;
Where all mirth is silenced,
　And the hearth is chill,
For one place is empty,
　And one voice is still.

Some hearts will be lighter
　While your captives roam
For their tender singing,
　Then recall them home;
When the sunny hours
　Into night depart,
Softly they will nestle
　In a quiet heart.

THE PEACE OF GOD.

We ask for Peace, O Lord!
　Thy children ask Thy Peace;
Not what the world calls rest,
　That toil and care should cease,
That through bright sunny hours
　Calm Life should fleet away,
And tranquil night should fade
　In smiling day; —
It is not for such Peace that we
　would pray.

We ask for Peace, O Lord!
　Yet not to stand secure,
Girt round with iron Pride,
　Contented to endure:
Crushing the gentle strings
　That human hearts should know,
Untouched by others' joy
　Or others' woe; —
Thou, O dear Lord, wilt never
　teach us so.

We ask Thy Peace, O Lord!
　Through storm, and fear, and strife,
To light and guide us on,
　Through a long, struggling life:

While no success or gain
　Shall cheer the desperate fight,
Or nerve, what the world calls,
　Our wasted might: —
Yet pressing through the darkness to the light.

It is Thine own, O Lord,
　Who toil while others sleep;
Who sow with loving care
　What other hands shall reap:
They lean on Thee entranced,
　In calm and perfect rest:
Give us that Peace, O Lord,
　Divine and blest,
Thou keepest for those hearts
　who love Thee best.

LIFE IN DEATH AND DEATH IN LIFE.

I.

If the dread day that calls thee hence
　Through a red mist of fear should loom,
(Closing in deadliest night and gloom
Long hours of aching, dumb suspense,)
　And leave me to my lonely doom, —

I think, belovéd, I could see
　In thy dear eyes the loving light
Glaze into vacancy and night,

And still say, "God is good to me,
  And all that He decrees is right."

That, watching thy slow struggling breath,
  And answering each imperfect sign,
I still could pray thy prayer and mine,
And tell thee, dear, though this was death,
  That God was love, and love divine.

Could hold thee in my arms, and lay
  Upon my heart thy weary head,
And meet thy last smile ere it fled;
Then hear, as in a dream, one say,
  "Now all is over, — she is dead."

Could smooth thy garments with fond care,
  And cross thy hands upon thy breast,
  And kiss thine eyelids down to rest,
And yet say no word of despair,
  But, through my sobbing, "It is best."

Could stifle down the gnawing pain,
  And say, "We still divide our life,
She has the rest, and I the strife,
And mine the loss, and hers the gain:
  My ill with bliss for her is rife."

Then turn, and the old duties take —
  Alone now — yet with earnest will
  Gathering sweet, sacred traces still
To help me on, and, for thy sake,
  My heart and life and soul to fill.

I think I could check vain, weak tears,
  And toil, — although the world's great space
  Held nothing but one vacant place,
And see the dark and weary years
  Lit only by a vanished grace.

And sometimes, when the day was o'er,
  Call up the tender past again:
  Its painful joy, its happy pain,
And live it over yet once more,
  And say, "But few more years remain."

And then, when I had striven my best,
  And all around would smiling say,

"See how Time makes all
  grief decay,"
Would lie down thankfully to
  rest,
And seek thee in eternal day.

II.

But if the day should ever
  rise —
It could not and it cannot
  be —
Yet, if the sun should ever see,
Looking upon us from his skies,
  A day that took thy heart from
  me;

If loving thee still more and
  more,
And still so willing to be blind,
I should the bitter knowledge
  find,
That Time had eaten out the core
Of love, and left the empty
  rind;

If the poor lifeless words, at last,
  (The soul gone, that was once
  so sweet,)
  Should cease my eager heart
  to cheat,
And crumble back into the past,
  And show the whole a vain
  deceit;

If I should see thee turn away,
  And know that prayer, and
  time, and pain,
  Could no more thy lost love
  regain,

Than bid the hours of dying day
  Gleam in their mid-day noon
  again;

If I should loose thy hand, and
  know
  That henceforth we must
  dwell apart,
  Since I had seen thy love depart,
And only count the hours flow
  By the dull throbbing of my
  heart;

If I should gaze and gaze in vain
  Into thine eyes so deep and
  clear,
  And read the truth of all my
  fear
  Half mixed with pity for my
  pain,
  And sorrow for the vanished
  year;

If, not to grieve thee overmuch,
  I strove to counterfeit disdain,
  And weave me a new life again,
  Which thy life could not mar, or
  touch,
  And so smile down my bitter
  pain; —

The ghost of my dead Past would
  rise
  And mock me, and I could
  not dare
  Look to a future of despair,
Or even to the eternal skies,
  For I should still be lonely
  there.

All Truth, all Honor, then would seem
  Vain clouds, which the first wind blew by;
All Trust, a folly doomed to die;
All Life, a useless, empty dream;
  All Love — since thine had failed — a lie.

But see, thy tender smile has cast
  My fear away: this thought of mine
Is treason to my Love and thine;
For Love is Life, and Death at last
  Crowns it eternal and divine!

RECOLLECTIONS.

As strangers, you and I are here;
  We both as aliens stand
Where once, in years gone by, I dwelt
  No stranger in the land.
Then while you gaze on park and stream,
  Let me remain apart,
And listen to the awakened sound
  Of voices in my heart.

Here, where upon the velvet lawn
  The cedar spreads its shade,
And by the flower-beds all around
  Bright roses bloom and fade,
Shrill merry childish laughter rings,
  And baby voices sweet,
And by me, on the path, I hear
  The tread of little feet.

Down the dark avenue of limes,
  Whose perfume loads the air,
Whose boughs are rustling overhead,
  (For the west-wind is there,)
I hear the sound of earnest talk,
  Warnings and counsels wise,
And the quick questioning that brought
  Such gentle, calm replies.

Still the light bridge hangs o'er the lake,
  Where broad-leaved lilies lie,
And the cool water shows again
  The cloud that moves on high; —
And one voice speaks, in tones I thought
  The past forever kept;
But now I know, deep in my heart
  Its echoes only slept.

I hear, within the shady porch,
  Once more, the measured sound
Of the old ballads that were read,
  While we sat listening round;
The starry passion-flower still
  Up the green trellis climbs;
The tendrils waving seem to keep
  The cadence of the rhymes.

I might have striven, and striven
    in vain,
Such visions to recall,
Well known and yet forgotten;
    now
I see, I hear, them all!
The Present pales before the Past,
    Who comes with angel wings;
As in a dream I stand, amidst
    Strange yet familiar things!

Enough; so let us go, mine eyes
    Are blinded by their tears;
A voice speaks to my soul to-day
    Of long-forgotten years.
And yet the vision in my heart,
    In a few hours more,
Will fade into the silent past,
    Silently as before.

ILLUSION.

Where the golden corn is bend-
    ing,
And the singing reapers pass,
Where the chestnut woods are
    sending
Leafy showers upon the grass,

The blue river onward flowing
    Mingles with its noisy strife,
The murmur of the flowers
    growing,
And the hum of insect life.

I from that rich plain was gazing
    Towards the snowy moun-
    tains high,
Who their gleaming peaks were
    raising
Up against the purple sky.

And the glory of their shining,
    Bathed in clouds of rosy
    light,
Set my weary spirit pining
    For a home so pure and
    bright!

So I left the plain, and weary,
    Fainting, yet with hope sus-
    tained,
Toiled through pathways long
    and dreary
Till the mountain-top was
    gained.

Lo! the height that I had taken,
    As so shining from below,
Was a desolate, forsaken
    Region of perpetual snow.

I am faint, my feet are bleeding,
    All my feeble strength is worn,
In the plain no soul is heeding,
    I am here alone, forlorn.

Lights are shining, bells are toll-
    ing,
In the busy vale below;
Near me night's black clouds
    are rolling,
Gathering o'er a waste of
    snow.

So I watch the river winding
    Through the misty fading
    plain,

Bitter are the tear-drops blinding,
Bitter, useless toil and pain,—
Bitterest of all the finding
That my dream was false and vain!

A VISION.

Gloomy and black are the cypress-trees,
Drearily waileth the chill night breeze.
The long grass waveth, the tombs are white,
And the black clouds flit o'er the chill moonlight.
Silent is all save the dropping rain,
When slowly there cometh a mourning train;
The lone churchyard is dark and dim,
And the mourners raise a funeral hymn.

"Open, dark grave, and take her;
Though we have loved her so,
Yet we must now forsake her,
Love will no more awake her:
(O bitter woe!)
Open thine arms and take her
To rest below!

"Vain is our mournful weeping,
Her gentle life is o'er;
Only the worm is creeping,
Where she will soon be sleeping
Forevermore:
Nor joy nor love is keeping
For her in store!"

Gloomy and black are the cypress-trees,
And drearily wave in the chill night breeze.
The dark clouds part and the heavens are blue,
Where the trembling stars are shining through.

Slowly across the gleaming sky,
A crowd of white angels are passing by.
Like a fleet of swans they float along,
Or the silver notes of a dying song.
Like a cloud of incense their pinions rise,
Fading away up the purple skies.
But hush! for the silent glory is stirred
By a strain such as earth has never heard:

"Open, O Heaven! we bear her,
This gentle maiden mild,
Earth's griefs we gladly spare her,
From earthly joys we tear her,
Still undefiled;
And to thine arms we bear her,
Thine own, thy child.

"Open, O Heaven! no morrow
  Will see this joy o'ercast,
No pain, no tears, no sorrow,
  Her gentle heart will borrow;
    Sad life is past;
Shielded and safe from sorrow,
  At home at last."

But the vision faded and all was still,
  On the purple valley and distant hill.
No sound was there save the wailing breeze,
The rain, and the rustling cypress-trees.

PICTURES IN THE FIRE.

WHAT is it you ask me, darling?
  All my stories, child, you know;
I have no strange dreams to tell you,
  Pictures I have none to show.

Tell you glorious scenes of travel?
  Nay, my child, that cannot be,
I have seen no foreign countries,
  Marvels none on land or sea.

Yet strange sights in truth I witness,
  And I gaze until I tire;
Wondrous pictures, changing ever,
  As I look into the fire.

There, last night, I saw a cavern,
  Black as pitch; within it lay,
Coiled in many folds, a dragon,
  Glaring as if turned at bay.

And a knight in dismal armor
  On a wingéd eagle came,
To do battle with this dragon:
  And his crest was all of flame.

As I gazed the dragon faded,
  And, instead, sat Pluto crowned
By a lake of burning fire;
  Spirits dark were crouching round.

That was gone, and lo! before me,
  A cathedral vast and grim;
I could almost hear the organ
  Peal along the arches dim.

As I watched the wreathéd pillars,
  Groves of stately palms arose,
And a group of swarthy Indians
  Stealing on some sleeping foes.

Stay: a cataract glancing brightly
  Dashed and sparkled; and beside
Lay a broken marble monster,
  Mouth and eyes were staring wide.

Then I saw a maiden wreathing
  Starry flowers in garlands sweet;

Did she see the fiery serpent
  That was wrapped about her feet?

That fell crashing all and vanished;
  And I saw two armies close, —
I could almost hear the clarions,
  And the shouting of the foes.
They were gone; and lo! bright angels,
  On a barren mountain wild,
Raised appealing arms to Heaven,
  Bearing up a little child.

And I gazed, and gazed, and slowly
  Gathered in my eyes sad tears,
And the fiery pictures bore me
  Back through distant dreams of years.

Once again I tasted sorrow,
  With past joy was once more gay,
Till the shade had gathered round me —
  And the fire had died away.

THE SETTLERS.

Two stranger youths in the Far West,
  Beneath the ancient forest trees,
Pausing, amid their toil to rest,
  Spake of their home beyond the seas;
Spake of the hearts that beat so warmly,
  Of the hearts they loved so well,
In their chilly Northern country.
" Would," they cried, " some voice could tell
Where they are, our own beloved ones!"
They looked up to the evening sky
Half hidden by the giant branches,
  But heard no angel-voice reply.
All silent was the quiet evening;
Silent were the ancient trees;
They only heard the murmuring song
  Of the summer breeze,
  That gently played among
  The acacia-trees.

And did no warning spirit answer,
  Amid the silence all around:
" Before the lowly village altar
  She thou lovest may be found,
Thou, who trustest still so blindly,
  Know she stands a smiling bride!
Forgetting thee, she turneth kindly
  To the stranger at her side.
Yes, this day thou art forgotten,
  Forgotten, too, thy last farewell,
All the vows that she has spoken,
  And thy heart has kept so well.

Dream no more of a starry fu-
  ture,
  In thy home beyond the seas!"
But he only heard the gentle sigh
  Of the summer breeze,
  So softly passing by
  The acacia-trees.

And vainly, too, the other, looking
  Smiling up through hopeful
    tears,
Asked in his heart of hearts,
  "Where is she,
  She I love these many years?"
He heard no echo calling faintly:
  "Lo, she lieth cold and pale,
And her smile so calm and saintly
  Heeds not grieving sob or
    wail, —
Heeds not the lilies strewn upon
    her,
  Pure as she is, and as white,
Or the solemn chanting voices,
  Or the taper's ghastly light."
But silent still was the ancient
    forest,
  Silent were the gloomy trees;
He only heard the wailing sound
  Of the summer breeze,
  That sadly played around
  The acacia-trees!

HUSH!

"I can scarcely hear," she mur-
    mured,
  "For my heart beats loud and
    fast,
But surely, in the far, far dis-
    tance,
  I can hear a sound at last."
  "It is only the reapers sing-
    ing,
  As they carry home their
    sheaves;
  And the evening breeze has
    risen,
  And rustles the dying
    leaves."

"Listen! there are voices talk-
    ing."
Calmly still she strove to
    speak,
Yet her voice grew faint and
    trembling,
  And the red flushed in her
    cheek.
  "It is only the children
    playing
  Below, now their work is
    done,
  And they laugh that their
    eyes are dazzled
  By the rays of the setting
    sun."

Fainter grew her voice, and
    weaker,
  As with anxious eyes she cried,
"Down the avenue of chestnuts,
  I can hear a horseman ride."
  "It was only the deer that
    were feeding
  In a herd on the clover-
    grass,

They were startled, and fled
  to the thicket,
    As they saw the reapers
      pass."

Now the night arose in silence,
  Birds lay in their leafy nest,
And the deer couched in the
    forest,
  And the children were at rest:
    There was only a sound of
      weeping
      From watchers around a
        bed,
    But Rest to the weary spirit,
      Peace to the quiet Dead!

HOURS.

When the bright stars came out
    last night,
  And the dew lay on the flow-
    ers,
I had a vision of delight, —
  A dream of bygone hours.

Those hours that came and fled
    so fast,
  Of pleasure or of pain,
As phantoms rose from out the
    past
  Before my eyes again.

With beating heart did I behold
  A train of joyous hours.
Lit with the radiant light of old,
  And, smiling, crowned with
    flowers.

And some were hours of childish
    sorrow,
  A mimicry of pain,
That through their tears looked
    for a morrow
  They knew must smile again.

Those hours of hope that longed
    for life,
  And wished their part begun,
And ere the summons to the
    strife
  Dreamed that the field was
    won.

I knew the echo of their voice,
  The starry crowns they wore;
The vision made my soul rejoice
  With the old thrill of yore.

I knew the perfume of their
    flowers;
  The glorious shining rays
Around these happy, smiling
    hours
  Were lit in bygone days.

O stay, I cried, — bright visions,
    stay,
  And leave me not forlorn!
But, smiling still, they passed
    away,
  Like shadows of the morn.

One spirit still remained, and
    cried,
  "Thy soul shall ne'er for-
    get!"
He standeth ever by my side, —
  The phantom called Regret!

But still the spirits rose, and there
Were weary hours of pain,
And anxious hours of fear and care
Bound by an iron chain.

Dim shadows came of lonely hours,
That shunned the light of day,
And in the opening smile of flowers
Saw only quick decay.

Calm hours that sought the starry skies
For heavenly lore were there;
With folded hands and earnest eyes,
I knew the hours of prayer.

Stern hours that darkened the sun's light,
Heralds of coming woes,
With trailing wings, before my sight
From the dim past arose.

As each dark vision passed and spoke,
I prayed it to depart:
At each some buried sorrow woke
And stirred within my heart.

Until these hours of pain and care
Lifted their tearful eyes,
Spread their dark pinions in the air,
And passed into the skies.

THE TWO INTERPRETERS.

The clouds are fleeting by, father;
Look, in the shining west,
The great white clouds sail onward
Upon the sky's blue breast.
Look at a snowy eagle,
His wings are tinged with red,
And a giant dolphin follows him,
With a crown upon his head!"

The father spake no word, but watched
The drifting clouds roll by;
He traced a misty vision too
Upon the shining sky:
A shadowy form, with well-known grace
Of weary love and care,
Above the smiling child she held,
Shook down her floating hair.

"The clouds are changing now, father,
Mountains rise higher and higher!
And see where red and purple ships
Sail in a sea of fire!"
The father pressed the little hand
More closely in his own,
And watched a cloud-dream in the sky
That he could see alone:

Bright angels carrying far away
  A white form, cold and dead,
Two held the feet, and two bore
    up
  The flower-crowned, drooping
    head.

"See, father, see! a glory floods
  The sky, and all is bright,
And clouds of every hue and
    shade
  Burn in the golden light.
And now, above an azure lake,
  Rise battlements and towers,
Where knights and ladies climb
    the heights,
  All bearing purple flowers."

The father looked, and, with a
    pang
  Of love and strange alarm,
Drew close the little eager child
  Within his sheltering arm;
From out the clouds the mother
    looks
  With wistful glance below,
She seems to seek the treasure
    left
  On earth so long ago;
She holds her arms out to her
    child,
  His cradle-song she sings:
The last rays of the sunset gleam
  Upon her outspread wings.

Calm twilight veils the summer
    sky,
  The shining clouds are gone;
In vain the merry laughing child
  Still gayly prattles on;
In vain the bright stars, one by
    one,
  On the blue silence start,
A dreary shadow rests to-night
  Upon the father's heart.

COMFORT.

Hast thou o'er the clear heaven
    of thy soul
  Seen tempests roll?
Hast thou watched all the hopes
    thou wouldst have won
  Fade, one by one?
Wait till the clouds are past,
    then raise thine eyes
  To bluer skies.

Hast thou gone sadly through a
    dreary night,
  And found no light,
No guide, no star, to cheer thee
    through the plain,
  No friend, save pain?
Wait, and thy soul shall see,
    when most forlorn,
  Rise a new morn.

Hast thou beneath another's stern
    control
  Bent thy sad soul,
And wasted sacred hopes and
    precious tears?
  Yet calm thy fears,
For thou canst gain, even from
    the bitterest part,
  A stronger heart.

Has Fate o'erwhelmed thee with
  some sudden blow?
    Let thy tears flow;
But know when storms are past,
  the heavens appear
More pure, more clear;
And hope, when farthest from
  their shining rays,
    For brighter days.

Hast thou found life a cheat, and
  worn in vain
    Its iron chain?
Has thy soul bent beneath earth's
  heavy bond?
    Look thou beyond;
If life is bitter—*there* forever
  shine
    Hopes more divine.

Art thou alone, and does thy
  soul complain
    It lives in vain?
Not vainly does he live who can
  endure.
    O be thou sure,
That he who hopes and suffers
  here, can earn
    A sure return.

Hast thou found naught within
  thy troubled life
    Save inward strife?
Hast thou found all she promised
  thee, Deceit,
    And Hope a cheat?
Endure, and there shall dawn
  within thy breast
    Eternal rest!

HOME AT LAST.

Child, do not fear;
We shall reach our home to-
  night,
    For the sky is clear,
    And the waters bright;
And the breezes have scarcely
  strength
    To unfold that little cloud,
    That like a shroud
Spreads out its fleecy length;
  Then have no fear,
As we cleave our silver way
  Through the waters clear.

Fear not, my child!
Though the waves are white and
  high,
    And the storm blows wild
    Through the gloomy sky;
On the edge of the western sea,
  See that line of golden light,
    Is the haven bright
Where home is awaiting thee;
  Where, this peril past,
We shall rest from our stormy
  voyage
    In peace at last.

Be not afraid;
But give me thy hand, and see
    How the waves have made
    A cradle for thee.
Night is come, dear, and we shall
  rest;
    So turn from the angry skies,
    And close thine eyes,
And lay thy head on my breast:

Child, do not weep;
In the calm, cold, purple depths
There we shall sleep.

UNEXPRESSED.

DWELLS within the soul of every Artist
More than all his effort can express;
And he knows the best remains unuttered;
Sighing at what *we* call his success.

Vainly he may strive; he dare not tell us
All the sacred mysteries of the skies;
Vainly he may strive, the deepest beauty
Cannot be unveiled to mortal eyes.

And the more devoutly that he listens,
And the holier message that is sent,
Still the more his soul must struggle vainly,
Bowed beneath a noble discontent.

No great Thinker ever lived and taught you
All the wonder that his soul received;

No true Painter ever set on canvas
All the glorious vision he conceived.

No Musician ever held your spirit
Charmed and bound in his melodious chains,
But be sure he heard, and strove to render,
Feeble echoes of celestial strains.

No real Poet ever wove in numbers
All his dream; but the diviner part,
Hidden from all the world, spake to him only
In the voiceless silence of his heart.

So with Love: for Love and Art united
Are twin mysteries; different, yet the same:
Poor indeed would be the love of any
Who could find its full and perfect name.

Love may strive, but vain is the endeavor
All its boundless riches to unfold;
Still its tenderest, truest secret lingers
Ever in its deepest depths untold.

Things of Time have voices:
  speak and perish.
Art and Love speak; but their
    words must be
Like sighings of illimitable for-
    ests,
And waves of an unfathomable
    sea.

BECAUSE.

It is not because your heart is
    mine — mine only —
  Mine alone;
It is not because you chose me,
    weak and lonely,
  For your own;
Not because the earth is fairer,
    and the skies
    Spread above you
Are more radiant for the shining
    of your eyes —
  That I love you!

It is not because the world's per-
    plexéd meaning
    Grows more clear;
And the Parapets of Heaven,
    with angels leaning,
    Seem more near;
And Nature sings of praise with
    all her voices
    Since yours spoke,
Since within my silent heart,
    that now rejoices,
  Love awoke!

Nay, not even because your hand
    holds heart and life;
  At your will

Soothing, hushing all its discord,
    making strife
  Calm and still;
Teaching Trust to fold her wings,
    nor ever roam
    From her nest;
Teaching Love that her securest,
    safest home
  Must be Rest.

But because this human Love,
    though true and sweet —
  Yours and mine —
Has been sent by Love more ten-
    der, more complete,
    More divine;
That it leads our hearts to rest
    at last in Heaven,
    Far above you;
Do I take you as a gift that God
    has given —
  — And I love you!

REST AT EVENING.

When the weariness of Life is
    ended,
And the task of our long day is
    done,
And the props, on which our
    hearts depended,
All have failed or broken, one
    by one;
Evening and our Sorrow's shad-
    ow blended,
Telling us that peace is now be-
    gun.

How far back will seem the sun's
   first dawning,
And those early mists so cold and
   gray!
Half forgotten even the toil of
   morning,
And the heat and burden of the
   day:
Flowers that we were tending,
   and weeds scorning,
All alike withered and cast away.

Vain will seem the impatient
   heart, which waited
Toils that gathered but too quickly round;
And the childish joy, so soon
   elated
At the path we thought none else
   had found;
And the foolish ardor, soon
   abated
By the storm which cast us to
   the ground.

Vain those pauses on the road,
   each seeming
As our final home and resting-
   place;
And the leaving them, while
   tears were streaming
Of eternal sorrow down our
   face;
And the hands we held, fond
   folly dreaming
That no future could their touch
   efface.

All will then be faded: — night
   will borrow
Stars of light to crown our perfect rest;
And the dim vague memory of
   faint sorrow
Just remain to show us all was
   best,
Then melt into a divine to-morrow: —
O how poor a day to be so blest!

A RETROSPECT.

From this fair point of present
   bliss,
   Where we together stand,
Let me look back once more,
   and trace
   That long and desert land,
Wherein till now was cast my lot,
   and I could live, and thou
   wert not.

Strange that my heart could beat,
   and know
   Alternate joy and pain,
That suns could roll from east
   to west,
   And clouds could pass in rain,
And the slow hours without thee
   fleet, nor stay their noiseless
   silver feet.

What had I then? a Hope, that
   grew
   Each hour more bright and
   dear,

The flush upon the eastern skies
  That showed the sun was near:—
Now night has faded far away,
  my sun has risen, and it is day.

A dim Ideal of tender grace
  In my soul reigned supreme;
Too noble and too sweet I thought
To live, save in a dream;—
Within thy heart to-day it lies,
  and looks on me from thy dear eyes.

Some gentle spirit—Love I thought—
Built many a shrine of pain;
Though each false Idol fell to dust,
  The worship was not vain,
But a faint, radiant shadow cast
  back from our Love upon the Past.

And Grief, too, held her vigil there;
With unrelenting sway
Breaking my cloudy visions down,
  Throwing my flowers away:—
I owe to her fond care alone
that I may now be all thine own.

Fair Joy was there,—her fluttering wings
At times she strove to raise;

Watching through long and patient nights,
Listening long eager days:
I know now that her heart and mine were waiting, Love, to welcome thine.

Thus I can read thy name throughout,
And, now her task is done,
Can see that even that faded Past
  Was thine, belovéd one,
And so rejoice my Life may be all
  consecrated, dear, to thee.

TRUE OR FALSE.

So you think you love me, do you?
  Well, it may be so;
But there are many ways of loving
  I have learnt to know.
Many ways, and but one true way,
  Which is very rare;
And the counterfeits look brightest,
  Though they will not wear.

Yet they ring, almost, quite truly,
  Last (with care) for long;
But in time must break, may shiver
  At a touch of wrong:

Having seen what looked most
    real
Crumble into dust;
Now I chose that test and trial
    Should precede my trust.

I have seen a love demanding
    Time and hope and tears,
Chaining all the past, exacting
    Bonds from future years;
Mind and heart, and joy and
    sorrow,
    Claiming as its fee:
That was Love of Self, and
    never,
    Never Love of me!

I have seen a love forgetting
    All above, beyond,
Linking every dream and fancy
    In a sweeter bond;
Counting every hour worthless,
    Which was cold or free:—
That, perhaps, was — Love of
    Pleasure,
    But not Love of me!

I have seen a love whose pa-
    tience
    Never turned aside,
Full of tender, fond devices;
    Constant, even when tried;
Smallest boons were held as vic-
    tories,
    Drops that swelled the sea:
That I think was — Love of
    Power,
    But not Love of me!

I have seen a love disdaining
    Ease and pride and fame,
Burning even its own white pin-
    ions
    Just to feed its flame;
Reigning thus, supreme, trium-
    phant,
    By the soul's decree;
That was — Love of Love, I
    fancy,
    But not Love of me!

I have heard — or dreamt, it
    may be —
    What Love is when true;
How to test and how to try it,
    Is the gift of few:
These few say (or did I dream
    it?)
    That true Love abides
In these very things, but always
    Has a soul besides.

Lives among the false loves,
    knowing
    Just their peace and strife;
Bears the self-same look, but al-
    ways
    Has an inner life.
Only a true heart can find it,
    True as it is true,
Only eyes as clear and tender
    Look it through and through.

If it dies, it will not perish
    By Time's slow decay,
True Love only grows (they tell
    me)
    Stronger, day by day:

Pain — has been its friend and
   comrade;
Fate — it can defy;
Only by its own sword, sometimes
   Love can choose to die.

And its grave shall be more
   noble
And more sacred still,
Than a throne, where one less
   worthy
Reigns and rules at will.
Tell me then, do you dare offer
   This true Love to me? . . .
Neither you nor I can answer;
   We will — wait and see!

GOLDEN WORDS.

Some words are played on
   golden strings,
Which I so highly rate,
I cannot bear for meaner things
   Their sound to desecrate.

For every day they are not meet,
   Or for a careless tone;
They are for rarest, and most
   sweet,
And noblest use alone.

One word is Poet: which is
   flung
So carelessly away,
When such as you and I have
   sung,
We hear it, day by day.

Men pay it for a tender phrase
   Set in a cadenced rhyme:
I keep it as a crown of praise
   To crown the kings of time.

And Love, the slightest feel-
   ings, stirred
By trivial fancy, seek
Expression in that golden word
   They tarnish while they speak.

Nay, let the heart's slow, rare
   decree,
That word in reverence keep;
Silence herself should only be
   More sacred and more deep.

Forever: men have grown at
   length
To use that word, to raise
Some feeble protest into strength,
   Or turn some tender phrase.

It should be said in awe and fear
   By true heart and strong will,
And burn more brightly year by
   year,
   A starry witness still.

Honor: all trifling hearts are
   fond
   Of that divine appeal,
And men, upon the slightest
   bond,
   Set it as slighter seal.

That word should meet a noble foe
   Upon a noble field,
And echo — like a deadly blow
   Turned by a silver shield.

Trust me, the worth of words is
 such
They guard all noble things,
And that this rash irreverent
 touch
Has jarred some golden
 strings.

For what the lips have lightly
 said
The heart will lightly hold,
And things on which we daily
 tread
Are lightly bought and sold.

The sun of every day will bleach
 The costliest purple hue,
And so our common daily
 speech
Discolors what was true.

But as you keep some thoughts
 apart
In sacred honored care,
If in the silence of your heart,
 Their utterance too be rare;

Then, while a thousand words
 repeat
Unmeaning clamors all,
Melodious golden echoes sweet
 Shall answer when you call.

LEGENDS AND LYRICS.

A BOOK OF VERSES.

SECOND SERIES.

LEGENDS AND LYRICS.

A LEGEND OF PROVENCE.

The lights extinguished, by the hearth I leant,
Half weary with a listless discontent.
The flickering giant-shadows, gathering near,
Closed round me with a dim and silent fear.
All dull, all dark; save when the leaping flame,
Glancing, lit up a Picture's ancient frame.
Above the hearth it hung. Perhaps the night,
My foolish tremors, or the gleaming light,
Lent power to that Portrait dark and quaint,—
A Portrait such as Rembrandt loved to paint,—
The likeness of a Nun. I seemed to trace
A world of sorrow in the patient face,
In the thin hands folded across her breast:—
Its own and the room's shadow hid the rest.
I gazed and dreamed, and the dull embers stirred,
Till an old legend that I once had heard
Came back to me; linked to the mystic gloom
Of that dark Picture in the ghostly room.

In the far south, where clustering vines are hung;
Where first the old chivalric lays were sung;
Where earliest smiled that gracious child of France,
Angel and knight and fairy, called Romance,
I stood one day. The warm blue June was spread
Upon the earth; blue summer overhead,
Without a cloud to fleck its radiant glare,
Without a breath to stir its sultry air.
All still, all silent, save the sobbing rush
Of rippling waves, that lapsed in silver hush

A LEGEND OF PROVENCE.

Upon the beach; where, glittering towards the strand,
The purple Mediterranean kissed the land.

All still, all peaceful; when a convent chime
Broke on the mid-day silence for a time,
Then trembling into quiet, seemed to cease,
In deeper silence and more utter peace.
So as I turned to gaze, where gleaming white,
Half hid by shadowy trees from passers' sight,
The Convent lay, one who had dwelt for long
In that fair home of ancient tale and song,
Who knew the story of each cave and hill,
And every haunting fancy lingering still
Within the land, spake thus to me, and told
The Convent's treasured Legend, quaint and old: —

Long years ago, a dense and flowering wood,
Still more concealed where the white convent stood,
Borne on its perfumed wings the title came:
"Our Lady of the Hawthorns" is its name.
Then did that bell, which still rings out to-day,
Bid all the country rise, or eat, or pray.
Before that convent shrine, the haughty knight
Passed the lone vigil of his perilous fight;
For humbler cottage strife or village brawl,
The Abbess listened, prayed, and settled all.
Young hearts that came, weighed down by love or wrong,
Left her kind presence comforted and strong.
Each passing pilgrim, and each beggar's right
Was food, and rest, and shelter for the night.
But, more than this, the Nuns could well impart
The deepest mysteries of the healing art;
Their store of herbs and simples was renowned,
And held in wondering faith for miles around.
Thus strife, love, sorrow, good and evil fate,
Found help and blessing at the convent gate.

Of all the nuns, no heart was half so light,
No eyelids veiling glances half as bright,
No step that glided with such noiseless feet,
No face that looked so tender or so sweet,

No voice that rose in choir so pure, so clear,
No heart to all the others half so dear,
So surely touched by others' pain or woe,
(Guessing the grief her young life could not know,)
No soul in childlike faith so undefiled,
As Sister Angela's, the "Convent Child."
For thus they loved to call her. She had known
No home, no love, no kindred, save their own.
An orphan, to their tender nursing given,
Child, plaything, pupil, now the Bride of Heaven.
And she it was who trimmed the lamp's red light
That swung before the altar, day and night;
Her hands it was whose patient skill could trace
The finest broidery, weave the costliest lace ;
But most of all, her first and dearest care,
The office she would never miss or share,
Was every day to weave fresh garlands sweet,
To place before the shrine at Mary's feet.
Nature is bounteous in that region fair,
For even winter has her blossoms there.
Thus Angela loved to count each feast the best,
By telling with what flowers the shrine was dressed.
In pomp supreme the countless Roses passed,
Battalion on battalion thronging fast,
Each with a different banner, flaming bright,
Damask, or striped, or crimson, pink, or white,
Until they bowed before a newborn queen,
And the pure virgin Lily rose serene.
Though Angela always thought the Mother blest
Must love the time of her own hawthorn best,
Each evening through the year, with equal care,
She placed her flowers; then kneeling down in prayer,
As their faint perfume rose before the shrine,
So rose her thoughts, as pure and as divine.
She knelt until the shades grew dim without,
Till one by one the altar lights shone out,
Till one by one the Nuns, like shadows dim,
Gathered around to chant their vesper hymn ;
Her voice then led the music's wingéd flight,
And " Ave, Maris Stella " filled the night.

But wherefore linger on those days of peace?
When storms draw near, then quiet hours must cease.
War, cruel war, defaced the land, and came
So near the convent with its breath of flame,
That, seeking shelter, frightened peasants fled,
Sobbing out tales of coming fear and dread.
Till after a fierce skirmish, down the road,
One night came straggling soldiers, with their load
Of wounded, dying comrades; and the band,
Half pleading, yet as if they could command,
Summoned the trembling Sisters, craved their care,
Then rode away, and left the wounded there.
But soon compassion bade all fear depart,
And bidding every Sister do her part,
Some prepare simples, healing salves, or bands,
The Abbess chose the more experienced hands,
To dress the wounds needing most skilful care;
Yet even the youngest Novice took her share.
To Angela, who had but ready will
And tender pity, yet no special skill,
Was given the charge of a young foreign knight,
Whose wounds were painful, but whose danger slight.
Day after day she watched beside his bed,
And first in hushed repose the hours fled:
His feverish moans alone the silence stirred,
Or her soft voice, uttering some pious word.
At last the fever left him; day by day
The hours, no longer silent, passed away.
What could she speak of? First, to still his plaints,
She told him legends of the martyred Saints;
Described the pangs, which, through God's plenteous grace,
Had gained their souls so high and bright a place.
This pious artifice soon found success —
Or so she fancied — for he murmured less.
So she described the glorious pomp sublime,
In which the chapel shone at Easter time,
The Banners, Vestments, gold, and colors bright,
Counted how many tapers gave their light;
Then in minute detail went on to say,
How the High Altar looked on Christmas-day:

The kings and shepherds, all in green and red,
And a bright star of jewels overhead.
Then told the sign by which they all had seen
How even nature loved to greet her Queen,
For, when Our Lady's last procession went
Down the long garden, every head was bent,
And, rosary in hand, each Sister prayed;
As the long floating banners were displayed,
They struck the hawthorn boughs, and showers and showers
Of buds and blossoms strewed her way with flowers.
The knight unwearied listened; till at last,
He too described the glories of his past;
Tourney, and joust, and pageant bright and fair,
And all the lovely ladies who were there.
But half incredulous she heard. Could this —
This be the world? this place of love and bliss!
Where then was hid the strange and hideous charm,
That never failed to bring the gazer harm?
She crossed herself, yet asked, and listened still,
And still the knight described with all his skill
The glorious world of joy, all joys above,
Transfigured in the golden mist of love.
Spread, spread your wings, ye angel guardians bright,
And shield these dazzling phantoms from her sight!
But no; days passed, matins and vespers rang,
And still the quiet Nuns toiled, prayed, and sang,
And never guessed the fatal, coiling net
Which every day drew near, and nearer yet,
Around their darling; for she went and came
About her duties, outwardly the same.
The same? ah, no! even when she knelt to pray,
Some charmèd dream kept all her heart away.
So days went on, until the convent gate
Opened one night. Who durst go forth so late?
Across the moonlit grass, with stealthy tread,
Two silent, shrouded figures passed and fled.
And all was silent, save the moaning seas,
That sobbed and pleaded, and a wailing breeze
That sighed among the perfumed hawthorn-trees.

What need to tell that dream so bright and brief,
Of joy uncheckered by a dread of grief?
What need to tell how all such dreams must fade,
Before the slow, foreboding, dreaded shade,
That floated nearer, until pomp and pride,
Pleasure and wealth, were summoned to her side,
To bid, at least, the noisy hours forget,
And clamor down the whispers of regret.
Still Angela strove to dream, and strove in vain;
Awakened once, she could not sleep again.
She saw, each day and hour, more worthless grown
The heart for which she cast away her own;
And her soul learnt, through bitterest inward strife,
The slight, frail love for which she wrecked her life,
The phantom for which all her hope was given,
The cold bleak earth for which she bartered heaven!
But all in vain; would even the tenderest heart
Now stoop to take so poor an outcast's part?

Years fled, and she grew reckless more and more,
Until the humblest peasant closed his door,
And where she passed, fair dames, in scorn and pride,
Shuddered, and drew their rustling robes aside.
At last a yearning seemed to fill her soul,
A longing that was stronger than control:
Once more, just once again, to see the place
That knew her young and innocent; to retrace
The long and weary southern path; to gaze
Upon the haven of her childish days;
Once more beneath the convent roof to lie;
Once more to look upon her home — and die!
Weary and worn — her comrades, chill remorse
And black despair, yet a strange silent force
Within her heart, that drew her more and more —
Onward she crawled, and begged from door to door.
Weighed down with weary days, her failing strength
Grew less each hour, till one day's dawn at length,
As first its rays flooded the world with light,
Showed the broad waters, glittering blue and bright,

And where, amid the leafy hawthorn wood,
Just as of old the quiet cloister stood.
Would any know her? Nay, no fear. Her face
Had lost all trace of youth, of joy, of grace,
Of the pure, happy soul they used to know —
The novice Angela — so long ago.
She rang the convent bell. The well-known sound
Smote on her heart, and bowed her to the ground.
And she, who had not wept for long, dry years,
Felt the strange rush of unaccustomed tears;
Terror and anguish seemed to check her breath,
And stop her heart. O God! could this be death?
Crouching against the iron gate, she laid
Her weary head against the bars, and prayed:
But nearer footsteps drew, then seemed to wait;
And then she heard the opening of the grate,
And saw the withered face, on which awoke
Pity and sorrow, as the portress spoke,
And asked the stranger's bidding: "Take me in,"
She faltered, "Sister Monica, from sin,
And sorrow, and despair, that will not cease;
O, take me in, and let me die in peace!"
With soothing words the Sister bade her wait,
Until she brought the key to unbar the gate.
The beggar tried to thank her as she lay,
And heard the echoing footsteps die away.
But what soft voice was that which sounded near,
And stirred strange trouble in her heart to hear?
She raised her head; she saw — she seemed to know —
A face that came from long, long years ago:
Herself; yet not as when she fled away,
The young and blooming novice, fair and gay,
But a grave woman, gentle and serene:
The outcast knew it, — *what she might have been.*
But, as she gazed and gazed, a radiance bright
Filled all the place with strange and sudden light;
The Nun was there no longer, but instead,
A figure with a circle round its head,
A ring of glory; and a face, so meek,
So soft, so tender. . . . Angela strove to speak,

And stretched her hands out, crying, "Mary mild,
Mother of mercy, help me! — help your child!"
And Mary answered, "From thy bitter past,
Welcome, my child! O, welcome home at last!
I filled thy place. Thy flight is known to none,
For all thy daily duties I have done;
Gathered thy flowers, and prayed, and sung, and slept;
Didst thou not know, poor child, *thy place was kept?*
Kind hearts are here; yet would the tenderest one
Have limits to its mercy: God has none.
And man's forgiveness may be true and sweet,
But yet he stoops to give it. More complete
Is Love that lays forgiveness at thy feet,
And pleads with thee to raise it. Only Heaven
Means *crowned*, not *vanquished*, when it says, 'Forgiven!'"
Back hurried Sister Monica; but where
Was the poor beggar she left lying there?
Gone; and she searched in vain, and sought the place
For that wan woman, with the piteous face:
But only Angela at the gateway stood,
Laden with hawthorn blossoms from the wood.
And never did a day pass by again,
But the old portress, with a sigh of pain,
Would sorrow for her loitering: with a prayer
That the poor beggar, in her wild despair,
Might not have come to any ill; and when
She ended, "God forgive her!" humbly then
Did Angela bow her head, and say, "Amen!"
How pitiful her heart was! all could trace
Something that dimmed the brightness of her face
After that day, which none had seen before;
Not trouble — but a shadow — nothing more.

Years passed away. Then, one dark day of dread
Saw all the Sisters kneeling round a bed,
Where Angela lay dying; every breath
Struggling beneath the heavy hand of death.
But suddenly a flush lit up her cheek,
She raised her wan right hand, and strove to speak.

In sorrowing love they listened; not a sound
Or sigh disturbed the utter silence round.
The very tapers' flames were scarcely stirred,
In such hushed awe the Sisters knelt and heard.
And through that silence Angela told her life:
Her sin, her flight; the sorrow and the strife,
And the return; and then clear, low, and calm,
"Praise God for me, my sisters"; and the psalm
Rang up to heaven, far and clear and wide,
Again, and yet again, then sank and died;
While her white face had such a smile of peace,
They saw she never heard the music cease;
And weeping Sisters laid her in her tomb,
Crowned with a wreath of perfumed hawthorn bloom.

And thus the Legend ended. It may be
Something is hidden in the mystery,
Besides the lesson of God's pardon shown,
Never enough believed, or asked, or known.
Have we not all, amid life's petty strife,
Some pure ideal of a noble life
That once seemed possible? Did we not hear
The flutter of its wings, and feel it near,
And just within our reach? It was. And yet
We lost it in this daily jar and fret,
And now live idle in a vague regret.
But still *our place is kept*, and it will wait,
Ready for us to fill it, soon or late:
No star is ever lost we once have seen,
We always may be what we might have been.
Since Good, though only thought, has life and breath,
God's life — can always be redeemed from death;
And evil, in its nature, is decay,
And any hour can blot it all away;
The hopes that lost in some far distance seem,
May be the truer life, and this the dream.

ENVY.

He was the first always: Fortune
  Shone bright in his face.
I fought for years; with no effort
  He conquered the place:
We ran; my feet were all bleeding,
  But he won the race.

Spite of his many successes,
  Men loved him the same;
My one pale ray of good fortune
  Met scoffing and blame.
When we erred, they gave him pity,
  But me — only shame.

My home was still in the shadow,
  His lay in the sun:
I longed in vain: what he asked for
  It straightway was done.
Once I staked all my heart's treasure,
  We played — and he won.

Yes; and just now I have seen him,
  Cold, smiling, and blest,
Laid in his coffin. God help me!
  While he is at rest,
I am cursed still to live: — even
  Death loved him the best.

OVER THE MOUNTAIN.

Like dreary prison walls
  The stern, gray mountains rise,
Until their topmost crags
  Touch the far gloomy skies;
One steep and narrow path
  Winds up the mountain's crest,
And from our valley leads
  Out to the golden West.

I dwell here in content,
  Thankful for tranquil days;
And yet my eyes grow dim,
  As still I gaze and gaze
Upon that mountain pass,
  That leads — or so it seems —
To some far happy land,
  Known in a world of dreams.

And as I watch that path
  Over the distant hill,
A foolish longing comes
  My heart and soul to fill,
A painful, strange desire
  To break some weary bond;
A vague unuttered wish
  For what might lie beyond!

In that far world unknown,
  Over that distant hill,
May dwell the loved and lost,
  Lost — yet belovéd still;
I have a yearning hope,
  Half longing, and half pain,
That by that mountain pass
  They may return again.

Space may keep friends apart,
  Death has a mighty thrall;
There is another gulf
  Harder to cross than all;
Yet watching that far road,
  My heart beats full and fast:
If they should come once more,
  If they should come at last!

See, down the mountain-side
  The silver vapors creep;
They hide the rocky cliffs,
  They hide the craggy steep,
They hide the narrow path
  That comes across the hill: —
O foolish longing, cease,
  O beating Heart, be still!

BEYOND.

We must not doubt, or fear, or dread, that love for life is only given,
And that the calm and sainted dead will meet estranged and cold in heaven: —
O, Love were poor and vain indeed, based on so harsh and stern a creed.

True that this earth must pass away, with all the starry worlds of light,
With all the glory of the day, and calmer tenderness of night;
For in that radiant home can shine alone the immortal and divine.

Earth's lower things — her pride, her fame, her science, learning, wealth, and power —
Slow growths that through long ages came, or fruits of some convulsive hour,
Whose very memory must decay — Heaven is too pure for such as they.

They are complete: their work is done. So let them sleep in endless rest.
Love's life is only here begun, nor is, nor can be, fully blest;
It has no room to spread its wings, amid this crowd of meaner things.

Just for the very shadow thrown upon its sweetness here below,
The cross that it must bear alone, and bloody baptism of woe,
Crowned and completed through its pain, we know that it shall rise

So if its flame burn pure and bright, here, where our air is dark and dense,
And nothing in this world of night lives with a living so intense;
When it shall reach its home at length — how bright its light! how strong its strength!

And while the vain weak loves of earth (for such base counterfeits abound)
Shall perish with what gave them birth — their graves are green and fresh around,
No funeral song shall need to rise for the true Love that never dies.

If in my heart I now could fear that, risen again, we should not know
What was our Life of Life when here, — the hearts we loved so much below, —
I would arise this very day, and cast so poor a thing away.

But Love is no such soulless clod: living, perfected it shall rise
Transfigured in the light of God, and giving glory to the skies:
And that which makes this life so sweet shall render Heaven's joy complete.

A WARNING.

PLACE your hands in mine, dear,
  With their rose-leaf touch:
If you heed my warning,
  It will spare you much.

Ah! with just such smiling
  Unbelieving eyes,
Years ago I heard it: —
  You shall be more wise.

You have one great treasure,
  Joy for all your life;
Do not let it perish
  In one reckless strife.

Do not venture all, child,
  In one frail, weak heart;
So, through any shipwreck,
  You may save a part

Where your soul is tempted
  Most to trust your fate,
There, with double caution,
  Linger, fear, and wait.

Measure all you give, still
  Counting what you take;
Love for love, so placing
  Each an equal stake.

Treasure love; though ready
  Still to live without.
In your fondest trust, keep
  Just one thread of doubt.

Build on no to-morrow;
  Love has but to-day:
If the links seem slackening,
  Cut the bond away.

Trust no prayer nor promise;
  Words are grains of sand:
To keep your heart unbroken,
  Hold it in your hand.

That your love may finish
  Calm as it begun,
Learn this lesson better,
  Dear, than I have done.

Years hence, perhaps, this warning
  You shall give again,
In just the self-same words, dear,
  And — just as much — in vain.

MAXIMUS.

Many, if God should make them kings,
  Might not disgrace the throne
    He gave;
How few who could as well fulfil
  The holier office of a slave!

I hold him great who, for Love's
    sake,
  Can give, with generous, earnest will, —

Yet he who takes for Love's
    sweet sake,
  I think I hold more generous
    still.

I prize the instinct that can
    turn
  From vain pretence with proud
    disdain;
Yet more I prize a simple heart
  Paying credulity with pain.

I bow before the noble mind
  That freely some great wrong
    forgives;
Yet nobler is the one forgiven,
  Who bears that burden well,
    and lives.

It may be hard to gain, and still
  To keep a lowly steadfast
    heart;
Yet he who loses has to fill
  A harder and a truer part.

Glorious it is to wear the crown
  Of a deserved and pure success; —
He who knows how to fail has
    won
  A Crown whose lustre is not
    less.

Great may he be who can command
  And rule with just and tender
    sway;
Yet is diviner wisdom taught
  Better by him who can obey.

Blessèd are those who die for God,
  And earn the Martyr's crown of light;
Yet he who lives for God may be
  A greater Conqueror in His sight.

OPTIMUS.

There is a deep and subtle snare
Whose sure temptation hardly fails,
Which, just because it looks so fair,
Only a noble heart assails.

So all the more we need be strong
Against this false and seeming Right;
Which none the less is deadly wrong,
Because it glitters clothed in light.

When duties unfulfilled remain,
Or noble works are left unplanned,
Or when great deeds cry out in vain
On coward heart and trembling hand, —

Then will a seeming Angel speak : —
" The hours are fleeting — great the need —
If thou art strong and others weak,
Thine be the effort and the deed.

" Deaf are their ears who ought to hear ;
Idle their hands, and dull their soul ;
While sloth, or ignorance, or fear,
Fetters them with a blind control.

" Sort thou the tangled web aright ;
Take thou the toil, take thou the pain :
For fear the hour begin its flight,
While Right and Duty plead in vain."

And now it is I bid thee pause,
Nor let this Tempter bend thy will;
There are diviner, truer laws
That teach a nobler lesson still.

Learn that each duty makes its claim
Upon one soul : not each on all.
How, if God speaks thy Brother's name,
Dare thou make answer to the call ?

The greater peril in the strife,
The less this evil should be done ;
For as in battle, so in life,
Danger and honor still are one.

Arouse him then : — this is thy part :
Show him the claim ; point out the need ;

And nerve his arm, and cheer
  his heart;
Then stand aside, and say, "God
  speed!"

Smooth thou his path ere it is
  trod;
Burnish the arms that he must
  wield;
And pray, with all thy strength,
  that God
May crown him Victor of the
  field.

And then, I think, thy soul shall
  feel
A nobler thrill of true content,
Than if presumptuous, eager zeal
Had seized a crown for others
  meant.

And even that very deed shall
  shine
In mystic sense, divine and true,
More wholly and more purely
  thine —
Because it is another's too.

A LOST CHORD.

Seated one day at the Organ,
  I was weary and ill at ease,
And my fingers wandered idly
  Over the noisy keys.

I do not know what I was playing,
  Or what I was dreaming then;
But I struck one chord of music,
  Like the sound of a great
  Amen.

It flooded the crimson twilight,
  Like the close of an Angel's
  Psalm,
And it lay on my fevered spirit
  With a touch of infinite calm.

It quieted pain and sorrow,
  Like love overcoming strife;
It seemed the harmonious echo
  From our discordant life.

It linked all perpléxéd meanings
  Into one perfect peace,
And trembled away into silence
  As if it were loth to cease.

I have sought, but I seek it vainly,
  That one lost chord divine,
Which came from the soul of the
  Organ,
  And entered into mine.

It may be that Death's bright
  angel
  Will speak in that chord again,
It may be that only in Heaven
  I shall hear that grand Amen.

TOO LATE.

Hush! speak low; tread softly;
  Draw the sheet aside; —
Yes, she does look peaceful;
  With that smile she died.

Yet stern want and sorrow
    Even now you trace
On the wan, worn features
    Of the still white face.

Restless, helpless, hopeless,
    Was her bitter part;—
Now— how still the Violets
    Lie upon her Heart!

She who toiled and labored
    For her daily bread;
See the velvet hangings
    Of this stately bed.

Yes, they did forgive her;
    Brought her home at last;
Strove to cover over
    Their relentless past.

Ah, they would have given
    Wealth, and home, and pride,
To see her just look happy
    Once before she died!

They strove hard to please her,
    But, when death is near,
All you know is deadened,
    Hope, and joy, and fear.

And besides, one sorrow
    Deeper still— one pain
Was beyond them: healing
    Came to-day— in vain!

If she had but lingered
    Just a few hours more;
Or had this letter reached her
    Just one day before!

I can almost pity
    Even him to-day;
Though he let this anguish
    Eat her heart away.

Yet she never blamed him;—
    One day you shall know
How this sorrow happened;
    It was long ago.

I have read the letter;
    Many a weary year,
For one word she hungered,—
    There are thousands here.

If she could but hear it,
    Could but understand;
See,— I put the letter
    In her cold white hand.

Even these words, so longed for,
    Do not stir her rest;
Well, I should not murmur,
    For God judges best.

She needs no more pity,—
    But I mourn his fate,
When he hears his letter
    Came a day too late.

THE REQUITAL.

Loud roared the Tempest,
    Fast fell the sleet;
A little Child Angel
    Passed down the street,
With trailing pinions,
    And weary feet.

The moon was hidden;
  No stars were bright;
So she could not shelter
  In heaven that night,
For the Angels' ladders
  Are rays of light.

She beat her wings
  At each window-pane,
And pleaded for shelter,
  But all in vain;—
"Listen," they said,
  "To the pelting rain!"

She sobbed, as the laughter
  And mirth grew higher,
"Give me rest and shelter
  Beside your fire,
And I will give you
  Your heart's desire."

The dreamer sat watching
  His embers gleam,
While his heart was floating
  Down hope's bright stream;
. . . So he wove her wailing
  Into his dream.

The worker toiled on,
  For his time was brief;
The mourner was nursing
  Her own pale grief;
They heard not the promise
  That brought relief.

But fiercer the Tempest
  Rose than before,
When the Angel paused
  At a humble door,
And asked for shelter
  And help once more

A weary woman,
  Pale, worn, and thin,
With the brand upon her
  Of want and sin,
Heard the Child Angel
  And took her in.

Took her in gently,
  And did her best
To dry her pinions;
  And made her rest
With tender pity
  Upon her breast.

When the eastern morning
  Grew bright and red,
Up the first sunbeam
  The Angel fled;
Having kissed the woman
  And left her — dead.

RETURNED — "MISSING."

(FIVE YEARS AFTER.)

YES, I was sad and anxious,
  But now, dear, I am gay;
I know that it is wisest
  To put all hope away:—
Thank God that I have done so,
  And can be calm to-day!

For hope deferred — you know it —
  Once made my heart so sick:
Now, I expect no longer;
  It is but the old trick
Of hope, that makes me tremble,
  And makes my heart beat quick.

All day I sit here calmly;
  Not as I did before,
Watching for one whose footstep
  Comes never, never more. . . .
Hush! was that some one passing,
  Who paused beside the door?

For years I hung on chances,
  Longing for just one word;
At last I feel it: — silence
  Will never more be stirred. . .
Tell me once more that rumor
  You fancied you had heard.

Life has more things to dwell on
  Than just one useless pain,
Useless and past forever;
  But noble things remain,
And wait us all: . . . you too, dear,
  Do you think hope quite vain?

All others have forgotten,
  'T is right I should forget,
Nor live on a keen longing
  Which shadows forth regret: . . .
Are not the letters coming?
  The sun is almost set.

Now that my restless legion
  Of hopes and fears is fled,
Reading is joy and comfort . . .
  . . . This very day I read,
O, such a strange returning
  Of one whom all thought dead!

Not that *I* dream or fancy,
  You know all that is past;
Earth has no hope to give me,
  And yet — Time flies so fast
That all but the impóssible
  Might be brought back at last.

IN THE WOOD.

In the wood where shadows are deepest
  From the branches overhead,
Where the wild wood-strawberries cluster,
  And the softest moss is spread,
I met to-day with a fairy,
  And I followed her where she led.

Some magical words she uttered,
  I alone could understand,
For the sky grew bluer and brighter;
  While there rose on either hand
The cloudy walls of a palace
  That was built in Fairy-land.

And I stood in a strange enchantment;
  I had known it all before:
In my heart of hearts was the magic
  Of days that will come no more,
The magic of joy departed,
  That Time can never restore.

That never, ah, never, never,
  Never again can be: —
Shall I tell you what powerful fairy
  Built up this palace for me?
It was only a little white Violet
  I found at the root of a tree.

TWO WORLDS.

God's world is bathed in beauty,
  God's world is steeped in light;
It is the self-same glory
  That makes the day so bright,
Which thrills the earth with music,
  Or hangs the stars in night.

Hid in earth's mines of silver,
  Floating on clouds above, —
Ringing in Autumn's tempest,
  Murmured by every dove, —
One thought fills God's creation,
  His own great name of Love!

In God's world Strength is lovely,
  And so is Beauty strong,
And Light — God's glorious shadow —
  To both great gifts belong;
And they all melt into sweetness,
  And fill the earth with Song.

Above God's world bends Heaven,
  With day's kiss pure and bright,
Or folds her still more fondly
  In the tender shade of night;
And she casts back Heaven's sweetness,
  In fragrant love and light.

God's world has one great echo;
  Whether calm blue mists are curled,
Or lingering dew-drops quiver,
  Or red storms are unfurled;
The same deep love is throbbing
  Through the great heart of God's world.

Man's world is black and blighted,
  Steeped through with self and sin;
And should his feeble purpose
  Some feeble good begin,
The work is marred and tainted
  By Leprosy within.

Man's world is bleak and bitter;
  Wherever he has trod
He spoils the tender beauty
  That blossoms on the sod,

And blasts the loving Heaven
  Of the great, good world of
    God.

There Strength on coward weakness
  In cruel might will roll;
Beauty and Joy are cankers
  That eat away the soul;
And Love — O God, avenge it —
  The plague-spot of the whole.

Man's world is Pain and Terror;
  He found it pure and fair,
And wove in nets of sorrow
  The golden summer air.
Black, hideous, cold, and dreary,
  Man's curse, not God's, is there.

And yet God's world is speaking:
  Man will not hear it call;
But listens where the echoes
  Of his own discords fall,
Then clamors back to Heaven
  That God has done it all.

O God, man's heart is darkened,
  He will not understand!
Show him Thy cloud and fire;
  And, with Thine own right
    hand,
Then lead him through his desert,
  Back to Thy Holy Land!

A NEW MOTHER.

I was with my lady when she
  died:
I it was who guided her weak hand
  For a blessing on each little
    head,
Laid her baby by her on the
  bed,
Heard the words they could not
  understand.

And I drew them round my
  knee that night,
Hushed their childish glee, and
  made them say
  They would keep her words
    with loving tears,
  They would not forget her
    dying fears
Lest the thought of her should
  fade away.

I, who guessed what her last
  dread had been,
Made a promise to that still,
  cold face,
  That her children's hearts, at
    any cost,
  Should be with the mother
    they had lost,
When a stranger came to take
  her place.

And I knew so much! for I had
  lived
With my lady since her childhood: known
  What her young and happy
    days had been,
  And the grief no other eyes
    had seen
I had watched and sorrowed for
  alone.

Ah! she once had such a happy smile!
I had known how sorely she was tried:
Six short years before, her eyes were bright
As her little blue-eyed May's that night,
When she stood by her dead mother's side.

No, I will not say he was unkind;
But she had been used to love and praise.
He was somewhat grave,— perhaps, in truth,
Could not weave her joyous, smiling youth
Into all his stern and serious ways.

She, who should have reigned a blooming flower,
First in pride and honor, as in grace,—
She, whose will had once ruled all around,
Queen and darling of us all,— she found
Change indeed in that cold, stately place.

Yet she would not blame him, even to me,
Though she often sat and wept alone;
But she could not hide it near her death,
When she said with her last struggling breath,
"Let my babies still remain my own!"

I it was who drew the sheet aside,
When he saw his dead wife's face. That test
Seemed to strike right to his heart. He said,
In a strange, low whisper, to the dead,
"God knows, love, I did it for the best!"

And he wept — O yes, I will be just —
When I brought the children to him there,
Wondering sorrow in their baby eyes;
And he soothed them with his fond replies,
Bidding me give double love and care.

Ah, I loved them well for her dear sake:
Little Arthur, with his serious air;
May, with all her mother's pretty ways,
Blushing, and at any word of praise
Shaking out her sunny golden hair.

And the little one of all — poor child!
She had cost that dear and precious life.

Once Sir Arthur spoke my lady's name,
When the baby's gloomy christening came,
And he called her "Olga—like my wife!"

Save that time, he never spoke of her:
He grew graver, sterner, every day;
And the children felt it, for they dropped
Low their voices, and their laughter stopped,
While he stood and watched them at their play.

No, he never named their mother's name.
But I told them of her: told them all
She had been; so gentle, good, and bright;
And I always took them every night
Where her picture hung in the great hall.

There she stood: white daisies in her hand,
And her red lips parted as to speak
With a smile; the blue and sunny air
Seemed to stir her floating golden hair,
And to bring a faint blush on her cheek.

Well, so time passed on; a year was gone,
And Sir Arthur had been much away.
Then the news came! I shed many tears
When I saw the truth of all my fears
Rise before me on that bitter day.

Any one but her I could have borne!
But my lady loved her as her friend.
Through their childhood and their early youth,
How she used to count upon the truth
Of this friendship that would never end!

Older, graver than my lady was,
Whose young, gentle heart on her relied,
She would give advice, and praise, and blame,
And my lady leant on Margaret's name,
As her dearest comfort, help, and guide.

I had never liked her, and I think
That my lady grew to doubt her too,
Since her marriage; for she named her less,

Never saw her, and I used to guess
At some secret wrong I never knew.

That might be or not. But now, to hear
She would come and reign here in her stead,
With the pomp and splendor of a bride:
Would no thought reproach her in her pride
With the silent memory of the dead?

So, the day came, and the bells rang out,
And I laid the children's black aside;
And I held each little trembling hand,
As I strove to make them understand
They must greet their father's new-made bride.

Ah, Sir Arthur might look grave and stern,
And his lady's eyes might well grow dim,
When the children shrank in fear away, —
Little Arthur hid his face, and May
Would not raise her eyes, or speak to him.

When Sir Arthur bade them greet their "mother,"
I was forced to chide, yet proud to hear
How my little loving May replied,
With her mother's pretty air of pride, —
"Our dear mother has been dead a year!"

Ah, the lady's tears might well fall fast,
As she kissed them, and then turned away.
She might strive to smile or to forget,
But I think some shadow of regret
Must have risen to blight her wedding-day.

She had some strange touch of self-reproach;
For she used to linger day by day,
By the nursery door, or garden gate,
With a sad, calm, wistful look, and wait
Watching the three children at their play.

But they always shrank away from her
When she strove to comfort their alarms,

And their grave, cold silence
    to beguile:
Even little Olga's baby-smile
Quivered into tears when in her
    arms.

I could never chide them: for I
    saw
How their mother's memory grew
    more deep
  In their hearts. Each night I
    had to tell
  Stories of her whom I loved
    so well
When a child, to send them off
    to sleep.

But Sir Arthur — O, this was
    too hard! —
He, who had been always stern
    and sad
  In my lady's time, seemed to
    rejoice
  Each day more; and I could
    hear his voice
Even, sounding younger and
    more glad.

He might perhaps have blamed
    them, but his wife
Never failed to take the children's
    part:
  She would stay him with her
    pleading tone,
  Saying she would strive, and
    strive alone,
Till she gained each little way-
    ward heart.

And she strove indeed, and
    seemed to be
Always waiting for their love,
    in vain;
  Yet, when May had most her
    mother's look,
  Then the lady's calm, cold ac-
    cents shook
With some memory of reproach-
    ful pain.

Little May would never call her
    mother:
So, one day, the lady, bending
    low,
  Kissed her golden curls, and
    softly said,
  "Sweet one, call me Marga-
    ret, instead, —
Your dear mother used to call
    me so."

She was gentle, kind, and pa-
    tient too,
Yet in vain: the children held
    apart.
  Ah, their mother's gentle
    memory dwelt
  Near them, and her little or-
    phans felt
She had the first claim upon
    their heart.

So three years passed; then the
    war broke out;
And a rumor seemed to spread
    and rise;

First we guessed what sorrow must befall,
Then all doubt fled, for we read it all
In the depths of her despairing eyes.

Yes; Sir Arthur had been called away
To that scene of slaughter, fear, and strife, —
Now he seemed to know with double pain
The cold, bitter gulf that must remain
To divide his children from his wife.

Nearer came the day he was to sail,
Deeper grew the coming woe and fear,
When, one night, the children at my knee
Knelt to say their evening prayer to me,
I looked up and saw Sir Arthur near.

There they knelt with folded hands, and said
Low, soft words in stammering accents sweet;
In the firelight shone their golden hair
And white robes: my darlings looked so fair,
With their little bare and rosy feet!

There he waited till their low "Amen!"
Stopped the rosy lips raised for "Good night!" —
Drew them with a fond clasp, close and near,
As he bade them stay with him, and hear
Something that would make his heart more light.

Little Olga crept into his arms;
Arthur leant upon his shoulder; May
Knelt beside him, with her earnest eyes
Lifted up in patient, calm surprise, —
I can almost hear his words to-day.

"Years ago, my children, years ago,
When your mother was a child, she came
From her Northern home, and here she met
Love for love, and comfort for regret,
In one early friend, — you know her name.

"And this friend — a few years older — gave
Such fond care, such love, that day by day
The new home grew happy, joy complete,

Studies easier, and play more sweet,
While all childish sorrows passed away.

"And your mother — fragile, like my May —
Leant on this deep love, — nor leant in vain.
For this friend (strong, generous, noble heart!)
Gave the sweet, and took the bitter part, —
Brought her all the joy, and kept the pain.

"Years passed on, and then I saw them first:
It was hard to say which was most fair,
Your sweet mother's bright and blushing face,
Or the graver Margaret's stately grace;
Golden locks, or braided raven hair.

"Then it happened, by a strange, sad fate,
One thought entered into each young soul:
Joy for one — if for the other pain;
Loss for one — if for the other gain:
One must lose, and one possess the whole.

"And so this — this — what they cared for — came
And belonged to Margaret: was her own.
But she laid the gift aside, to take
Pain and sorrow for your mother's sake,
And none knew it but herself alone.

"Then she travelled far away, and none
The strange mystery of her absence knew.
Margaret's secret thought was never told:
Even your mother thought her changed and cold,
And for many years I thought so too.

"She was gone; and then your mother took
That poor gift which Margaret laid aside:
Flower, or toy, or trinket, matters not:
What it was had better be forgot . . .
It was just then she became my bride.

"Now, I think May knows the hope I have.
Arthur, darling, can you guess the rest?

Even my little Olga understands
Great gifts can be given by little hands,
Since of all gifts Love is still the best.

"Margaret is my dear and honored wife,
And I hold her so. But she can claim
From your hearts, dear ones, a loving debt
I can neither pay, nor yet forget:
You can give it in your mother's name.

"Earth spoils even Love, and here a shade
On the purest, noblest heart may fall:
Now your mother dwells in perfect light,
She will bless us, I believe, to-night, —
She is happy now, and she knows all."

Next day was farewell, — a day of tears;
Yet Sir Arthur, as he rode away,
And turned back to see his lady stand
With the children clinging to her hand,
Looked as if it were a happy day.

Ah, they loved her soon! The little one
Crept into her arms as to a nest;
Arthur always with her now; and May
Growing nearer to her every day: —
— Well, I loved my own dear lady best.

GIVE PLACE.

STARRY Crowns of Heaven
  Set in azure night!
Linger yet a little
  Ere you hide your light: —
    — Nay; let Starlight fade away,
  Heralding the day!

Snow-flakes pure and spotless,
  Still, O, still remain,
Binding dreary winter,
  In your silver chain: —
    — Nay; but melt at once and bring
  Radiant sunny Spring!

Blossoms, gentle blossoms,
  Do not wither yet;
Still for you the sun shines,
  Still the dews are wet: —
    — Nay; but fade and wither fast,
  Fruit must come at last!

Joy, so true and tender,
  Dare you not abide?
Will you spread your pinions,
  Must you leave our side?
    — Nay; an Angel's shining grace
  Waits to fill your place!

MY WILL.

SINCE I have no lands or houses,
  And no hoarded golden store,
What can I leave those who love me
  When they see my face no more?
Do not smile; I am not jesting,
  Though my words sound gay and light,
Listen to me, dearest Alice,
  I will make my Will to-night.

First for Mabel, — who will never
  Let the dust of future years
Dim the thought of me, but keep it
  Brighter still: perhaps with tears.
In whose eyes, whate'er I glance at,
  Touch, or praise, will always shine,
Through a strange and sacred radiance,
  By Love's Charter, wholly mine;

She will never lend to others
  Slenderest link of thought I claim,
I will, therefore, to her keeping
  Leave my memory and my name.

Bertha will do truer service
  To her kind than I have done,
So I leave to her young spirit
  The long Work I have begun.
Well! the threads are tangled, broken,
  And the colors do not blend,
She will bend her earnest striving
  Both to finish and amend:
And, when it is all completed,
  Strong with care and rich with skill,
Just because my hands began it,
  She will love it better still.

Ruth shall have my dearest token,
  The one link I dread to break,
The one duty that I live for,
  She, when I am gone, will take.
Sacred is the trust I leave her,
  Needing patience, prayer, and tears;
I have striven to fulfil it,
  As she knows, these many years.
Sometimes hopeless, faint, and weary,
  Yet a blessing shall remain

With the task, and Ruth will prize it,
For my many hours of pain.

What must I leave you, my Alice?
Nothing, Love, to do or bear,
Nothing that can dim your blue eyes
With the slightest cloud of care.
I will leave my heart to love you,
With the tender faith of old;
Still to comfort, warm, and light you,
Should your life grow dark or cold.
No one else, my child, can claim it;
Though you find old scars of pain,
They were only wounds, my darling,
There is not, I trust, one stain.

Are my gifts indeed so worthless
Now the slender sum is told?
Well, I know not: years may bless them
With a nobler price than gold.
Am I poor? ah no, most wealthy,
Not in these poor gifts you take,
But in the true hearts that tell me
You will keep them for my sake.

KING AND SLAVE.

If in my soul, dear,
An omen should dwell,
Bidding me pause, ere
I love thee too well;
If the whole circle
Of noble and wise,
With stern forebodings,
Between us should rise; —

I will tell *them*, dear,
That Love reigns — a King,
Where storms cannot reach him,
And words cannot sting;
He counts it dishonor
His faith to recall;
He trusts; — and forever
He gives — and gives all!

I will tell *thee*, dear,
That Love is — a Slave,
Who dreads thought of freedom,
As life dreads the grave;
And if doubt or peril
Of change there may be,
Such fear would but drive him
Still nearer to thee!

A CHANT.

"*Benedictus qui venit in nomine Domini.*"

I.

Who is the Angel that cometh?
Life!
Let us not question what he brings,
Peace or Strife;

Under the shade of his mighty
wings,
    One by one,
  Are his secrets told;
    One by one,
Lit by the rays of each morning
sun,
  Shall a new flower its petals
unfold,
  With the mystery hid in its
heart of gold.
We will arise and go forth to
greet him,
  Singly, gladly, with one accord; —
"Blessed is he that cometh
  In the name of the Lord!"

II.

Who is the Angel that cometh?
    Joy!
Look at his glittering rainbow
wings, —
    No alloy
Lies in the radiant gifts he
brings;
  Tender and sweet,
  He is come to-day,
  Tender and sweet:
While chains of love on his
silver feet
Will hold him in lingering fond
delay.
But greet him quickly, he will
not stay,
Soon he will leave us; but
though for others
All his brightest treasures are
stored, —

"Blessed is he that cometh
  In the name of the Lord!"

III.

Who is the Angel that cometh?
    Pain!
Let us arise and go forth to greet
him;
    Not in vain
Is the summons come for us to
meet him;
  He will stay,
  And darken our sun;
  He will stay
A desolate night, a weary day.
  Since in that shadow our
work is done,
  And in that shadow our
crowns are won,
Let us say still, while his bitter
chalice
  Slowly into our hearts is
poured, —
"Blessed is he that cometh
  In the name of the Lord!"

IV.

Who is the Angel that cometh?
    Death!
But do not shudder and do not
fear;
  Hold your breath,
For a kingly presence is drawing
near.
  Cold and bright
  Is his flashing steel,
  Cold and bright

The smile that comes like a
    starry light
  To calm the terror and grief
    we feel;
He comes to help and to save
    and heal:
Then let us, baring our hearts
    and kneeling,
  Sing, while we wait this An-
    gel's sword, —
" Blessed is he that cometh
    In the name of the Lord!"

DREAM-LIFE.

LISTEN, friend, and I will tell
    you
  Why I sometimes seem so
    glad,
Then, without a reason, chang-
    ing,
  Soon become so grave and
    sad.

Half my life I live a beggar,
  Ragged, helpless, and alone;
But the other half a monarch,
  With my courtiers round my
    throne.

Half my life is full of sorrow,
  Half of joy, still fresh and
    new;
One of these lives is a fancy,
  But the other one is true.

While I live and feast on glad-
    ness,
  Still I feel the thought remain,
This must soon end, — nearer,
    nearer,
  Comes the life of grief and
    pain.

While I live a wretched beggar,
  One bright hope my lot can
    cheer;
Soon, soon thou shalt have thy
    kingdom,
  Brighter hours are drawing
    near.

So you see my life is twofold,
  Half a pleasure, half a grief;
Thus all joy is somewhat tem-
    pered,
  And all sorrow finds relief.

Which, you ask me, is the real life,
  Which the dream, — the joy,
    or woe?
Hush, friend! it is little matter,
  And, indeed — I never know.

REST.

SPREAD, spread thy silver wings,
    O Dove!
And seek for rest by land and
    sea,
And bring the tidings back to me
For thee and me and those I
    love.

Look how my Dove soars far away;
Go with her, heart of mine, I pray;
Go where her fluttering silver pinions
Follow the track of the crimson day.

Is rest where cloudlets slowly creep,
And sobbing winds forget to grieve,
And quiet waters gently heave,
As if they rocked the ship to sleep?
Ah no! that southern vapor white
Will bring a tempest ere the night,
And thunder through the quiet heaven,
Lashing the sea in its angry might.

The battle-field lies still and cold,
While stars that watch in silent light
Gleam here and there on weapons bright,
In weary sleepers' slackened hold;
Nay, though they dream of no alarm,
One bugle sound will stir that calm,
And all the strength of two great nations,
Eager for battle, will rise and arm.

Pause where the Pilgrims' day is done,
Where scrip and staff aside are laid,
And, resting in the silent shade,
They watch the slowly sinking sun.
Ah no! that worn and weary band
Must journey long before they stand,
With bleeding feet, and hearts rejoicing,
Kissing the dust of the Holy Land.

Then find a soul who meets at last
A noble prize but hard to gain,
Or joy long pleaded for in vain,
Now sweeter for a bitter past.
Ah no! for Time can rob her yet,
And even should cruel Time forget,
Then Death will come, and, unrelenting,
Brand her with sorrowful long regret.

Seek farther, farther yet, O Dove!
Beyond the Land, beyond the Sea,
There shall be rest for thee and me,
For thee and me and those I love.
I heard a promise gently fall,
I heard a far-off Shepherd call

The weary and the broken-hearted,
  Promising rest unto each and all—

It is not marred by outward strife,
It is not lost in calm repose,
It heedeth neither joys nor woes,
Is not disturbed by death or life;
  Through, and beyond them, lies our Rest:
Then cease, O Heart, thy longing quest!
And thou, my Dove, with silver pinions
  Flutter again to thy quiet nest!

THE TYRANT AND THE CAPTIVE.

It was midnight when I listened,
  And I heard two Voices speak;
One was harsh, and stern, and cruel,
  And the other soft and weak:
Yet I saw no Vision enter,
  And I heard no steps depart,
Of this Tyrant and his Captive, . . .
Fate it might be and a *Heart*.

Thus the stern Voice spake in triumph: —
  "I have shut your life away
From the radiant world of nature,
  And the perfumed light of day.
You, who loved to steep your spirit
  In the charm of Earth's delight,
See no glory of the daytime,
  And no sweetness of the night."

But the soft Voice answered calmly: —
  "Nay, for when the March winds bring
Just a whisper to my window,
  I can dream the rest of Spring;
And to-day I saw a swallow
  Flitting past my prison bars,
And my cell has just one corner
  Whence at night I see the stars."

But its bitter taunt repeating,
  Cried the harsh Voice: —
"Where are they,
All the friends of former hours,
  Who forget your name to-day?
All the links of love are shattered,
  Which you thought so strong before;
And your very heart is lonely,
  And alone since loved no more."

But the low Voice spoke still lower: —
  "Nay, I know the golden chain
Of my love is purer, stronger,
  For the cruel fire of pain:

They remember me no longer,
  But I, grieving here alone,
Bind their souls to me forever
  By the love within my own."

But the Voice cried: — "Once remember
  You devoted soul and mind
To the welfare of your brethren,
  And the service of your kind.
Now, what sorrow can you comfort?
You, who lie in helpless pain,
With an impotent compassion
Fretting out your life in vain."

"Nay"; and then the gentle answer
  Rose more loud, and full, and clear:
"For the sake of all my brethren
  I thank God that I am here!
Poor had been my Life's best efforts,
  Now I waste no thought or breath, —
For the prayer of those who suffer
  Has the strength of Love and Death."

THE CARVER'S LESSON.

Trust me, no mere skill of subtle tracery,
  No mere practice of a dexterous hand,
Will suffice, without a hidden spirit,
  That we may, or may not, understand.

And those quaint old fragments that are left us
  Have their power in this, — the Carver brought
Earnest care, and reverent patience, only
  Worthily to clothe some noble thought.

Shut then in the petals of the flowers,
  Round the stems of all the lilies twine,
Hide beneath each bird's or angel's pinion,
  Some wise meaning or some thought divine.

Place in stony hands that pray forever
  Tender words of peace, and strive to wind
Round the leafy scrolls and fretted niches
  Some true, loving message to your kind.

Some will praise, some blame, and, soon forgetting,
  Come and go, nor even pause to gaze;
Only now and then a passing stranger
  Just may loiter with a word of praise.

But I think, when years have floated onward,
And the stone is gray, and dim, and old,
And the hand forgotten that has carved it,
And the heart that dreamt it still and cold;

There may come some weary soul, o'erladen
With perplexéd struggle in his brain,
Or, it may be, fretted with life's turmoil,
Or made sore with some perpetual pain.

Then, I think those stony hands will open,
And the gentle lilies overflow,
With the blessing and the loving token
That you hid there many years ago.

And the tendrils will unroll, and teach him
How to solve the problem of his pain;
And the birds' and angels' wings shake downward
On his heart a sweet and tender rain.

While he marvels at his fancy, reading
Meaning in that quaint and ancient scroll,
Little guessing that the loving Carver
Left a message for his weary soul.

THREE ROSES.

Just when the red June Roses blow
She gave me one, — a year ago.
A Rose whose crimson breath revealed
The secret that its heart concealed,
And whose half-shy, half-tender grace
Blushed back upon the giver's face.
A year ago — a year ago —
To hope was not to know.

Just when the red June Roses blow
I plucked her one, — a month ago:
Its half-blown crimson to eclipse,
I laid it on her smiling lips;
The balmy fragrance of the south
Drew sweetness from her sweeter mouth.
Swiftly do golden hours creep, —
To hold is not to keep.

The red June Roses now are past,
This very day I broke the last, —

And now its perfumed breath is hid,
With her, beneath a coffin-lid;
There will its petals fall apart,
And wither on her icy heart:—
  At three red Roses' cost
  My world was gained and lost.

MY PICTURE GALLERY.

I.

You write and think of me, my friend, with pity;
While you are basking in the light of Rome,
Shut up within the heart of this great city,
Too busy and too poor to leave my home.

II.

You think my life debarred all rest or pleasure,
Chained all day to my ledger and my pen;
Too sickly even to use my little leisure
To bear me from the strife and din of men.

III.

Well, it is true; yet, now the days are longer,
At sunset I can lay my writing down,
And slowly crawl (summer has made me stronger)
Just to the nearest outskirt of the town.

IV.

There a wide Common, blackened though and dreary
With factory smoke, spreads outward to the West;
I lie down on the parched-up grass, if weary,
Or lean against a broken wall to rest.

V.

So might a King, turning to Art's rich treasure,
At evening, when the cares of state were done,
Enter his royal gallery, drinking pleasure
Slowly from each great picture, one by one.

VI.

Towards the West I turn my weary spirit,
And watch my pictures: one each night is mine.
Earth and my soul, sick of day's toil, inherit
A portion of that luminous peace divine.

VII.

There I have seen a sunset's crimson glory,
Burn as if earth were one great Altar's blaze;

Or, like the closing of a piteous
 story,
Light up the misty world with
 dying rays.

VIII.

There I have seen the clouds,
 in pomp and splendor,
Their gold and purple banners
 all unfurl;
There I have watched colors,
 more faint and tender
Than pure and delicate tints
 upon a pearl.

IX.

Skies strewn with roses fading,
 fading slowly,
While one star trembling watched
 the daylight die;
Or deep in gloom a sunset, hidden wholly,
Save through gold rents torn in
 a violet sky.

X.

Or parted clouds, as if asunder
 riven
By some great angel, and beyond a space
Of far-off tranquil light; the gates
 of Heaven
Will lead as grandly to as calm
 a place.

XI.

Or stern dark walls of cloudy
 mountain ranges
Hid all the wonders that we knew
 must be;

While, far on high, some little
 white clouds' changes
Revealed the glory they alone
 could see.

XII.

Or in wild wrath the affrighted
 clouds lay shattered,
Like treasures of the lost Hesperides,
All in a wealth of ruined splendor scattered,
Save one strange light on distant
 silver seas.

XIII.

What land or time can claim the
 Master Painter,
Whose art could teach him half
 such gorgeous dyes?
Or skill so rare, but purer hues
 and fainter
Melt every evening in my western
 skies.

XIV.

So there I wait, until the shade
 has lengthened,
And night's blue misty curtain
 floated down;
Then, with my heart calmed, and
 my spirit strengthened,
I crawl once more back to the
 sultry town.

XV.

What Monarch, then, has nobler
 recreations
Than mine? Or where the great
 and classic Land

Whose wealth of Art delights the
    gathered nations
That owns a Picture Gallery half
    as grand ?

SENT TO HEAVEN.

I HAD a Message to send her,
    To her whom my soul loved
    best;
But I had my task to finish,
    And she was gone home to
    rest.

To rest in the far bright heaven:
    O, so far away from here,
It was vain to speak to my dar-
    ling,
    For I knew she could not
    hear !

I had a message to send her,
    So tender, and true, and
    sweet,
I longed for an Angel to bear it,
    And lay it down at her feet.

I placed it, one summer evening,
    On a Cloudlet's fleecy breast;
But it faded in golden splendor,
    And died in the crimson west.

I gave it the Lark, next morning,
    And I watched it soar and
    soar ;
But its pinions grew faint and
    weary,
    And it fluttered to earth once
    more.

To the heart of a Rose I told it ;
    And the perfume, sweet and
    rare,
Growing faint on the blue bright
    ether,
    Was lost in the balmy air.

I laid it upon a Censer,
    And I saw the incense rise ;
But its clouds of rolling silver
    Could not reach the far blue
    skies.

I cried, in my passionate long-
    ing : —
    " Has the earth no Angel-
    friend
Who will carry my love the mes-
    sage
    That my heart desires to
    send ? "

Then I heard a strain of music,
    So mighty, so pure, so clear,
That my very sorrow was silent,
    And my heart stood still to
    hear.

And I felt, in my soul's deep
    yearning,
    At last the sure answer stir : —
" The music will go up to
    Heaven,
    And carry my thought to her."

It rose in harmonious rushing
　Of mingled voices and strings,
And I tenderly laid my message
　On the Music's outspread wings.

I heard it float farther and farther,
　In sound more perfect than speech;
Farther than sight can follow,
　Farther than soul can reach.

And I know that at last my message
　Has passed through the golden gate:
So my heart is no longer restless,
　And I am content to wait.

NEVER AGAIN.

"Never again!" vow hearts when reunited,
　"Never again shall Love be cast aside;
Forever now the shadow has departed;
　Nor bitter sorrow, veiled in scornful pride,
Shall feign indifference, or affect disdain, —
Never, O Love, again, never again!"

"Never again!" so sobs, in broken accents,
　A soul laid prostrate at a holy shrine, —
"Once more, once more forgive, O Lord, and pardon,
　My wayward life shall bend to love divine;
And nevermore shall sin its whiteness stain, —
Never, O God, again, never again!"

"Never again!" so speaketh one forsaken,
　In the blank desolate passion of despair, —
"Never again shall the bright dream I cherished
　Delude my heart, for bitter truth is there, —
The angel, Hope, shall still thy cruel pain
Never again, my heart, never again!"

"Never again!" so speaks the sudden silence,
　When round the hearth gathers each well-known face,
But one is missing, and no future presence,
　However dear, can fill that vacant place;
Forever shall the burning thought remain, —
"Never, beloved, again! never again!"

"Never again!" so — but beyond
    our hearing —
Ring out far voices fading up
    the sky;
Never again shall earthly care
    and sorrow
    Weigh down the wings that
    bear those souls on high;
"Listen, O earth, and hear that
    glorious strain, —
Never, never again! never
    again!"

LISTENING ANGELS.

BLUE against the bluer heavens
    Stood the mountain, calm and
    still,
Two white Angels, bending
    earthward,
    Leant upon the hill.

Listening leant those silent An-
    gels,
    And I also longed to hear
What sweet strain of earthly
    music
    Thus could charm their ear.

I heard the sound of many trum-
    pets
    In a warlike march draw
    nigh;
Solemnly a mighty army
    Passed in order by.

But the clang had ceased; the
    echoes
    Soon had faded from the hill;
While the Angels, calm and ear-
    nest,
    Leant and listened still.

Then I heard a fainter clamor,
    Forge and wheel were clashing
    near,
And the Reapers in the meadow
    Singing loud and clear.

When the sunset came in glory,
    And the toil of day was o'er,
Still the Angels leant in silence,
    Listening as before.

Then, as daylight slowly van-
    ished,
    And the evening mists grew
    dim,
Solemnly from distant voices
    Rose a vesper hymn.

When the chant was done, and
    lingering
    Died upon the evening air,
From the hill the radiant Angels
    Still were listening there.

Silent came the gathering dark-
    ness,
    Bringing with it sleep and
    rest;
Save a little bird was singing
    Near her leafy nest.

Through the sounds of war and labor
She had warbled all day long,
While the Angels leant and listened
Only to her song.

But the starry night was coming;
When she ceased her little lay,
From the mountain-top the Angels
Slowly passed away.

GOLDEN DAYS.

GOLDEN days — where are they?
  Pilgrims east and west
Cry; if we could find them
  We would pause and rest:
We would pause and rest a little
  From our long and weary ways: —
Where are they, then, where are they —
  Golden days?

Golden days — where are they?
  Ask of childhood's years,
Still untouched by sorrow,
  Still undimmed by tears:
Ah, they seek a phantom Future,
  Crowned with brighter, starry rays; —
Where are they, then, where are they —
  Golden days?

Golden days — where are they?
  Has Love learnt the spell
That will charm them hither,
  Near our hearth to dwell?
Insecure are all her treasures,
  Restless is her anxious gaze: —
Where are they, then, where are they —
  Golden Days?

Golden days — where are they?
  Farther up the hill
I can hear the echo
  Faintly calling still:
Faintly calling, faintly dying,
  In a far-off misty haze: —
Where are they, then, where are they —
  Golden days?

PHILIP AND MILDRED.

Lingering fade the rays of daylight, and the listening air is chilly;
    Voice of bird and forest murmur, insect hum and quivering spray,
Stir not in that quiet hour: through the valley, calm and stilly,
    All in hushed and loving silence watch the slow departing Day.

Till the last faint western cloudlet, faint and rosy, ceases blushing,
    And the blue grows deep and deeper where one trembling planet shines,
And the day has gone forever— then, like some great ocean rushing,
    The sad night wind wails lamenting, sobbing through the moaning pines.

Such, of all day's changing hours, is the fittest and the meetest
    For a farewell hour — and parting looks less bitter and more blest;
Earth seems like a shrine for sorrow, Nature's mother voice is sweetest,
    And her hand seems laid in chiding on the unquiet throbbing breast.

Words are lower, for the twilight seems rebuking sad repining,
    And wild murmur and rebellion, as all childish and in vain;
Breaking through dark future hours clustering starry hopes seem shining,
    Then the calm and tender midnight folds her shadow round the pain.

So they paced the shady lime-walk in that twilight dim and holy,
    Still the last farewell deferring, she could hear or he should say;
Every word, weighed down by sorrow, fell more tenderly and slowly —
    This, which now beheld their parting, should have been their wedding-day.

Should have been : her dreams of childhood, never straying, never faltering,
   Still had needed Philip's image to make future life complete ;
Philip's young hopes of ambition, ever changing, ever altering,
   Needed Mildred's gentle presence even to make successes sweet.

This day should have seen their marriage ; the calm crowning and assurance
   Of two hearts, fulfilling rather, and not changing, either life :
Now they must be rent asunder, and her heart must learn endurance,
   For he leaves their home, and enters on a world of work and strife.

But her gentle spirit long had learnt, unquestioning, submitting,
   To revere his youthful longings, and to marvel at the fate
That gave such a humble office, all unworthy and unfitting,
   To the genius of the village, who was born for something great.

When the learnéd Traveller came there who had gained renown at college,
   Whose abstruse research had won him even European fame,
Questioned Philip, praised his genius, marvelled at his self-taught knowledge,
   Could she murmur if he called him up to London and to fame ?

Could she waver when he bade her take the burden of decision,
   Since his troth to her was plighted, and his life was now her own ?
Could she doom him to inaction ? could she, when a new-born vision
   Rose in glory for his future, check it for her sake alone ?

So her little trembling fingers, that had toiled with such fond pleasure,
   Paused, and laid aside, and folded the unfinished wedding gown ;
Faltering earnestly assurance, that she too could, in her measure,
   Prize for him the present honor, and the future's sure renown.

Now they pace the shady lime-walk, now the last words must be spoken,
   Words of trust, for neither dreaded more than waiting and delay ;

Was not love still called eternal, — could a plighted vow be broken ? —
See the crimson light of sunset fades in purple mist away.

"Yes, my Mildred," Philip told her, "one calm thought of joy and blessing,
Like a guardian spirit by me, through the world's tumultuous stir,
Still will spread its wings above me, and now urging, now repressing,
With my Mildred's voice will murmur thoughts of home, and love, and her.

"It will charm my peaceful leisure, sanctify my daily toiling,
With a right none else possesses, touching my heart's inmost string;
And to keep its pure wings spotless I shall fly the world's touch, soiling
Even in thought this Angel Guardian of my Mildred's Wedding Ring.

"Take it, dear; this little circlet is the first link, strong and holy,
Of a life-long chain, and holds me from all other love apart;
Till the day when you may wear it as my wife — my own — mine wholly —
Let me know it rests forever near the beating of your heart."

Dawn of day saw Philip speeding on his road to the Great City,
Thinking how the stars gazed downward just with Mildred's patient eyes;
Dreams of work, and fame, and honor struggling with a tender pity,
Till the loving Past receding saw the conquering Future rise.

Daybreak still found Mildred watching, with the wonder of first sorrow,
How the outward world unaltered shone the same this very day;
How unpitying and relentless busy life met this new morrow,
Earth, and sky, and man unheeding that her joy had passed away.

Then the round of weary duties, cold and formal, came to meet her,
With the life within departed that had given them each a soul;
And her sick heart even slighted gentle words that came to greet her;
For Grief spread its shadowy pinions, like a blight upon the whole.

Jar one chord, the harp is silent; move one stone, the arch is shattered;
  One small clarion-cry of sorrow bids an arméd host awake;
One dark cloud can hide the sunlight; loose one string, the pearls are scattered;
  Think one thought, a soul may perish; say one word, a heart may break!

Life went on, he two lives running side by side; the outward seeming,
  And the truer and diviner hidden in the heart and brain;
Dreams grow holy, put in action; work grows fair through starry dreaming;
  But where each flows on unmingling, both are fruitless and in vain.

Such was Mildred's life; her dreaming lay in some far-distant region,
  All the fairer, all the brighter, that its glories were but guessed;
And the daily round of duties seemed an unreal, airy legion,—
  Nothing true save Philip's letters and the ring upon her breast.

Letters telling how he struggled, for some plan or vision aiming,
  And at last how he just grasped it as a fresh one spread its wings;
How the honor or the learning, once the climax, now were claiming,
  Only more and more, becoming merely steps to higher things.

Telling her of foreign countries: little store had she of learning,
  So her earnest, simple spirit answered as he touched the string;
Day by day, to these bright fancies all her silent thoughts were turning,
  Seeing every radiant picture framed within her golden Ring.

O poor heart! love, if thou willest; but, thine own soul still possessing,
  Live thy life: not a reflection or a shadow of his own:
Lean as fondly, as completely, as thou willest,—but confessing
  That thy strength is God's, and therefore can, if need be, stand alone.

Little means were there around her to make farther, wider ranges,
  Where her loving gentle spirit could try any stronger flight;
And she turned aside, half fearing that fresh thoughts were fickle changes,—
  That she *must* stay as he left her on that farewell summer night.

Love should still be guide and leader, like a herald should have risen,
    Lighting up the long dark vistas, conquering all opposing fates;
But new claims, new thoughts, new duties found her heart a silent prison,
    And found Love, with folded pinions, like a jailer by the gates.

Yet why blame her? it had needed greater strength than she was given
    To have gone against the current that so calmly flowed along;
Nothing fresh came near the village save the rain and dew of heaven,
    And her nature was too passive, and her love perhaps too strong.

The great world of thought, that rushes down the years, and onward sweeping
    Bears upon its mighty billows in its progress each and all,
Flowed so far away, its murmur did not rouse them from their sleeping;
    Life and Time and Truth were speaking, but they did not hear their call.

Years flowed on; and every morning heard her prayer grow lower, deeper,
    As she called all blessings on him, and bade every ill depart,
And each night when the cold moonlight shone upon that quiet sleeper,
    It would show her ring that glittered with each throbbing of her heart.

Years passed on. Fame came for Philip in a full, o'erflowing measure;
    He was spoken of and honored through the breadth of many lands,
And he wrote it all to Mildred, as if praise were only pleasure,
    As if fame were only honor, when he laid them in her hands.

Mildred heard it without wonder, as a sure result expected,
    For how could it fail, since merit and renown go side by side?
And the neighbors, who first fancied genius ought to be suspected,
    Might at last give up their caution, and could own him now with pride.

Years flowed on. These empty honors led to others they called better,
    He had saved some slender fortune, and might claim his bride at last:

Mildred, grown so used to waiting, felt half startled by the letter
  That now made her future certain, and would consecrate her past.

And he came: grown sterner, older — changed indeed: a grave reliance
  Had replaced his eager manner, and the quick short speech of old:
He had gone forth with a spirit half of hope and half defiance;
  He returned with proud assurance half disdainful and half cold.

Yet his old self seemed returning while he stood sometimes, and listened
  To her calm, soft voice, relating all the thoughts of these long years;
And if Mildred's heart was heavy, and at times her blue eyes glistened,
  Still in thought she would not whisper aught of sorrow or of fears.

Autumn with its golden cornfields, autumn with its storms and showers,
  Had been there to greet his coming with its forests gold and brown;
And the last leaves still were falling, fading still the year's last flowers,
  When he left the quiet village, and took back his bride to town.

Home, — the home that she had pictured many a time in twilight, dwelling
  On that tender, gentle fancy, folded round with loving care;
Here was home, — the end, the haven; and what spirit voice seemed telling,
  That she only held the casket, with the gem no longer there?

Sad it may be to be longing, with a patience faint and weary,
  For a hope deferred, — and sadder still to see it fade and fall;
Yet to grasp the thing we long for, and, with sorrow sick and dreary,
  Then to find how it can fail us, is the saddest pain of all.

What was wanting? He was gentle, kind, and generous still, deferring
  To her wishes always; nothing seemed to mar their tranquil life:
There are skies so calm and leaden that we long for storm-winds stirring,
  There is peace so cold and bitter, that we almost welcome strife.

Darker grew the clouds above her, and the slow conviction clearer,
  That he gave her home and pity, but that heart and soul and mind

Were beyond her now; he loved her, and in youth he had been near her,
    But he now had gone far onward, and had left her there behind.

Yes, beyond her: yes, quick-hearted, her Love helped her in revealing
    It was worthless, while so mighty; was too weak, although so strong;
There were courts she could not enter, depths she could not sound;
    yet feeling
It was vain to strive or struggle, vainer still to mourn or long.

He would give her words of kindness, he would talk of home, but
    seeming
With an absent look, forgetting if he held or dropped her hand;
And then turn with eager pleasure to his writing, reading, dreaming,
    Or to speak of things with others that she could not understand.

He had paid, and paid most nobly, all he owed; no need of blaming;
    It had cost him something, maybe, that no future could restore:
In her heart of hearts she knew it; Love and Sorrow, not complaining,
    Only suffered all the deeper, only loved him all the more.

Sometimes then a stronger anguish, and more cruel, weighed upon
    her,
That, through all those years of waiting, he had slowly learnt the
    truth;
He had known himself mistaken, but that, bound to her in honor,
    He renounced his life, to pay her for the patience of her youth.

But a star was slowly rising from that mist of grief, and brighter
    Grew her eyes, for each slow hour surer comfort seemed to bring;
And she watched with strange sad smiling how her trembling hands
    grew slighter,
And how thin her slender finger, and how large her wedding-ring.

And the tears dropped slowly on it, as she kissed that golden token
    With a deeper love, it may be, than was in the far-off past;
And remembering Philip's fancy, that so long ago was spoken,
    Thought her Ring's bright angel guardian had stayed near her to
    the last.

Grieving sorely, grieving truly, with a tender care and sorrow,
  Philip watched the slow, sure fading of his gentle, patient wife;
Could he guess with what a yearning she was longing for the morrow,
  Could he guess the bitter knowledge that had wearied her of life?

Now with violets strewn upon her, Mildred lies in peaceful sleeping;
  All unbound her long, bright tresses, and her throbbing heart at rest,
And the cold, blue rays of moonlight, through the open casement creeping,
  Show the ring upon her finger, and her hands crossed on her breast.

Peace at last. Of peace eternal is her calm, sweet smile a token.
  Has some angel lingering near her let a radiant promise fall?
Has he told her Heaven unites again the links that Earth has broken?
  For on Earth so much is needed, but in Heaven Love is all!

BORROWED THOUGHTS.

I. FROM "LAVATER."

TRUST him little who doth raise
  To one height both great and small,
And sets the sacred crown of praise,
  Smiling, on the head of all.

Trust him less who looks around
  To censure all with scornful eyes,
And in everything has found
  Something that he dare despise.

But for one who stands apart,
  Stirred by naught that can befall,
With a cold, indifferent heart,—
  Trust him least and last of all.

II. FROM "PHANTASTES."

I HAVE a bitter Thought, a Snake
  That used to sting my life to pain.
I strove to cast it far away,
  But every night and every day
  It crawled back to my heart again!

It was in vain to live or strive,
  To think or sleep, to work or pray;
At last I bade this thing accursed

Gnaw at my heart, and do its
    worst,
And so I let it have its way.

Thus said I, "I shall never fall
    Into a false and dreaming
    peace,
And then awake, with sudden
    start,
To feel it biting at my heart,
    For now the pain can never
    cease."

But I gained more; for I have
    found
    That such a snake's enven-
    omed charm
Must always, always find a part,
Deep in the centre of my heart,
    Which it can never wound or
    harm.

It is coiled round my heart to-
    day.
    It sleeps at times, this cruel
    snake,
And while it sleeps it never
    stings: —
Hush! let us talk of other things,
    Lest it should hear me and
    awake.

III. FROM "LOST ALICE."

Yes, dear, our Love is slain;
    In the cold grave forevermore it
    lies,
Never to wake again,

Or light our sorrow with its
    starry eyes:
And so — regret is vain.

One hour of pain and dread,
We killed our Love, we took its
    life away
    With the false words we
    said;
And so we watch it, since that
    cruel day,
    Silent, and cold, and dead.

We should have seen it
    shine
Long years beside us. Time and
    Death might try
To touch that life divine,
Whose strength could every other
    stroke defy
    Save only thine and mine.

No longing can restore
Our dead again. Vain are the
    tears we weep,
    And vainly we deplore
Our buried Love: its grave lies
    dark and deep
    Between us evermore.

IV. FROM * * *

Within the kingdom of my
    Soul
I bid you enter, Love, to-day;
Submit my life to your control,
    And give my Heart up to your
    sway.

My Past, whose light and life is flown,
Shall live through memory for you still;
Take all my Present for your own,
And mould my Future to your will.

One only thought remains apart,
And will forever so remain;
There is one Chamber in my heart
Where even you might knock in vain.

A haunted Chamber: — long ago
I closed it, and I cast the key
Where deep and bitter waters flow,
Into a vast and silent sea.

Dear, it is haunted. All the rest
Is yours; but I have shut that door
Forever now. 'T is even best
That I should enter it no more.

No more. It is not well to stay
With ghosts; their very look would scare
Your joyous, loving smile away; —
So never try to enter there.

Check, if you love me, all regret
That this one thought remains apart: —

Now let us smile, dear, and forget
The haunted Chamber in my Heart.

LIGHT AND SHADE.

THOU hast done well to kneel and say,
"Since He who gave can take away,
And bid me suffer, I obey."

And also well to tell thy heart,
That good lies in the bitterest part,
And thou wilt profit by her smart.

But bitter hours come to all:
When even truths like these will pall,
Sick hearts for humbler comfort call.

Then I would have thee strive to see
That good and evil come to thee,
As one of a great family.

And as material life is planned,
That even the loneliest one must stand
Dependent on his brother's hand;

So links more subtle and more fine
Bind every other soul to thine
In one great brotherhood divine.

Nor with thy share of work be
    vexed;
Though incomplete, and even
    perplext,
It fits exactly to the next.

What seems so dark to thy dim
    sight
May be a shadow, seen aright,
Making some brightness doubly
    bright.

The flash that struck thy tree —
    no more
To shelter thee — lets Heaven's
    blue floor
Shine where it never shone be-
    fore.

Thy life that has been dropped
    aside
Into Time's stream, may stir the
    tide
In rippled circles spreading wide.

The cry wrung from thy spirit's
    pain
May echo on some far-off plain,
And guide a wanderer home
    again.

Fail — yet rejoice; because no
    less
The failure that makes thy dis-
    tress
May teach another full success.

It may be that in some great
    need
Thy life's poor fragments are
    decreed
To help build up a lofty deed.

Thy heart should throb in vast
    content,
Thus knowing that it was but
    meant
As chord in one great instru-
    ment;

That even the discord in thy
    soul
May make completer music roll
From out the great harmonious
    whole.

It may be, that when all is light,
Deep set within that deep de-
    light
Will be to know *why* all was
    right;

To hear life's perfect music rise,
And, while it floods the happy
    skies,
Thy feeble voice to recognize.

Then strive more gladly to fulfil
Thy little part. This darkness
    still
Is light to every loving will.

And trust, as if already plain,
How just thy share of loss and
    pain
Is for another fuller gain.

I dare not limit time or place
Touched by thy life: nor dare I
    trace
Its far vibrations into space.

One only knows. Yet if the fret
Of thy weak heart, in weak re-
    gret
Needs a more tender comfort yet:

Then thou mayst take thy lone-
    liest fears,
The bitterest drops of all thy
    tears,
The dreariest hours of all thy
    years;

And through thy anguish there
    outspread,
May ask that God's great love
    would shed
Blessings on one belovéd head.

And thus thy soul shall learn to
    draw
Sweetness from out that loving
    law
That sees no failure and no flaw,

Where all is good. And life is
    good,
Were the one lesson understood
Of its most sacred brotherhood.

A CHANGELING.

A LITTLE changeling spirit
    Crept to my arms one day:
I had no heart or courage
    To drive the child away.

So all day long I soothed her,
    And hushed her on my breast;
And all night long her wailing
    Would never let me rest.

I dug a grave to hold her,
    A grave both dark and deep;
I covered her with violets,
    And laid her there to sleep.

I used to go and watch there,
    Both night and morning
    too:—
It was my tears, I fancy,
    That kept the violets blue.

I took her up: and once more
    I felt the clinging hold,
And heard the ceaseless wailing
    That wearied me of old.

I wandered, and I wandered,
    With my burden on my breast,
Till I saw a church-door open,
    And entered in to rest.

In the dim, dying daylight,
    Set in a flowery shrine,
I saw the Virgin Mother
    Holding her Child divine.

I knelt down there in silence,
    And on the altar-stone
I laid my wailing burden,
    And came away — alone.

And now that little spirit,
　That sobbed so all day long,
Is grown a shining Angel,
　With wings both wide and strong.

She watches me from Heaven
　With loving, tender care,
And one day she has promised
　That I shall find her there.

DISCOURAGED.

Where the little babbling streamlet
　First brings forth to light,
Trickling through soft velvet mosses,
　Almost hid from sight;
Vowed I with delight, —
"River, I will follow thee,
Through thy wanderings to the Sea!"

Gleaming 'mid the purple heather,
　Downward then it sped,
Glancing through the mountain gorges,
　Like a silver thread,
As it quicker fled,
Louder music in its flow,
Dashing to the vale below.

Then its voice grew lower, gentler,
　And its pace less fleet,
Just as though it loved to linger
　Round the rushes' feet,
As they stooped to meet
Their clear images below,
Broken by the ripples' flow.

Purple Willow-herb bent over
　To her shadow fair;
Meadow-sweet, in feathery clusters,
　Perfumed all the air;
Silver-weed was there,
And in one calm, grassy spot,
Starry, blue Forget-me-not.

Tangled weeds, below the waters,
　Still seemed drawn away;
Yet the current, floating onward,
　Was less strong than they; —
Sunbeams watched their play,
With a flickering light and shade,
Through the screen the Alders made.

Broader grew the flowing River;
　To its grassy brink
Slowly, in the slanting sun-rays,
　Cattle trooped to drink;
The blue sky, I think,
Was no bluer than that stream,
Slipping onward, like a dream.

Quicker, deeper then it hurried,
　Rushing fierce and free;
But I said, "It should grow calmer
　Ere it meets the Sea,
The wide purple Sea,

Which I weary for in vain,
Wasting all my toil and pain."

But it rushed still quicker, fiercer,
    In its rocky bed,
Hard and stony was the pathway
    To my tired tread;
"I despair," I said,
"Of that wide and glorious Sea
That was promised unto me."

So I turned aside, and wandered
    Through green meadows near,
Far away, among the daisies,
    Far away, for fear
Lest I still should hear
The loud murmur of its song,
As the River flowed along.

Now I hear it not : — I loiter
    Gayly as before;
Yet I sometimes think, — and thinking
Makes my heart so sore, —
Just a few steps more,
And there might have shone for me,
Blue and infinite, the Sea.

IF THOU COULDST KNOW.

I THINK if thou couldst know,
    O soul that will complain,
What lies concealed below
    Our burden and our pain;
How just our anguish brings
Nearer those longed-for things
We seek for now in vain, —
I think thou wouldst rejoice, and not complain.

I think if thou couldst see,
    With thy dim mortal sight,
How meanings, dark to thee,
    Are shadows hiding light;
Truth's efforts crossed and vexed,
Life's purpose all perplexed, —
If thou couldst see them right,
I think that they would seem all clear, and wise, and bright.

And yet thou canst not know,
    And yet thou canst not see;
Wisdom and sight are slow
    In poor humanity.
If thou couldst *trust*, poor soul,
In Him who rules the whole,
Thou wouldst find peace and rest :
Wisdom and sight are well, but Trust is best.

THE WARRIOR TO HIS DEAD BRIDE.

IF in the fight my arm was strong,
    And forced my foes to yield, —
If conquering and unhurt I came
    Back from the battle-field, —
It is because thy prayers have been
My safeguard and my shield.

My comrades smile to see my arm
  Spare or protect a foe,
They think thy gentle pleading voice
  Was silenced long ago;
But pity and compassion, love,
  Were taught me first by woe.

Thy heart, my own, still beats in Heaven
  With the same love divine
That made thee stoop to such a soul,
  So hard, so stern as mine, —
My eyes have learnt to weep, beloved,
  Since last they looked on thine

I hear thee murmur words of peace
  Through the dim midnight air,
And a calm falls from the angel stars
  And soothes my great despair, —
The heavens themselves look brighter, love,
  Since thy sweet soul is there.

And if my heart is once more calm,
  My step is once more free,
It is because each hour I feel
  Thou prayest still for me ;
Because no fate or change can come
  Between my soul and thee.

It is because my heart is stilled,
  Not broken by despair,

Because I see the grave is bright,
  And death itself is fair : —
I dread no more the wrath of Heaven, —
  I have an angel there !

A LETTER.

Dear, I tried to write you such a letter
As would tell you all my heart to-day.
Written Love is poor ; one word were better ;
Easier, too, a thousand times, to say.

I can tell you all : fears, doubts unheeding,
While I can be near you, hold your hand,
Looking right into your eyes, and reading
Reassurance that you understand.

Yet I wrote it through, then lingered, thinking
Of its reaching you, — what hour, what day ;
Till I felt my heart and courage sinking
With a strange, new, wondering dismay.

" Will my letter fall," I wondered sadly,
" On her mood like some discordant tone,

A LETTER.

Or be welcomed tenderly and
    gladly?
Will she be with others, or alone?

" It may find her too absorbed to
    read it,
Save with hurried glance and
    careless air:
Sad and weary, she may scarcely
    heed it;
Gay and happy, she may hardly
    care.

" Shall I — dare I — risk the
    chances?" slowly
Something — was it shyness,
    love, or pride? —
Chilled my heart, and checked
    my courage wholly;
So I laid it wistfully aside.

Then I leant against the case-
    ment, turning
Tearful eyes towards the far-off
    west,
Where the golden evening light
    was burning,
Till my heart throbbed back
    again to rest.

And I thought: " Love's soul is
    not in fetters,
Neither space nor time keeps
    souls apart;
Since I cannot — dare not —
    send my letters,
Through the silence I will send
    my heart.

" If, perhaps now, while my
    tears are falling,
She is dreaming quietly alone,
She will hear my Love's far echo
    calling,
Feel my spirit drawing near her
    own.

" She will hear, while twilight
    shades enfold her,
All the gathered Love she knows
    so well, —
Deepest Love my words have
    ever told her,
Deeper still — all I could never
    tell.

" Wondering at the strange,
    mysterious power
That has touched her heart, then
    she will say:
' Some one whom I love, this
    very hour,
Thinks of me, and loves me, far
    away.'

" If, as well may be, to-night
    has found her
Full of other thoughts, with
    others by,
Through the words and claims
    that gather round her
She will hear just one half-
    smothered sigh;

" Or will marvel why, without
    her seeking,
Suddenly the thought of me re-
    curs;

Or, while listening to another speaking,
Fancy that my hand is holding hers."

So I dreamed, and watched the stars' far splendor
Glimmering on the azure darkness, start, —
While the star of trust rose bright and tender,
Through the twilight shadows of my heart.

A COMFORTER.

I.

" Will she come to me, little Effie,
  Will she come in my arms to rest,
And nestle her head on my shoulder,
  While the sun goes down in the west?

II.

" I and Effie will sit together,
  All alone, in this great armchair : —
Is it silly to mind it, darling,
  When Life is so hard to bear ?

III.

" No one comforts me like my Effie,
  Just I think that she does not try, —
Only looks with a wistful wonder
  Why grown people should ever cry ;

IV.

" While her little soft arms close tighter
  Round my neck in their clinging hold : —
Well, I must not cry on your hair, dear,
  For my tears might tarnish the gold.

V.

" I am tired of trying to read, dear ;
  It is worse to talk and seem gay :
There are some kinds of sorrow, Effie,
  It is useless to thrust away.

VI.

" Ah, advice may be wise, my darling,
  But one always knows it before ;
And the reasoning down one's sorrow
  Seems to make one suffer the more.

VII.

" But my Effie won't reason, will she ?
  Or endeavor to understand ;

Only holds up her mouth to kiss
  me,
  As she strokes my face with
    her hand.

VIII.

"If you break your plaything
  yourself, dear,
  Don't you cry for it all the
    same?
I don't think it is such a com-
  fort,
  One has only one's self to
    blame.

IX.

"People say things cannot be
  helped, dear,
  But then that is the reason
    why;
For if things could be helped or
  altered,
  One would never sit down to
    cry:

X.

"They say, too, that tears are
  quite useless
  To undo, amend, or restore,—
When I think *how* useless, my
  Effie;
  Then my tears only fall the
    more.

XI.

"All to-day I struggled against
  it;
  But that does not make sor-
    row cease;

And now, dear, it is such a
  comfort
  To be able to cry in peace.

XII.

"Though wise people would call
    that folly,
  And remonstrate with grave sur-
    prise;
We won't mind what they say,
    my Effie;—
  We never professed to be wise.

XIII.

"But my comforter knows a
    lesson
  Wiser, truer than all the
    rest:—
That to help and to heal a sor-
    row,
  Love and silence are always
    best.

XIV.

"Well, who is my comforter,—
    tell me?
  Effie smiles, but she will not
    speak:
Or look up through the long
    curled lashes
  That are shading her rosy
    cheek.

XV.

"Is she thinking of talking fishes,
  The bluebird, or magical tree?

Perhaps I am thinking, my darling,
Of something that never can be.

XVI.

"You long — don't you, dear?
— for the Genii,
Who were slaves of lamps and of rings;
And, I — I am sometimes afraid, dear,
I want as impossible things.

XVII.

"But hark! there is Nurse calling Effie!
It is bedtime, so run away;
And I must go back, or the others
Will be wondering why I stay.

XVIII.

"So good night to my darling Effie;
Keep happy, sweetheart, and grow wise: —
There's one kiss for her golden tresses,
And two for her sleepy eyes."

UNSEEN.

THERE are more things in Heaven and Earth than we
Can dream of, or than nature understands;
We learn not through our poor philosophy
What hidden chords are touched by unseen hands.

The present hour repeats upon its strings
Echoes of some vague dream we have forgot;
Dim voices whisper half-remembered things,
And when we pause to listen — answer not.

Forebodings come: we know not how, or whence,
Shadowing a nameless fear upon the soul,
And stir within our hearts a subtler sense
Than light may read, or wisdom may control.

And who can tell what secret links of thought
Bind heart to heart? Unspoken things are heard,
As if within our deepest selves was brought
The soul, perhaps, of some unuttered word.

But, though a veil of shadow hangs between
That hidden life and what we see and hear,
Let us revere the power of the Unseen,
And know a world of mystery is near.

A REMEMBRANCE OF AUTUMN.

Nothing stirs the sunny silence,—
  Save the drowsy humming of the bees
    Round the rich ripe peaches on the wall,
  And the south-wind sighing in the trees,
    And the dead leaves rustling as they fall:
While the swallows, one by one, are gathering,
  All impatient to be on the wing,
  And to wander from us, seeking
    Their belovéd Spring!

Cloudless rise the azure heavens!
  Only vaporous wreaths of snowy white
    Nestle in the gray hill's rugged side;
  And the golden woods are bathed in light,
    Dying, if they must, with kingly pride:
While the swallows, in the blue air wheeling,
  Circle now an eager, fluttering band,
  Ready to depart and leave us
    For a brighter land!

But a voice is sounding sadly,
  Telling of a glory that has been;
  Of a day that faded all too fast:—
See afar through the blue air serene,
  Where the swallows wing their way at last,
And our hearts perchance as sadly wandering,
  Vainly seeking for a long-lost day,
  While we watch the far-off swallows,
    Flee with them away!

THREE EVENINGS IN A LIFE.

I.

Yes, it looked dark and dreary,
  That long and narrow street:
Only the sound of the rain,
  And the tramp of passing feet,
The duller glow of the fire,
  And gathering mists of night,
To mark how slow and weary
  The long day's cheerless flight!

II.

Watching the sullen fire,
  Hearing the dismal rain,
Drop after drop, run down
  On the darkening window pane:
Chill was the heart of Alice,
  Chill as that winter day,—

For the star of her life had risen
  Only to fade away.

III.

The voice that had been so strong
  To bid the snare depart,
The true and earnest will,
  The calm and steadfast heart,
Were now weighed down by sorrow,
  Were quivering now with pain;
The clear path now seemed clouded,
  And all her grief in vain.

IV.

Duty, Right, Truth, who promised
  To help and save their own,
Seemed spreading wide their pinions
  To leave her there alone.
So, turning from the Present
  To well-known days of yore,
She called on them to strengthen
  And guard her soul once more.

V.

She thought how in her girlhood
  Her life was given away,
The solemn promise spoken
  She kept so well to-day;
How to her brother Herbert
  She had been help and guide,
And how his artist nature
  On her calm strength relied.

VI.

How through life's fret and turmoil
  The passion and fire of art
In him was soothed and quickened
  By her true sister heart;
How future hopes had always
  Been for his sake alone;
And now — what strange new feeling
  Possessed her as its own?

VII.

Her home — each flower that breathed there,
  The wind's sigh, soft and low,
Each trembling spray of ivy,
  The river's murmuring flow,
The shadow of the forest,
  Sunset, or twilight dim, —
Dear as they were, were dearer
  By leaving them for him.

VIII.

And each year as it found her
  In the dull, feverish town,
Saw self still more forgotten,
  And selfish care kept down
By the calm joy of evening
  That brought him to her side,
To warn him with wise counsel,
  Or praise with tender pride.

IX.

Her heart, her life, her future,
  Her genius, only meant
Another thing to give him,
  And be therewith content.

To-day, what words had stirred
    her,
Her soul could not forget?
What dream had filled her spirit
    With strange and wild regret?

X.

To leave him for another, —
    Could it indeed be so?
Could it have cost such anguish
    To bid this vision go?
Was this her faith? Was Herbert
The second in her heart?
Did it need all this struggle
    To bid a dream depart?

XI.

And yet, within her spirit
    A far-off land was seen,
A home, which might have held
    her,
A love, which might have
    been.
And Life — not the mere being
    Of daily ebb and flow,
But Life itself — had claimed her,
    And she had let it go!

XII.

Within her heart there echoed
    Again the well-known tone
That promised this bright future,
    And asked her for her own:
Then words of sorrow, broken
    By half-reproachful pain:
And then a farewell, spoken
    In words of cold disdain.

XIII.

Where now was the stern purpose
That nerved her soul so long?
Whence came the words she
    uttered,
    So hard, so cold, so strong?
What right had she to banish
    A hope that God had given?
Why must she choose earth's
    portion,
    And turn aside from Heaven?

XIV.

To-day! Was it this morning?
    If this long, fearful strife
Was but the work of hours,
    What would be years of life?
Why did a cruel Heaven
    For such great suffering call?
And why — O still more cruel! —
    Must her own words do all?

XV.

Did she repent? O Sorrow!
    Why do we linger still
To take thy loving message,
    And do thy gentle will?
See, her tears fall more slowly,
    The passionate murmurs cease,
And back upon her spirit
    Flow strength, and love, and
    peace.

XVI.

The fire burns more brightly,
    The rain has passed away,
Herbert will see no shadow
    Upon his home to-day:

Only that Alice greets him
  With doubly tender care,
Kissing a fonder blessing
  Down on his golden hair.

II.

I.

THE Studio is deserted,
  Palette and brush laid by,
The sketch rests on the easel,
  The paint is scarcely dry;
And Silence — who seems always
  Within her depths to bear
The next sound that will utter —
  Now holds a dumb despair.

II.

So Alice feels it: listening
  With breathless, stony fear,
Waiting the dreadful summons
  Each minute brings more near:
When the young life, now ebbing,
  Shall fail, and pass away
Into that mighty shadow
  Who shrouds the house to-day.

III.

But why — when the sick-chamber
  Is on the upper floor —
Why dares not Alice enter
  Within the close-shut door?
If he — her all — her Brother,
  Lies dying in that gloom,
What strange mysterious power
  Has sent her from the room?

IV.

It is not one week's anguish
  That can have changed her so;
Joy has not died here lately,
  Struck down by one quick blow;
But cruel months have needed
  Their long relentless chain,
To teach that shrinking manner
  Of helpless, hopeless pain.

V.

The struggle was scarce over
  Last Christmas eve had brought;
The fibres still were quivering
  Of the one wounded thought,
When Herbert — who, unconscious,
  Had guessed no inward strife—
Bade her, in pride and pleasure,
  Welcome his fair young wife.

VI.

Bade her rejoice, and smiling,
  Although his eyes were dim,
Thanked God he thus could pay her
  The care she gave to him.
This fresh bright life would bring her
  A new and joyous fate —
O Alice, check the murmur
  That cries, "Too late! too late!"

VII.

Too late! Could she have known it
 A few short weeks before,
That his life was completed,
 And needing hers no more,
She might — O sad repining!
 What "might have been" forget;
"It was not" should suffice us
 To stifle vain regret.

VIII.

He needed her no longer,
 Each day it grew more plain;
First with a startled wonder,
 Then with a wondering pain.
Love: why, his wife best gave it;
 Comfort: durst Alice speak
Or counsel, when resentment
 Flushed on the young wife's cheek?

IX.

No more long talks by firelight
 Of childish times long past,
And dreams of future greatness
 Which he must reach at last;
Dreams, where her purer instinct
 With truth unerring told,
Where was the worthless gilding,
 And where refinéd gold.

X.

Slowly, but surely ever,
 Dora's poor jealous pride,
Which she called love for Herbert,
 Drove Alice from his side;
And, spite of nervous effort
 To share their altered life,
She felt a check to Herbert,
 A burden to his wife.

XI.

This was the least; for Alice
 Feared, dreaded, *knew* at length
How much his nature owed her
 Of truth, and power, and strength;
And watched the daily failing
 Of all his nobler part:
Low aims, weak purpose, telling
 In lower, weaker art.

XII.

And now, when he is dying,
 The last words she could hear
Must not be hers, but given
 The bride of one short year.
The last care is another's;
 The last prayer must not be
The one they learnt together
 Beside their mother's knee.

XIII.

Summoned at last: she kisses
 The clay-cold stiffening hand;
And, reading pleading efforts
 To make her understand,
Answers, with solemn promise,
 In clear but trembling tone,
To Dora's life henceforward
 She will devote her own.

XIV.

Now all is over. Alice
 Dares not remain to weep,

But soothes the frightened Dora
  Into a sobbing sleep.
The poor weak child will need
    her: ...
O, who can dare complain,
When God sends a new Duty
  To comfort each new Pain!

III.

I.

THE House is all deserted
  In the dim evening gloom,
Only one figure passes
  Slowly from room to room;
And, pausing at each doorway,
  Seems gathering up again
Within her heart the relics
  Of bygone joy and pain.

II.

There is an earnest longing
  In those who onward gaze,
Looking with weary patience
  Towards the coming days.
There is a deeper longing,
  More sad, more strong, more keen :
Those know it who look backward,
  And yearn for what has been.

III.

At every hearth she pauses,
  Touches each well-known chair;
Gazes from every window,
  Lingers on every stair.

What have these months brought Alice
  Now one more year is past?
This Christmas eve shall tell us,
  The third one and the last.

IV.

The wilful, wayward Dora,
  In those first weeks of grief,
Could seek and find in Alice
  Strength, soothing, and relief.
And Alice — last sad comfort
  True woman-heart can take —
Had something still to·suffer
  And bear for Herbert's sake.

V.

Spring, with her western breezes,
  From Indian islands bore
To Alice news that Leonard
  Would seek his home once more.
What was it, — joy, or sorrow?
  What were they, — hopes, or fears?
That flushed her cheeks with crimson,
  And filled her eyes with tears?

VI.

He came. And who so kindly
  Could ask and hear her tell
Herbert's last hours; for Leonard
  Had known and loved him well.
Daily he came; and Alice,
  Poor weary heart, at length,

Weighed down by others' weak-
    ness,
  Could lean upon his strength.

VII.

Yet not the voice of Leonard
  Could her true care beguile,
That turned to watch, rejoicing,
  Dora's reviving smile.
So, from that little household
  The worst gloom passed away,
The one bright hour of evening
  Lit up the livelong day.

VIII.

Days passed. The golden sum-
    mer
  In sudden heat bore down
Its blue, bright, glowing sweet-
    ness
  Upon the scorching town.
And sights and sounds of country
  Came in the warm soft tune
Sung by the honeyed breezes
  Borne on the wings of June.

IX.

One twilight hour, but earlier
  Than usual, Alice thought
She knew the fresh sweet fra-
    grance
  Of flowers that Leonard
    brought;
Through opened doors and win-
    dows
  It stole up through the gloom,
And with appealing sweetness
  Drew Alice from her room.

X.

Yes, he was there; and, pausing
  Just near the opened door,
To check her heart's quick beat-
    ing,
  She heard — and paused still
    more —
His low voice — Dora's an-
    swers —
  His pleading — Yes, she knew
The tone — the words — the ac-
    cents;
  She once had heard them too.

XI.

"Would Alice blame her?"
    Leonard's
  Low, tender answer came:
"Alice was far too noble
  To think or dream of blame."
"And was he sure he loved
    her?"
  "Yes, with the one love given
Once in a lifetime only,
  With one soul and one heav-
    en!"

XII.

Then came a plaintive mur-
    mur, —
  "Dora had once been told
That he and Alice — " "Dear-
    est,
  Alice is far too cold
To love; and I, my Dora,
  If once I fancied so,
It was a brief delusion,
  And over — long ago."

XIII.

Between the Past and Present,
　On that bleak moment's height,
She stood. As some lost traveller,
　By a quick flash of light
Seeing a gulf before him,
　With dizzy, sick despair,
Reels backward, but to find it
　A deeper chasm there.

XIV.

The twilight grew still darker,
　The fragrant flowers more sweet,
The stars shone out in heaven,
　The lamps gleamed down the street;
And hours passed in dreaming
　Over their new-found fate,
Ere they could think of wondering
　Why Alice was so late.

XV.

She came, and calmly listened;
　In vain they strove to trace
If Herbert's memory shadowed
　In grief upon her face.
No blame, no wonder showed there,
　No feeling could be told;
Her voice was not less steady,
　Her manner not more cold.

XVI.

They could not hear the anguish
　That broke in words of pain
Through the calm summer midnight,—
　"My Herbert—mine again!"
Yes, they have once been parted,
　But this day shall restore
The long-lost one: she claims him;
　"My Herbert—mine once more!"

XVII.

Now Christmas eve returning
　Saw Alice stand beside
The altar, greeting Dora,
　Again a smiling bride;
And now the gloomy evening
　Sees Alice pale and worn,
Leaving the house forever,
　To wander out forlorn.

XVIII.

Forlorn—nay, not so. Anguish
　Shall do its work at length;
Her soul, passed through the fire,
　Shall gain still purer strength.
Somewhere there waits for Alice
　An earnest, noble part;
And meanwhile God is with her,—
　God, and her own true heart!

THE WIND.

The wind went forth o'er land and sea,
　Loud and free;

Foaming waves leapt up to
    meet it,
Stately pines bowed down to
    greet it;
While the wailing sea
And the forest's murmured sigh
    Joined the cry
Of the wind that swept o'er land
    and sea.

The wind that blew upon the sea
    Fierce and free,
Cast the bark upon the shore,
Whence it sailed the night be-
    fore
Full of hope and glee;
And the cry of pain and death
    Was but a breath,
Through the wind that roared
    upon the sea.

The wind was whispering on the
    lea
    Tenderly;
But the white rose felt it pass,
And the fragile stalks of grass
    Shook with fear to see
All her trembling petals shed,
    As it fled
So gently by,— the wind upon
    the lea.

Blow, thou wind, upon the sea
    Fierce and free,
And a gentler message send,
Where frail flowers and grasses
    bend,
    On the sunny lea;

For thy bidding still is one,
    Be it done
In tenderness or wrath, on land
    or sea!

EXPECTATION.

THE King's three daughters
    stood on the terrace,
The hanging terrace, so broad
    and green,
Which keeps the sea from the
    marble Palace:
There was Princess May, and
    Princess Alice,
And the youngest Princess,
    Gwendoline.

Sighed Princess May, "Will it
    last much longer,
Time throbs so slow and my
    Heart so quick;
And O, how long is the day in
    dying!
Weary am I of waiting and
    sighing,
For Hope deferred makes the
    spirit sick."

But Princess Gwendoline smiled
    and kissed her:—
"Am I not sadder than you, my
    Sister?
Expecting joy is a happy pain.
The Future's fathomless mine of
    treasures,

All countless hordes of possible
   pleasures,
Might bring their store to my
   feet in vain."

Sighed Princess Alice as night
   grew nearer : —
"So soon, so soon, is the daylight fled!
And O, how fast comes the dark
   to-morrow,
Who hides, perhaps, in her veil
   of sorrow
The terrible hour I wait and
   dread!"

But Princess Gwendoline kissed
   her, sighing : —
"It is only Life that can fear
   dying;
Possible loss means possible gain.
Those who still dread are not
   quite forsaken;
But not to fear, because all is
   taken,
Is the loneliest depth of human
   pain."

AN IDEAL.

While the gray mists of early
   dawn
   Were lingering round the hill,
And the dew was still upon the
   flowers,
   And the earth lay calm and
   still,

A wingéd Spirit came to me,
Noble, and radiant, and free.

Folding his blue and shining
   wings,
   He laid his hand on mine.
I know not if I felt, or heard
   The mystic word divine,
Which woke the trembling air
   to sighs,
And shone from out his starry
   eyes.

The word he spoke within my
   heart
   Stirred life unknown before,
And cast a spell upon my soul
   To chain it evermore;
Making the cold, dull earth look
   bright,
And skies flame out in sapphire
   light.

When noon ruled from the heav-
   ens, and man
   Through busy day toiled on,
My Spirit drooped his shining
   wings;
   His radiant smile was gone;
His voice had ceased, his grace
   had flown,
His hand grew cold within my
   own.

Bitter, O bitter tears I wept,
   Yet still I held his hand,
Hoping with vague unreasoning
   hope:
   I would not understand

That this pale Spirit nevermore
Could be what he had been before.

Could it be so? My heart stood
   still.
   Yet he was by my side.
I strove; but my despair was
   vain;
   Vain too was love and pride.
Could he have changed to me
   so soon?
My day was only at its noon.

Now stars are rising one by one,
   Through the dim evening air;
Near me a household Spirit waits,
   With tender loving care;
He speaks and smiles, but never
   sings,
Long since he lost his shining
   wings.

With thankful, true content, I
   know
   This is the better way;
Is not a faithful spirit mine —
   Mine still — at close of
   day?...
Yet will my foolish heart repine
For that bright morning dream
   of mine.

OUR DEAD.

Nothing is our own: we hold
   our pleasures
Just a little while, ere they are
   fled:

One by one life robs us of our
   treasures;
Nothing is our own except our
   Dead.

They are ours, and hold in faithful keeping,
Safe forever, all they took away.
Cruel life can never stir that
   sleeping,
Cruel time can never seize that
   prey.

Justice pales; truth fades; stars
   fall from heaven;
Human are the great whom we
   revere:
No true crown of honor can be
   given,
Till we place it on a funeral bier.

How the Children leave us: and
   no traces
Linger of that smiling angel
   band;
Gone, forever gone; and in their
   their places
Weary men and anxious women
   stand.

Yet we have some little ones,
   still ours;
They have kept the baby smile
   we know,
Which we kissed one day, and
   hid with flowers,
On their dead white faces, long
   ago.

When our Joy is lost — and life
  will take it —
Then no memory of the past
  remains;
Save with some strange, cruel
  sting, to make it
Bitterness beyond all present
  pains.

Death, more tender-hearted,
  leaves to sorrow
Still the radiant shadow, fond
  regret:
We shall find, in some far, bright
  to-morrow,
Joy that he has taken, living yet.

Is Love ours, and do we dream
  we know it,
Bound with all our heart-strings,
  all our own?
Any cold and cruel dawn may
  show it,
Shattered, desecrated, over-
  thrown.

Only the dead Hearts forsake us
  never;
Death's last kiss has been the
  mystic sign
Consecrating Love our own forever,
Crowning it eternal and divine.

So when Fate would fain besiege
  our city,
Dim our gold, or make our
  flowers fall,

Death, the Angel, comes in love
  and pity,
And, to save our treasures, claims
  them all.

———

A WOMAN'S ANSWER.

I WILL not let you say a Woman's part
 Must be to give exclusive love
  alone;
Dearest, although I love you so,
  my heart
 Answers a thousand claims
  besides your own.

I love — what do I not love?
  earth and air
 Find space within my heart,
  and myriad things
You would not deign to heed are
  cherished there,
 And vibrate on its very inmost strings.

I love the Summer with her ebb
  and flow
 Of light, and warmth, and
  music, that have nurst
Her tender buds to blossoms . . .
  and you know
 It was in summer that I saw
  you first.

I love the Winter dearly, too, . . .
   but then
  I owe it so much; on a winter's day,
Bleak, cold, and stormy, you returned again,
  When you had been those weary months away.

I love the Stars like friends; so many nights
  I gazed at them, when you were far from me,
Till I grew blind with tears . . . . those far-off lights
  Could watch you, whom I longed in vain to see.

I love the Flowers; happy hours lie
  Shut up within their petals close and fast:
You have forgotten, dear; but they and I
  Keep every fragment of the golden Past.

I love, too, to be loved; all loving praise
  Seems like a crown upon my Life, — to make
It better worth the giving, and to raise
  Still nearer to your own the heart you take.

I love all good and noble souls; — I heard
  One speak of you but lately, and for days,
Only to think of it, my soul was stirred
  In tender memory of such generous praise.

I love all those who love you; all who owe
  Comfort to you: and I can find regret
Even for those poorer hearts who once could know
  And once could love you, and can now forget.

Well, is my heart so narrow, — I, who spare
  Love for all these? Do I not even hold
My favorite books in special tender care,
  And prize them as a miser does his gold?

The Poets that you used to read to me
  While summer twilights faded in the sky;
But most of all I think Aurora Leigh,
  Because — because — do you remember why?

Will you be jealous? Did you guess before
  I loved so many things? — Still you the best: —
Dearest, remember that I love you more,
  O, more a thousand times, than all the rest!

THE STORY OF THE FAITHFUL SOUL.

FOUNDED ON AN OLD FRENCH LEGEND.

The fettered Spirits linger
  In purgatorial pain,
With penal fires effacing
  Their last faint earthly stain,
Which Life's imperfect sorrow
  Had tried to cleanse in vain.

Yet, on each feast of Mary
  Their sorrow finds release,
For the Great Archangel Michael
  Comes down and bids it cease;
And the name of these brief respites
  Is called "Our Lady's Peace."

Yet once — so runs the Legend —
  When the Archangel came,
And all these holy spirits
  Rejoiced at Mary's name,
One voice alone was wailing,
  Still wailing on the same.

And though a great Te Deum
  The happy echoes woke,
This one discordant wailing
  Through the sweet voices broke:
So when St. Michael questioned,
  Thus the poor spirit spoke: —

"I am not cold or thankless,
  Although I still complain;
I prize our Lady's blessing,
  Although it comes in vain
To still my bitter anguish,
  Or quench my ceaseless pain.

"On earth a heart that loved me
  Still lives and mourns me there,
And the shadow of his anguish
  Is more than I can bear;
All the torment that I suffer
  Is the thought of his despair.

"The evening of my bridal
  Death took my Life away;
Not all Love's passionate pleading
  Could gain an hour's delay.
And he I left has suffered
  A whole year since that day.

"If I could only see him, —
  If I could only go
And speak one word of comfort
  And solace, — then I know
He would endure with patience,
  And strive against his woe."

Thus the Archangel answered: —
  "Your time of pain is brief,
And soon the peace of Heaven
  Will give you full relief;
Yet if his earthly comfort
  So much outweighs your grief,

"Then through a special mercy
  I offer you this grace, —
You may seek him who mourns you,
  And look upon his face,
And speak to him of comfort
  For one short minute's space.

"But when that time is ended,
　Return here, and remain
A thousand years in torment,
　A thousand years in pain :
Thus dearly must you purchase
　The comfort he will gain."

* * * *

The Lime-trees' shade at evening
　Is spreading broad and wide;
Beneath their fragrant arches,
　Pace slowly, side by side,
In low and tender converse,
　A Bridegroom and his Bride.

The night is calm and stilly,
　No other sound is there
Except their happy voices:
　What is that cold bleak air
That passes through the Lime-trees,
　And stirs the Bridegroom's hair?

While one low cry of anguish,
　Like the last dying wail
Of some dumb, hunted creature,
　Is borne upon the gale : —
Why does the Bridegroom shudder
　And turn so deathly pale?

* * * *

Near Purgatory's entrance
　The radiant Angels wait;
It was the great St. Michael
　Who closed that gloomy gate,
When the poor wandering spirit
　Came back to meet her fate.

"Pass on," thus spoke the Angel:
" Heaven's joy is deep and vast;
Pass on, pass on, poor Spirit,
　For Heaven is yours at last;
In that one minute's anguish
　Your thousand years have passed."

A CONTRAST.

CAN you open that ebony Casket?
　Look, this is the key : but stay,
Those are only a few old letters
　Which I keep, — to burn some day. .

Yes, that Locket is quaint and ancient;
　But leave it, dear, with the ring,
And give me the little Portrait
　Which hangs by a crimson string.

I have never opened that Casket
　Since, many long years ago,
It was sent me back in anger
　By one whom I used to know.

But I want you to see the Portrait:
　I wonder if you can trace
A look of that smiling creature
　Left now in my faded face.

It was like me once; but remember
  The weary, relentless years,
And Life, with its fierce brief tempests,
  And its long, long rain of tears.

Is it strange to call it my Portrait?
  Nay, smile, dear, for well you may,
To think of that radiant Vision
  And of what I am to-day.

With restless, yet confident longing,
  How those blue eyes seem to gaze
Into deep and exhaustless treasures,
  All hid in the coming days.

With that trust which leans on the Future,
  And counts on her promised store,
Until she has taught us to tremble
  And hope, — but to trust no more.

How that young, light heart would have pitied
  Me now — if her dreams had shown
A quiet and weary woman
  With all her illusions flown.

Yet I — who shall soon be resting,
  And have passed the hardest part —
Can look back with a deeper pity
  On that young, unconscious heart.

It is strange; but Life's currents drift us
  So surely and swiftly on,
That we scarcely notice the changes,
  And how many things are gone:

And forget, while to-day absorbs us,
  How old mysteries are unsealed;
How the old, old ties are loosened,
  And the old, old wounds are healed.

And we say that our Life is fleeting
  Like a story that Time has told;
But we fancy that we — we only —
  Are just what we were of old.

So now and then it is wisdom
  To gaze, as I do to-day,
At a half-forgotten relic
  Of a Time that is passed away.

The very look of that Portrait,
  The perfume that seems to cling
To those fragile and faded letters,
  And the Locket, and the Ring,

If they only stirred in my spirit
  Forgotten pleasure and pain, —
Why, memory is often bitter,
  And almost always in vain;

But the contrast of bygone hours
  Comes to rend a veil away, —
And I marvel to see the stranger
  Who is living in me to-day.

THE BRIDE'S DREAM.

The stars are gleaming;
  The maiden sleeps, —
What is she dreaming?
  For see — she weeps.
By her side is an Angel
  With folded wings;
While the Maiden slumbers,
  The Angel sings:
He sings of a Bridal,
  Of Love, of Pain,
Of a heart to be given, —
  And all in vain;
(See, her cheek is flushing,
  As if with pain;)
He telleth of sorrow,
  Regrets and fears,
And the few vain pleasures
  We buy with tears;
And the bitter lesson
  We learn from years.

The stars are gleaming
  Upon her brow:
What is she dreaming
  So calmly now?
By her side is the Angel
  With folded wings;
She smiles in her slumber
  The while he sings.
He sings of a Bridal,
  Of Love divine;
Of a heart to be laid
  On a sacred shrine;
Of a crown of glory,
  Where seraphs shine;
Of the deep, long rapture
  The chosen know
Who forsake for Heaven
  Vain joys below,
Who desire no pleasure,
  And fear no woe.

The Bells are ringing,
  The sun shines clear,
The Choir is singing,
  The guests are here.
Before the High Altar
  Behold the Bride;
And a mournful Angel
  Is by her side.
She smiles, all content
  With her chosen lot, —
(Is her last night's dreaming
  So soon forgot?)
And oh, may the Angel
  Forsake her not!
For on her small hand
  There glitters plain

The first sad link
Of a life-long chain; —
And she needs his guiding
Through paths of pain.

THE ANGEL'S BIDDING.

NOT a sound is heard in the Convent;
The Vesper Chant is sung,
The sick have all been tended,
The poor nun's toils are ended
Till the Matin bell has rung.
All is still, save the Clock, that is ticking
So loud in the frosty air,
And the soft snow, falling as gently
As an answer to a prayer.
    But an Angel whispers,
    " O Sister,
    You must rise from your bed to pray;
    In the silent, deserted chapel,
    You must kneel till the dawn of day;
    For, far on the desolate moorland,
    So dreary, and bleak, and white,
    There is one, all alone and helpless,
    In peril of death to-night.

" No sound on the moorland to guide him,
No star in the murky air;
And he thinks of his home and his loved ones
With the tenderness of despair;
He has wandered for hours in the snow-drift,
And he strives to stand in vain,
And so lies down to dream of his children,
And never to rise again.
    Then kneel in the silent chapel
    Till the dawn of to-morrow's sun,
    And ask of the Lord you worship
    For the life of that desolate one;
    And the smiling eyes of his children
    Will gladden his heart again,
    And the grateful tears of God's poor ones
    Will fall on your soul like rain !

" Yet, leave him alone to perish,
And the grace of your God implore,
With all the strength of your spirit,
For one who needs it more.
Far away, in the gleaming city,
Amid perfume, and song, and light,
A soul that Jesus has ransomed
Is in peril of sin to-night.

"The Tempter is close beside him,
  And his danger is all forgot,
And the far-off voices of child-
    hood
  Call aloud, but he hears them
    not;
He sayeth no prayer, and his
    mother —
  He thinks not of her to-day,
And he will not look up to
    heaven,
  And his Angel is turning
    away.

"Then pray for a soul in peril,
  A soul for which Jesus died;
Ask, by the cross that bore Him,
  And by her who stood beside;
And the Angels of God will
    thank you,
  And bend from their thrones
    of light,
To tell you that Heaven rejoices
  At the deed you have done to-
    night."

SPRING.

Hark! the hours are softly call-
    ing,
  Bidding Spring arise,
To listen to the rain-drops falling
  From the cloudy skies,
To listen to Earth's weary
    voices,
  Louder every day,
Bidding her no longer linger
  On her charmèd way;
But hasten to her task of beauty
  Scarcely yet begun;
By the first bright day of Summer
  It should all be done.
She has yet to loose the fountain
  From its iron chain;
And to make the barren moun-
    tain
  Green and bright again;
She must clear the snow that
    lingers
  Round the stalks away,
And let the snow-drop's trem-
    bling whiteness
  See the light of day.
She must watch, and warm, and
    cherish
  Every blade of green,
Till the tender grass appearing
  From the earth is seen;
She must bring the golden crocus
  From her hidden store;
She must spread broad showers
    of daisies
  Each day more and more.
In each hedge-row she must
    hasten
  Cowslips sweet to set;
Primroses in rich profusion,
  With bright dew-drops wet,
And under every leaf, in shadow
  Hide a violet!
Every tree within the forest
  Must be decked anew;
And the tender buds of promise
  Should be peeping through,
Folded deep, and almost hidden,
  Leaf by leaf beside,

What will make the Summer's
   glory,
     And the Autumn's pride.
She must weave the loveliest car-
   pets,
     Checkered sun and shade,
Every wood must have such path-
   ways,
     Laid in every glade;
She must hang laburnum
   branches
     On each archéd bough; —
And the white and purple lilac
     Should be waving now;
She must breathe, and cold winds
   vanish
     At her breath away;
And then load the air around her
     With the scent of May!
Listen then, O Spring! nor
   linger
     On thy charméd way;
Have pity on thy prisoned flowers
     Wearying for the day.
Listen to the rain-drops falling
     From the cloudy skies;
Listen to the hours calling,
     Bidding thee arise.

EVENING HYMN.

The shadows of the evening
   hours
     Fall from the darkening sky;
Upon the fragrance of the flowers
     The dews of evening lie;
Before thy throne, O Lord of
   heaven,
     We kneel at close of day;
Look on thy children from on
   high,
     And hear us while we pray.

The sorrows of thy servants,
   Lord,
     O do not thou despise;
But let the incense of our prayers
     Before thy mercy rise;
The brightness of the coming
   night
     Upon the darkness rolls:
With hopes of future glory chase
     The shadows on our souls.

Slowly the rays of daylight fade;
     So fade within our heart
The hopes in earthly love and joy,
     That one by one depart:
Slowly the bright stars, one by
   one,
     Within the heavens shine; —
Give us, O Lord, fresh hopes in
   Heaven,
     And trust in things divine.

Let peace, O Lord, thy peace, O
   God,
     Upon our souls descend;
From midnight fears and perils,
   thou
     Our trembling hearts defend;
Give us a respite from our toil,
     Calm and subdue our woes;
Through the long day we suffer,
   Lord,
     O give us now repose!

THE INNER CHAMBER.

In the outer Court I was singing,
  Was singing the whole day long;
From the inner chamber were ringing
  Echoes repeating my song.

And I sang till it grew immortal;
  For that very song of mine,
When re-echoed behind the Portal,
  Was filled with a life divine.

Was the Chamber a silver round
  Of arches, whose magical art
Drew in coils of musical sound,
  And cast them back on my heart?

Was there hidden within a lyre
  Which, as air breathed over its strings,
Filled my song with a soul of fire,
  And sent back my words with wings?

Was some seraph imprisoned there,
  Whose Voice made my song complete,
And whose lingering, soft despair
  Made the echo so faint and sweet?

Long I trembled and paused,—then parted
  The curtains with heavy fringe;
And, half fearing, yet eager-hearted,
  Turned the door on its golden hinge.

Now I sing in the court once more,
  I sing and I weep all day,
As I kneel by the close-shut door,
  For I know what the echoes say.

Yet I sing not the song of old,
  Ere I knew whence the echo came,
Ere I opened the door of gold;
  But the music sounds just the same.

Then take warning, and turn away;
  Do not ask of that hidden thing,
Do not guess what the echoes say,
  Or the meaning of what I sing.

HEARTS.

I.

A trinket made like a Heart, dear,
  Of red gold, bright and fine,
Was given to me for a keepsake,
  Given to me for mine.

And another heart, warm and tender,
  As true as a heart could be ;
And every throb that stirred it
  Was always and all for me.

Sailing over the waters,
  Watching the far blue land,
I dropped my golden heart, dear,
  Dropped it out of my hand!

It lies in the cold, blue waters,
  Fathoms and fathoms deep,
The golden heart which I promised,
  Promised to prize and keep.

Gazing at Life's bright visions,
  So false, and fair, and new,
I forgot the other heart, dear,
  Forgot it and lost it too!

I might seek that heart forever,
  I might seek and seek in vain ; —
And for one short, careless hour,
  I pay with a life of pain.

II.

The Heart ? — Yes, I wore it
  As sign and as token
Of a love that once gave it,
  A vow that was spoken ;
But a love, and a vow, and a heart
  Can be broken.

The Love ? — Life and Death
  Are crushed into a day,
So what wonder that Love
  Should as soon pass away, —
What wonder I saw it
  Fade, fail, and decay ?

The Vow ? — why what was it ?
  It snapped like a thread ;
Who cares for the corpse
  When the spirit is fled ?
Then I said, "Let the Dead rise
  And bury its dead,

"While the true, living future
  Grows pure, wise, and strong."
So I cast the gold heart
  I had worn for so long
In the Lake, and bound on it
  A Stone — and a Wrong!

III.

Look, this little golden Heart
  Was a true-love shrine
For a tress of hair ; I held them,
  Heart and tress, as mine,
Like the Love which gave the token : —
See, to-day the Heart is broken!

Broken is the golden heart,
  Lost the tress of hair;
Ah, the shrine is empty, vacant,
  Desolate and bare!
So the token should depart,
When Love dies within the heart.

Fast and deep the river floweth,
  Floweth to the west;
I will cast the golden trinket
  In its cold dark breast: —
Flow, O river, deep and fast,
Over all the buried past!

TWO LOVES.

DEEP within my heart of hearts, dear,
  Bound with all its strings,
Two Loves are together reigning,
  Both are crowned like Kings;
While my life, still uncomplaining,
  Rests beneath their wings.

So they both will rule my heart, dear,
  Till it cease to beat;
No sway can be deeper, stronger,
  Truer, more complete;
Growing, as it lasts the longer,
  Sweeter, and more sweet.

Once all life and time transfigures;
  Piercing through and through
Meaner things with magic splendor,
  Old, yet ever new:
This — so strong and yet so tender —
Is . . . my Love for you.

Should it fail, — forgive my doubting
  In this world of pain, —
Yet my other Love would ever
  Steadfastly remain;
And I know that I could never
  Turn to that in vain.

Though its radiance may be fainter,
  Yet its task is wide;
For it lives to comfort sorrows,
  Strengthen, calm, and guide,
And from Trust and Honor borrows
  All its peace and pride.

Will you blame my dreaming, even
  If the first were flown?
Ah, I would not live without it,
  It is all your own:
And the other — can you doubt it? —
  Yours, and yours alone.

A WOMAN'S LAST WORD.

WELL — the links are broken,
  All is past;

This farewell, when spoken,
    Is the last.
I have tried and striven
    All in vain;
Such bonds must be riven,
    Spite of pain,
And never, never, never
    Knit again.

So I tell you plainly,
    It must be:
I shall try, not vainly,
    To be free;
Truer, happier chances
    Wait me yet,
While you, through fresh fancies,
    Can forget; —
And life has nobler uses
    Than Regret.

All past words retracing,
    One by one,
Does not help effacing
    What is done.
Let it be. O, stronger
    Links can break!
Had we dreamed still longer
    We could wake, —
Yet let us part in kindness
    For Love's sake.

Bitterness and sorrow
    Will at last,
In some bright to-morrow,
    Heal their past;
But future hearts will never
    Be as true

As mine was — is ever,
    Dear, for you . . . .
. . Then must we part, when loving
    As we do?

PAST AND PRESENT.

"LINGER," I cried, " O radiant Time! thy power
Has nothing more to give; life is complete:
Let but the perfect Present, hour by hour,
Itself remember and itself repeat.

"And Love, — the future can but mar its splendor,
Change can but dim the glory of its youth;
Time has no star more faithful or more tender
To crown its constancy or light its truth."

But Time passed on in spite of prayer or pleading,
Through storm and peril; but that life might gain
A Peace through strife all other peace exceeding,
Fresh joy from sorrow, and new hope from pain.

And since Love lived when all
  save Love was dying,
And, passed through fire, grew
  stronger than before: —
Dear, you know why, in double
  faith relying,
I prize the Past much, but the
  Present more.

FOR THE FUTURE.

I wonder did you ever count
The value of one human fate;
Or sum the infinite amount
Of one heart's treasures, and
  the weight
Of Life's one venture, and the
  whole concentrate purpose
  of a soul.

And if you ever paused to
  think
That all this in your hands I
  laid
Without a fear: — did you
  not shrink
From such a burden? half
  afraid,
Half wishing that you could divide the risk, or cast it all
  aside.

While Love has daily perils,
  such
As none foresee and none control;
And hearts are strung so that
  one touch,
Careless or rough, may jar the
  whole,
You well might feel afraid to
  reign with absolute power
  of joy and pain.

You well might fear — if
  Love's sole claim
Were to be happy: but true Love
Takes joy as solace, not as aim,
And looks beyond, and looks
  above;
And sometimes through the bit-
  terest strife first learns to
  live her highest life.

Earth forges joy into a chain
Till fettered Love forgets its
  strength,
Its purpose, and its end; —
  but Pain
Restores its heritage at length,
And bids Love rise again and be
  eternal, mighty, pure, and
  free.

If then your future life should
  need
A strength my Love can only
  gain
Through suffering, or my heart
  be freed
Only by sorrow from some
  stain,
Then you shall give, and I will
  take, this Crown of fire for
  Love's dear sake.

September 8, 1860.

A CHAPLET OF VERSES.

PUBLISHED FOR THE BENEFIT OF

THE PROVIDENCE ROW NIGHT REFUGE

FOR

HOMELESS WOMEN AND CHILDREN.

INTRODUCTION.

There is scarcely any charitable institution which should excite such universal, such unhesitating sympathy, as a Night Refuge for the Homeless Poor.

A shelter through the bleak winter nights, leave to rest in some poor shed instead of wandering through the pitiless streets, is a boon we could hardly deny to a starving dog. And yet we have all known that in this country, in this town, many of our miserable fellow-creatures were pacing the streets through the long weary nights, without a roof to shelter them, without food to eat, with their poor rags soaked in rain, and only the bitter winds of Heaven for companions; women and children utterly forlorn and helpless, either wandering about all night, or crouching under a miserable archway, or, worst of all, seeking in death or sin the refuge denied them elsewhere. It is a marvel that we could sleep in peace in our warm, comfortable homes with this horror at our very door.

But at last some efforts were made to efface this stain upon our country, public sympathy was appealed to, and a few "Refuges" were opened, to shelter our homeless poor through the winter nights.

In the autumn of 1860 there was no Catholic Refuge in the kingdom; and excellent as were the Protestant Refuges, their resources were quite inadequate to meet the claims upon them.

In this country, as we all know, the very poorest and most destitute are in many cases Catholics; and doubtless our Priests, to whom no form of sin or sorrow is strange, must see in a special manner, and in innumerable results, the sufferings, dangers, and temptations of the homeless. The Rev. Dr. Gilbert therefore resolved to open a Catholic Night Refuge in his parish, and to his zealous charity and unwearied efforts are due the foundation and success of the PROVIDENCE ROW NIGHT REFUGE FOR HOMELESS WOMEN AND CHILDREN; the first Catholic Refuge in England or Ireland, and still the only one in England.

The Sisters of Mercy had long been aiding their pastors in the schools of the parish, and when this new opening for their charity was suggested to them, they unhesitatingly accepted a task, worthy indeed of the holy name they bear. They were seeking for some house more suitable for a Convent than the one they had hitherto occupied in Broad Street; and when Dr. Gilbert saw the large stable at the back of 14 Finsbury Square, he felt that here was a suitable place for his long-cherished plan of a Night Refuge. It was separated from the house by a yard, and opened on a narrow street at the back, already called, with a happy appropriateness, Providence Row. To Finsbury Square therefore the community removed, and it was not long before the stable was fitted up with wooden beds and benches, the few preparations were completed, and on the 7th of October, 1860, the Refuge was opened. At first there were but fourteen beds, but contributions flowed in from Protestants as well as Catholics, and in February, 1861, thirty-one more beds were added, making in all forty-five. But as many of the poor women have children with them, rarely less than sixty persons are each night admitted. Up to the present time, fourteen thousand seven hundred and eighty-five nights' lodgings have been given, with the same number of suppers and breakfasts.

From six to eight are the hours of admission; but this is indeed a needless rule, for a crowd of ragged women, with pale, weary children clinging to them, are waiting patiently long before the doors are opened, and the place is filled at once.

Means for washing are given them, they rest themselves in warmth, light, and peace, and at eight o'clock each person receives half a pound of bread and a large basin of excellent gruel. Night prayers are said by one of the Sisters, and then the poor wanderers lie down in their rude but clean and comfortable beds. They have the same meal in the morning.

Those who come on Saturday evening remain till Monday, receiving on Sunday, besides the usual breakfast and supper, an extra half-pound of bread, and a good supply of meat soup. There is no distinction of creed; Protestants and Catholics are alike admitted. There are but two conditions of admittance, — that the applicants be homeless and of good character. This is the only Refuge which makes character a condition; and it is found that, in spite of all precautions, much harm arises in the other Refuges to the young and innocent, from the bad language and evil example of the degraded class with whom they are brought in contact.

Each evening (and on Sundays more fully) simple instructions on the Catechism are given by one of the Sisters; but this the Protestants do not attend; they frequently ask leave to be present, but it is not permitted, (without the special permission of one of the clergy,) as the instructions on the practice of our faith would be to them comparatively useless and unmeaning.

The temporary shelter and food which is given in Providence Row is not the only, perhaps often not the greatest, benefit bestowed upon the poor forlorn inmates. They find advice, sympathy, and help from the kind Sisters; and the very telling their troubles to one who is there to serve and tend them, not for any earthly reward, but from Christian love and pity, must be a rest to their weary hearts, a comfort in their sore want and distress. It is touching to see their eager desire to be allowed to help the Sister in the cleaning, cooking, etc., and the half-ashamed thankfulness with which they watch her busied in her service.

One of the Nuns sleeps every night in the Refuge, and no unruly sound, no whisper of murmur or disrespect, ever rises against her gentle sway. Nay, even more, when she has the sad task of selecting among the waiting crowd the number who may enter, choosing generally those with children and those who have not applied before, the rest submit without a murmur. Though the little ones are hardly counted, but creep in by their mothers' sides, there are still many — sometimes thirty or forty nightly — turned away for want of space. They have had a glimpse of warmth and light, and then it is the cruel office of the kind Nun to bar the door against them; but no angry word, no remonstrance, meets her sorrowful refusal; they turn once more to their weary wanderings in the dark, bleak streets. And so will many have to do, night after night, until the Refuge is enlarged. The present space will hold no more beds, but to build an additional dormitory is the earnest desire and intention of Dr. Gilbert.

No salaries are received by any who have charge of the Refuge.

Among the many causes for gratitude we have to our good Religious, surely it is not one of the least, that what we can spare in the cause of charity goes solely and directly to its object; the more difficult and more perfect share of the good work being taken by them out of love to God and his poor.

The Refuge is open from the month of October to April.

It is placed under the special patronage of Our Blessed Lady, and Blessed Benedict Labré.

May the Mother who wandered homeless through inhospitable Bethlehem, and the Saint who was a beggar and an outcast upon the face of the earth, watch over this Refuge for the poor and desolate, and obtain from the charity of the faithful the aid which it so sorely needs.

I may add, that donations for the Refuge will be thankfully received by the Rev. Dr. Gilbert, 22 Finsbury Circus, or by the Rev. Mother, at the Convent, 14 Finsbury Square, E. C.

We all meditate long and often on the many kinds of sufferings borne for us by our Blessed Redeemer; but perhaps, if we consider a moment, we shall most of us confess, that the one we think of least often, the one we compassionate least of all, is the only one of which he deigned to tell us himself, and for which he himself appealed to our pity in the Divine complaint, "The foxes have holes, and the birds of the air have nests, but the Son of Man *has not where to lay his head.*"

A. A. P.

May, 1862.

A CHAPLET OF VERSES.

THE ARMY OF THE LORD.

I.

To fight the battle of the Cross, Christ's chosen ones are sent, —
Good soldiers and great victors, — a noble armament.
They use no earthly weapon, they know not spear or sword,
Yet right and true and valiant is the army of the Lord.

II.

Fear them, ye mighty ones of earth; fear them, ye demon foes;
Slay them and think to conquer, but the ranks will always close:
In vain do Earth and Hell unite their power and skill to try,
They fight better for their wounds, and they conquer when they die.

III.

The soul of every sinner is the victory they would gain;
They would bind each rebel heart in their Master's golden chain:
Faith is the shield they carry, and the two-edged sword they bear
Is God's strongest, mightiest weapon, and they call it Love and
    Prayer.

IV.

Where the savage hordes are dwelling by the Ganges' sacred tide,
Through the trackless Indian forests, St. Francis is their guide;
Where crime and sin are raging, to conquer they are gone; —
They do conquer as they go, for St. Philip leads them on.

V.

They are come where all are kneeling at the shrines of wealth and pride,
And an old and martyred Bishop is their comrade and their guide:
To tell the toil-worn negro of freedom and repose,
O'er the vast Atlantic's bosom they are called by sweet St. Rose.

VI.

They are gone where Love is frozen, and Faith grown calm and cold,
Where the world is all triumphant, and the sheep have left the fold,
Where His children scorn His blessings, and His sacred Shrines despise, —
And the beacon of the warriors is the light in Mary's eyes.

VII.

The bugle for their battle is the matin bell for prayer;
And for their noble standard Christ's holy Cross they bear;
His sacred name their war-cry, 't is in vain what ye can do,
They *must* conquer, for your Angels are leaguing with them too.

VIII.

Would you know, O World, these warriors? Go where the poor, the old,
Ask for pardon and for heaven, and you offer food and gold;
With healing and with comfort, with words of peace and prayer,
Bearing His greatest gift to man, — Christ's chosen priests are there.

IX.

Where sin and crime are dwelling, hid from the light of day,
And life and hope are fading at Death's cold touch away,
Where dying eyes in horror see the long-forgotten past,
Christ's servants claim the sinner, and gain his soul at last.

X.

Where the rich and proud and mighty God's message would defy,
In warning and reproof His anointed ones stand by:
Bright are the crowns of glory God keepeth for His own,
Their life one sigh for heaven, and their aim His will alone.

XI.

And see sweet Mercy's sister, where the poor and wretched dwell,
In gentle accents telling of Him she loves so well;
Training young hearts to serve their Lord, and place their hope in Heaven,
Bidding her erring sisters love much and be forgiven.

XII.

And where in cloistered silence dim the Brides of Jesus dwell,
Where purest incense rises up from every lowly cell,
They plead not vainly, — they have chosen and gained the better part,
And given their gentle life away to Him who has their heart.

XIII.

And some there are among us — the path which they have trod
Of sin and pain and anguish has led at last to God:
They plead, and Christ will hear them, that the poor slaves who pine
In the bleak dungeon they have left, may see His truth divine.

XIV.

O, who can tell how many hearts are altars to His praise,
From which the silent prayer ascends through patient nights and days:
The sacrifice is offered still in secret and alone,
O World, ye do not know them, but He can help His own.

XV.

They are with us, His true soldiers, they come in power and might;
Glorious the crown which they shall gain after the heavenly fight;
And you, perchance, who scoff, may yet their rest and glory share,
As the rich spoil of their battle and the captives of their prayer.

XVI.

O, who shall tell the wonder of that great day of rest,
When even in this place of strife His soldiers are so blest:
O World, O Earth, why strive ye? join the low chant they sing, —
"O Grave, where is thy victory! O Death, where is thy sting!"

THE STAR OF THE SEA.

How many a mighty ship
   The stormy waves o'erwhelm ;
Yet our frail bark floats on,
   Our Angel holds the helm :
Dark storms are gathering round,
   And dangerous winds arise,
Yet see ! one trembling star
   Is shining in the skies ; —
And we are safe who trust in thee,
   Star of the Sea !

A long and weary voyage
   Have we to reach our home,
And dark and sunken rocks
   Are hid in silver foam ;
Each moment we may sink,
   But steadily we sail,
Our wingéd Pilot smiles,
   And says we shall not fail : —
And so we kneel and call on thee,
   Star of the Sea !

Yes, for those shining rays
   Shall beam upon the main,
Shall guide us safely on,
   Through fear and doubt and pain :
And see — the stormy wind
   Our little sail has caught,
The tempest others fear
   Shall drive us into port : —
Through Life's dark voyage we trust in thee,
   Star of the Sea !

The shore now looms in sight,
   The far-off golden strand,
Yet many a freight is wrecked
   And lost in sight of land ;
Then guide us safely home,
   Through that last hour of strife,
And welcome us to land,
   From the long voyage of life : —
In death and life we call on thee,
   Star of the Sea !

THE SACRED HEART.

What wouldst thou have, O soul,
   Thou weary soul ?
Lo ! I have sought for rest
On the Earth's heaving breast,
   From pole to pole.
Sleep — I have been with her,
   But she gave dreams ;
Death — nay, the rest he gives
   Rest only seems.
Fair nature knows it not —
   The grass is growing ;
The blue air knows it not —
   The winds are blowing :
Not in the changing sky,
   The stormy sea,
Yet somewhere in God's wide world
   Rest there must be.
Within thy Saviour's Heart
   Place all thy care,

And learn, O weary soul,
  Thy Rest is there.

What wouldst thou, trembling
    soul?
  Strength for the strife, —
Strength for this fiery war
  That we call Life.
Fears gather thickly round;
  Shadowy foes,
Like unto arméd men,
  Around me close.
What am I, frail and poor,
  When griefs arise?
No help from the weak earth,
  Or the cold skies.
Lo! I can find no guards,
  No weapons borrow;
Shrinking, alone I stand,
  With mighty sorrow.
Courage, thou trembling soul,
  Grief thou must bear,
Yet thou canst find a strength
  Will match despair;
Within thy Saviour's Heart —
  Seek for it there.

What wouldst thou have, sad
    soul,
  Oppressed with grief? —
Comfort: I seek in vain,
  Nor find relief.
Nature, all pitiless,
  Smiles on my pain;
I ask my fellow-men,
  They give disdain.
I asked the babbling streams,
  But they flowed on;
I asked the wise and good,
  But they gave none.
Though I have asked the stars,
  Coldly they shine.
They are too bright to know
  Grief such as mine.
I asked for comfort still,
  And I found tears,
And I have sought in vain
  Long, weary years.
Listen, thou mournful soul,
  Thy pain shall cease;
Deep in His sacred Heart
  Dwells joy and peace.

Yes, in that Heart divine
  The Angels bright
Find, through eternal years,
  Still new delight.
From thence his constancy
  The martyr drew,
And there the virgin band
  Their refuge knew.
There, racked by pain without,
  And dread within,
How many souls have found
  Heaven's bliss begin.
Then leave thy vain attempts
  To seek for peace;
The world can never give
  One soul release:
But in thy Saviour's Heart
  Securely dwell,
No pain can harm thee, hid
  In that sweet cell.
Then fly, O coward soul,
  Delay no more:
What words can speak the joy
  For thee in store?

THE NAMES OF OUR LADY.

Through the wide world thy children raise
    Their prayers, and still we see
Calm are the nights and bright the days
    Of those who trust in thee.

Around thy starry crown are wreathed
    So many names divine:
Which is the dearest to my heart,
    And the most worthy thine?

Star of the Sea: we kneel and pray
    When tempests raise their voice;
Star of the Sea! the haven reached,
    We call thee and rejoice.

Help of the Christian: in our need
    Thy mighty aid we claim;
If we are faint and weary, then
    We trust in that dear name.

Our Lady of the Rosary:
    What name can be so sweet
As what we call thee when we place
    Our chaplets at thy feet.

Bright Queen of Heaven: when we are sad,
    Best solace of our pains;—
It tells us, though on earth we toil,
    Our Mother lives and reigns.

Our Lady of Mount Carmel: thus
    Sometimes thy name is known;
It tells us of the badge we wear,
    To live or die thine own.

Our Lady dear of Victories:
    We see our faith oppressed,
And, praying for our erring land,
    We love that name the best.

Refuge of Sinners: many a soul,
    By guilt cast down, and sin,
Has learned through this dear name of thine
    Pardon and peace to win.

Health of the Sick: when anxious hearts
    Watch by the sufferer's bed,
On this sweet name of thine they lean,
    Consoled and comforted.

Mother of Sorrows: many a heart
    Half broken by despair
Has laid its burden by the cross,
    And found a mother there.

Queen *of all Saints:* the Church
 appeals
For her loved dead to thee;
She knows they wait in patient
 pain
A bright eternity.

Fair Queen of Virgins : thy pure
 band,
The lilies round thy throne,
Love the dear title which they
 bear
Most that it is thine own.

True Queen of Martyrs : if we
 shrink
From want, or pain, or woe,
We think of the sharp sword
 that pierced
Thy heart, and call thee so.

Mary : the dearest name of all,
The holiest and the best;
The first low word that Jesus
 lisped
Laid on His mother's breast.

Mary, the name that Gabriel
 spoke,
The name that conquers hell :
Mary, the name that through
 high heaven
The angels love so well.

Mary, — our comfort and our
 hope, —
O may that word be given
To be the last we sigh on earth, —
The first we breathe in heaven.

A CHAPLET OF FLOWERS.

DEAR, set the casement open,
 The evening breezes blow
Sweet perfumes from the flowers
 I cannot see below.

I can but catch the waving
 Of chestnut boughs that pass,
Their shadow must have covered
 The sun-dial on the grass.

So go and bring the flowers
 I love best to my room,
My failing strength no longer
 Can bear me where they bloom.

You know I used to love them,
 But ah ! they come too late, —
For see, my hands are trembling
 Beneath their dewy weight.

So I will watch you weaving
 A chaplet for me, dear,
Of all my favorite flowers,
 As I could do last year.

First, take those crimson roses, —
 How red their petals glow !
Red as the blood of Jesus,
 Which heals our sin and woe.

See in each heart of crimson
 A deeper crimson shine :
So in the foldings of our hearts
 Should glow a love divine.

Next place those tender violets,
  Look how they still regret
The cell where they were hid-
    den, —
  The tears are on them yet.

How many souls — His loved
    ones —
  Dwell lonely and apart,
Hiding from all but One above
  The fragrance of their heart.

Then take that virgin lily,
  How holily she stands!
You know the gentle angels
  Bear lilies in their hands.

Yet crowned with purer radiance
  A deeper love they claim,
Because their queen-like white-
    ness
  Is linked with Mary's name.

And now this spray of ivy:
  You know its gradual clasp
Uproots strong trees, and towers
  Fall crumbling in its grasp.

So God's dear grace around us
  With secret patience clings,
And slow, sure power, that
    loosens
  Strongholds on human things.

Then heliotrope, that turneth
  Towards her lord the sun, —
Would that our thoughts as
    fondly
  Sought our belovéd One.

Nay, if that branch be fading,
  Cast not one blossom by,
Its little task is ended
  And it does well to die.

And let some field flowers even
  Be wreathed among the rest,
I think the infant Jesus
  Would love such ones the best.

These flowers are all too bril-
    liant,
  So place calm heart's-ease
    there,
God's last and sacred treasure
  For all who wait and bear.

Then lemon-leaves, whose sweet-
    ness
  Grows sweeter than before
When bruised, and crushed, and
    broken,
  — Hearts need that lesson
    more.

Yet stay, — one crowning glory,
  All His, and yet all ours;
The dearest, tenderest thought of
    all,
  Is still the Passion-flower's.

So take it now, — nay, heed not
  My tears that on it fall;
I thank Him for the flowers,
  As I can do for all.

And place it on the altar,
  Where oft, in days long flown,
I knelt by His dear Mother,
  And knew she was my own.

The bells ring out her praises,
  The evening shades grow
    dim;
Go there and say a prayer for me,
  And sing Our Lady's hymn.

While I lie here, and ask her
    help
  In that last, longed-for day —
When the Belovéd of my heart
  Will call my soul away.

KYRIE ELEISON.

In joy, in pain, in sorrow,
  Father, Thy hand we see;
But some among Thy children
  Deny this faith and Thee.
They will not ask Thy mercy,
  But we kneel for them in
    prayer;
Are they not still Thy children?
  Pity, O God! and spare.
Thy peace, O Lord, has never
  On their desolate pathway
    shone,
Darkness is all around them:
  Kyrie Eleison!

For them the starry heavens
  No hymn of worship raise;
For them, earth's innocent flow-
    ers
  Breathe not Thy silent praise;
In heaven they know no Saviour,
  No Father, and no Friend,
And life is all they hope for,
  And Death they call the end;
Their eyes, O Lord! are blinded
  To the glories of the sun,
To the shining of the sea-star —
  Kyrie Eleison!

By the love Thy saints have
    shown Thee,
  And the sorrows they have
    borne,
Leave not these erring creatures
  To wander thus forlorn.
By Thy tender name of Sa-
    viour, —
  The name they have denied;
By Thy bitter death and passion,
  And the Cross which they de-
    ride;
By the anguish Thou hast suf-
    fered,
  And the glory Thou hast won;
By Thy love and by Thy pity —
  Christe Eleison!

Pray for them, glorious seraphs,
  And ye, bright angel band,
Who chant His praises ever,
  And in His presence stand;
And thou, O gentle Mother,
  Queen of the starry sky;
Ye Saints whose toils are over,
  Join your voices to our cry, —
In Thy terror or Thy mercy,
  Call them ere life is done,
For His sake who died to save
    them,
  Kyrie Eleison!

THE ANNUNCIATION.

How pure, and frail, and white,
   The snowdrops shine!
Gather a garland bright
   For Mary's shrine.

For, born of winter snows,
   These fragile flowers
Are gifts to our fair Queen
   From Spring's first hours.

For on this blessèd day
   She knelt at prayer;
When, lo! before her shone
   An Angel fair.

"Hail, Mary!" thus he cried,
   With reverent fear:
She, with sweet wondering eyes,
   Marvelled to hear.

Be still, ye clouds of Heaven!
   Be silent, Earth!
And hear an Angel tell
   Of Jesus' birth,

While she, whom Gabriel hails
   As full of grace,
Listens with humble faith
   In her sweet face.

Be still, Pride, War, and Pomp,
   Vain Hopes, vain Fears,
For now an Angel speaks,
   And Mary hears.

"Hail, Mary!" lo, it rings
   Through ages on;
"Hail, Mary!" it shall sound,
   Till Time is done.

"Hail, Mary!" infant lips
   Lisp it to-day;
"Hail, Mary!" with faint smile
   The dying say.

"Hail, Mary!" many a heart
   Broken with grief,
In that angelic prayer
   Has found relief.

And many a half-lost soul,
   When turnep at bay,
With those triumphant words
   Has won the day.

"Hail, Mary, Queen of Heaven!"
   Let us repeat,
And place our snowdrop wreath
   Here at her feet.

AN APPEAL.

"THE IRISH CHURCH MISSION FOR CONVERTING THE CATHOLICS."

SPARE her, O cruel England!
   Thy Sister lieth low;
Chained and oppressed she lieth
   Spare her that cruel blow.

AN APPEAL.

We ask not for the freedom
  Heaven has vouchsafed to thee,
Nor bid thee share with Ireland
  The empire of the sea;
Her children ask no shelter, —
  Leave them the stormy sky;
They ask not for thy harvests,
  For they know how to die:
Deny them, if it please thee,
  A grave beneath the sod: —
But we do cry, O England,
  Leave them their faith in God!

Take, if thou wilt, the earnings
  Of the poor peasant's toil,
Take all the scanty produce
  That grows on Irish soil,
To pay the alien preachers
  Whom Ireland will not hear,
To pay the scoffers at a Creed
  Which Irish hearts hold dear:
But leave them, cruel England,
  The gift their God has given,
Leave them their ancient worship,
  Leave them their faith in Heaven.

You come and offer Learning, —
  A mighty gift, 't is true;
Perchance the greatest blessing
  That now is known to you.
But not to see the wonders
  Sages of old beheld
Can they peril a priceless treasure,
  The Faith their Fathers held;
For in learning and in science
  They may forget to pray, —
God will not ask for knowledge
  On the great judgment day.

When, in their wretched cabins,
  Racked by the fever pain,
And the weak cries of their children
  Who ask for food in vain;
When starving, naked, helpless,
  From the shed that keeps them warm
Man has driven them forth to perish,
  In a less cruel storm; —
Then, then, we plead for mercy,
  Then, Sister, hear our cry!
For all we ask, O England,
  Is — leave them there to die!
Cursed is the food and raiment
  For which a soul is sold;
Tempt not another Judas
  To barter God for gold.
You offer food and shelter
  If they their faith deny: —
What do you gain, O England,
  By such a shallow lie? ....
We will not judge the tempted, —
  May God blot out their shame, —
He sees the misery round them,
  He knows man's feeble frame;
His pity still may save them,
  In His strength they must trust
Who calls us all His children,
  Yet knows we are but dust.

Then leave them the kind tending
  Which helped their childish years;
Leave them the gracious comfort
  Which dries the mourner's tears;

Leave them to that great mother
   In whose bosom they were born;
Leave them the holy mysteries
   That comfort the forlorn:
And, amid all their trials,
   Let the Great Gift abide,
Which you, O prosperous England,
   Have dared to cast aside.
Leave them the pitying Angels
   And Mary's gentle aid,
For which earth's dearest treasures
   Were not too dearly paid.
Take back your bribes, then, England,
   Your gold is black and dim,
And if God sends plague and famine,
   They can die and go to Him.

THE JUBILEE OF 1850.

[The titles of the "Island of Saints" and the "Dower of our Lady," though more frequently applied to Ireland, were often given to England in former times.]

Bless God, ye happy Lands,
   For your more favored lot:
Our England dwells apart,
   Yet O forget her not.
While, with united joy,
   This day you all adore,
Remember what she was,
   Though her voice is heard no more.
Pray for our desolate land,
   Left in her pride and power: —
She was the Isle of Saints,
She was Our Lady's Dower.

Look on her ruined Altars;
   He dwelleth there no more:
Think what her empty churches
   Have been in times of yore;
She knows the names no longer
   Of her own sainted dead,
Denies the faith they held,
   And the cause for which they bled.
Then pray for our desolate land,
   Left in her pride and power: —
She was the Isle of Saints,
She was Our Lady's Dower!

Pray that her vast Cathedrals,
   Deserted, empty, bare,
May once more echo accents
   Of Love, and Faith, and Prayer;
That the holy sign may bless us,
   On wood, and field, and plain,
And Jesus, Mary, Joseph,
   May dwell with us again.
Pray, ye more faithful nations,
   In this most happy hour: —
She was the Isle of Saints,
She was Our Lady's Dower.

Beg of our Lord to give her
  The gift she cast aside,
And in His mercy pardon
  Her faithlessness and pride:
Pray to her Saints, who worship
  Before God's mercy Throne;
Look where our Queen is dwelling,
  Ask her to claim her own,
    To give her the proud titles
    Lost in an evil hour: —
    She was the Isle of Saints,
    She was Our Lady's Dower.

CHRISTMAS FLOWERS.

The Earth is so bleak and deserted,
  So cold the winds blow,
That no bud or no blossom will venture
  To peep from below;
But, longing for springtime, they nestle
  Deep under the snow.

O, in May how we honored Our Lady,
  Her own month of flowers!
How happy we were with our garlands
  Through all the spring hours!
All her shrines, in the church or the wayside,
  Were made into bowers.

And in August — her glorious Assumption;
  What feast was so bright!
What clusters of virginal lilies,
  So pure and so white!
Why, the incense could scarce overpower
  Their perfume that night.

And through her dear feasts of October
  The roses bloomed still;
Our baskets were laden with flowers,
  Her vases to fill:
Oleanders, geraniums, and myrtles,
  We chose at our will.

And we know when the Purification,
  Her first feast, comes round,
The early spring flowers, to greet it,
  Just opening are found;
And pure, white, and spotless, the snowdrop
  Will pierce the dark ground.

And now, in this dreary December,
  Our glad hearts are fain
To see if Earth comes not to help us;
  We seek all in vain:
Not the tiniest blossom is coming
  Till Spring breathes again.

And the bright feast of Christmas
    is dawning,
And Mary is blest;
For now she will give us her
    Jesus,
Our dearest, our best,
And see where she stands, the
    Maid-Mother,
Her Babe on her breast!

And not one poor garland to give
    her,
And yet now, behold,
How the Kings bring their gifts,
    — myrrh, and incense,
And bars of pure gold:
And the Shepherds have brought
    for the Baby
Some lambs from their folds.

He stretches His tiny hands to-
    wards us,
He brings us all grace;
And look at His Mother who
    holds Him, —
The smile on her face
Says they welcome the humblest
    gifts
In the manger we place.

Where love takes, let love give;
    and so doubt not:
Love counts but the will,
And the heart has its flowers of
    devotion
No Winter can chill;
They who cared for "good-will"
    that first Christmas
Will care for it still.

In the Chaplet on Jesus and
    Mary,
From our hearts let us call,
At each Ave Maria we whisper
A rosebud shall fall,
And at each Gloria Patri a lily,
    The crown of them all!

A DESIRE.

O, TO have dwelt in Bethlehem
    When the star of the Lord
    shone bright!
To have sheltered the holy wan-
    derers
    On that blesséd Christmas
    night;
To have kissed the tender way-
    worn feet
Of the Mother undefiled,
And, with reverent wonder and
    deep delight,
    To have tended the Holy
    Child!

Hush! such a glory was not for
    thee;
    But that care may still be
    thine;
For are there not little ones still
    to aid
For the sake of the Child di-
    vine?
Are there no wandering Pilgrims
    now,
    To thy heart and thy home to
    take?

And are there no mothers whose
    weary hearts
You can comfort for Mary's
    sake?

O to have knelt at Jesus' feet,
    And to have learnt His heavenly lore!
To have listened the gentle lessons He taught
    On mountain, and sea, and shore!
While the rich and the mighty
    knew Him not,
To have meekly done His will: —
Hush! for the worldly reject Him yet,
    You can serve and love Him still.
Time cannot silence His mighty words,
    And though ages have fled away,
His gentle accents of love divine
    Speak to your soul to-day.

O to have solaced that weeping one
    Whom the righteous dared despise!
To have tenderly bound up her scattered hair,
    And have dried her tearful eyes!
Hush! there are broken hearts to soothe,
    And penitent tears to dry,

While Magdalen prays for you and them,
    From her home in the starry sky.

O to have followed the mournful way
    Of those faithful few forlorn!
And grace, beyond even an angel's hope,
    The Cross for our Lord have borne!
To have shared in His tender mother's grief,
    To have wept at Mary's side,
To have lived as a child in her home, and then
    In her loving care have died!

Hush! and with reverent sorrow still,
    Mary's great anguish share;
And learn, for the sake of her Son divine,
    Thy cross, like His, to bear.
The sorrows that weigh on thy soul unite
    With those which thy Lord has borne,
And Mary will comfort thy dying hour,
    Nor leave thy soul forlorn.

O to have seen what we now adore,
    And, though veiled to faithless sight,
To have known, in the form that Jesus wore,
    The Lord of Life and Light!

Hush! for He dwells among us
    still,
And a grace can yet be thine,
Which the scoffer and doubter
    can never know, —
The Presence of the Divine.
Jesus is with His children yet,
    For His word can never deceive;
Go where His lowly Altars rise,
    And worship, and believe.

OUR DAILY BREAD.

Give us our daily Bread,
    O God, the bread of strength!
For we have learnt to know
    How weak we are at length.
As children we are weak,
    As children must be fed; —
Give us Thy Grace, O Lord,
    To be our daily Bread.

Give us our daily Bread, —
    The bitter bread of grief.
We sought earth's poisoned feasts
    For pleasure and relief;
We sought her deadly fruits,
    But now, O God, instead,
We ask Thy healing grief
    To be our daily Bread.

Give us our daily Bread
    To cheer our fainting soul;
The feast of comfort, Lord,
    And peace, to make us whole:
For we are sick of tears,
    The useless tears we shed; —
Now give us comfort, Lord,
    To be our daily Bread.

Give us our daily Bread,
    The Bread of Angels, Lord,
By us, so many times,
    Broken, betrayed, adored:
His Body and His Blood; —
The feast that Jesus spread:
Give Him — our life, our all —
    To be our daily Bread!

THREEFOLD.

Mother of grace and mercy,
    Behold how burdens three
Weigh down my weary spirit,
    And drive me here — to Thee.
Three gifts I place forever
    Before thy shrine:
The threefold offering of my love,
    Mary, to thine!

The Past: with all its memories,
    Of pain — that stings me yet;
Of sin — that brought repentance;
    Of joy — that brought regret.
That which has been: — forever
    So bitter-sweet —
I lay in humblest offering
    Before thy feet.

The Present: that dark shadow
  Through which we toil to-day;
The slow drops of the chalice
  That must not pass away.
Mother! I dare not struggle,
  Still less despair:
I place my Present in thy hands,
  And leave it there.

The Future: holding all things
  Which I can hope or fear,
Brings sin and pain, it may be,
  Nearer and yet more near.
Mother! this doubt and shrinking
  Will not depart,
Unless I trust my Future
  To thy dear Heart.

Making the Past my lesson,
  Guiding the Present right,
Ruling the misty Future, —
  Bless them and me to-night.
What may be, and what must be,
  And what has been,
In thy dear care forever
  I leave, my Queen!

CONFIDO ET CONQUIESCO.

"*Scit; potest; vult: quid est quod timeamus?*" — S. IGNATIUS.

FRET not, poor soul: while doubt
    and fear
  Disturb thy breast,
The pitying angels, who can see
How vain thy wild regret must be,
  Say, Trust and Rest.

Plan not, nor scheme, — but
    calmly wait;
  His choice is best.
While blind and erring is thy
    sight,
His wisdom sees and judges right,
  So Trust and Rest.

Strive not, nor struggle: thy
    poor might
  Can never wrest
The meanest thing to serve thy
    will;
All power is His alone: Be still,
  And Trust and Rest.

Desire not: self-love is strong
  Within thy breast;
And yet He loves thee better still,
So let Him do His loving will,
  And Trust and Rest.

What dost thou fear? His wisdom reigns
  Supreme confessed;
His power is infinite; his love
Thy deepest, fondest dreams
    above; —
  So Trust and Rest.

ORA PRO ME.

AVE MARIA! bright and pure,
  Hear, O hear me when I pray!

Pains and pleasures try the pilgrim
On his long and weary way;
Fears and perils are around me, —
    Ora pro me.

Mary, see my heart is burdened,
    Take, O take the weight away,
Or help me, that I may not murmur
If it is a cross you lay
On my weak and trembling heart,
— but
    Ora pro me.

Mary, Mary, Queen of Heaven!
    Teach, O teach me to obey:
Lead me on, though fierce temptations
Stand and meet me in the way;
When I fail and faint, my mother,
    Ora pro me.

Then shall I — if thou, O Mary,
    Art my strong support and stay —
Fear nor feel the threefold danger
Standing forth in dread array;
Now and ever shield and guard me,
    Ora pro me.

When my eyes are slowly closing,
    And I fade from earth away,
And when Death, the stern destroyer,
Claims my body as his prey, —
Claim my soul, and then, sweet Mary,
    Ora pro me.

THE CHURCH IN 1849.

O MIGHTY Mother, hearken! for thy foes
    Gather around thee, and exulting cry
That thine old strength is gone and thou must die,
Pointing with fierce rejoicing to thy woes.
And is it so? The raging whirlwind blows
    No stronger now than it has done of yore:
    Rebellion, strife, and sin have been before;
The same companions whom thy Master chose.
We too rejoice: we know thy might is more
    When to the world thy glory seemeth dim;
Nor can Hell's gates prevail to conquer Thee,
    Who hearest over all the voice of Him
Who chose thy first and greatest Prince should be
A fisher on the Lake of Galilee.

FISHERS OF MEN.

THE boats are out, and the storm is high;
    We kneel on the shore and pray:

The Star of the Sea shines still in
    the sky,
And God is our help and stay.

The fishers are weak, and the
    tide is strong,
    And their boat seems slight
        and frail;
But St. Peter has steered it for
    them so long,
    It would weather a rougher
        gale.

St. John the Belovéd sails with
    them too,
    And his loving words they
        hear;
So with tender trust the boat's
    brave crew
    Neither doubt, or pause, or fear.

He who sent them fishing is with
    them still,
    And He bids them cast their
        net;
And He has the power their boat
    to fill,
    So we know He will do it yet.

They have cast their nets again
    and again,
    And now call to us on shore;
If our feeble prayers seem only
    in vain,
    We will pray and pray the
        more.

Though the storm is loud, and
    our voice is drowned
By the roar of the wind and
    sea,
We know that more terrible
    tempests found
    Their Ruler, O Lord, in Thee!

See, they do not pause, they are
    toiling on,
    Yet they cast a loving glance
On the star above, and ever anon
    Look up through the blue ex-
        panse.

O Mary, listen! for danger is
    nigh,
    And we know thou art near
        us then;
For thy Son's dear servants to
    thee we cry,
    Sent out as fishers of men.

O, watch, — as of old thou didst
    watch the boat
    On the Galilean lake, —
And grant that the fishers may
    keep afloat
    Till the nets, o'ercharged, shall
        break.

THE OLD YEAR'S BLESSING.

I AM fading from you,
    But one draweth near,
Called the Angel-guardian
    Of the coming year.

If my gifts and graces
　Coldly you forget,
Let the New-Year's Angel
　Bless and crown them yet.

For we work together;
　He and I are one:
Let him end and perfect
　All I leave undone.

I brought Good Desires,
　Though as yet but seeds;
Let the New-Year make them
　Blossom into Deeds.

I brought Joy to brighten
　Many happy days;
Let the New-Year's Angel
　Turn it into Praise.

If I gave you Sickness,
　If I brought you Care,
Let him make one Patience,
　And the other Prayer.

Where I brought you Sorrow,
　Through his care, at length,
It may rise triumphant
　Into future Strength.

If I brought you Plenty,
　All wealth's bounteous charms,
Shall not the New Angel
　Turn them into Alms?

I gave Health and Leisure,
　Skill to dream and plan;

Let him make them nobler;—
　Work for God and Man.

If I broke your Idols,
　Showed you they were dust,
Let him turn the Knowledge
　Into heavenly Trust.

If I brought Temptation,
　Let sin die away
Into boundless Pity
　For all hearts that stray.

If your list of Errors
　Dark and long appears,
Let this new-born Monarch
　Melt them into Tears.

May you hold this Angel
　Dearer than the last,—
So I bless his Future,
　While he crowns my Past.

EVENING CHANT.

Strew before our Lady's Picture
　Roses,—flushing like the sky
Where the lingering western cloudlets
　Watch the daylight die.

Violets steeped in dreamy odors,
　Humble as the Mother mild,
Blue as were her eyes when watching
　O'er her sleeping Child.

Strew white Lilies, pure and spotless,
  Bending on their stalks of green,
Bending down with tender pity,—
  Like our Holy Queen.

Let the flowers spend their fragrance
  On our Lady's own dear shrine,
While we claim her gracious helping
  Near her Son divine.

Strew before our Lady's picture
  Gentle flowers, fair and sweet;
Hope, and Fear, and Joy, and Sorrow,
  Place, too, at her feet.

Hark! the Angelus is ringing, —
  Ringing through the fading light,
In the heart of every Blossom
  Leave a prayer to-night.

All night long will Mary listen,
  While our pleadings fond and deep
On their scented breath are rising
  For us — while we sleep.

Scarcely through the starry silence
  Shall one trembling petal stir,
While they breathe their own sweet fragrance
  And our prayers — to Her.

Peace to every heart that loves her!
  All her children shall be blest:
While She prays and watches for us,
  We will trust and rest.

A CHRISTMAS CAROL.

The moon that now is shining
  In skies so blue and bright,
Shone ages since on Shepherds
  Who watched their flocks by night.
There was no sound upon the earth,
  The azure air was still,
The sheep in quiet clusters lay
  Upon the grassy hill.

When lo! a white-winged Angel
  The watchers stood before,
And told how Christ was born on earth,
  For mortals to adore;
He bade the trembling Shepherds
  Listen, nor be afraid,
And told how in a manger
  The glorious Child was laid.

When suddenly in the Heavens
  Appeared an Angel band,
(The while in reverent wonder
  The Syrian Shepherds stand.)

And all the bright host chanted
  Words that shall never cease,—
Glory to God in the highest,
  On earth good-will and peace!

The vision in the heavens
  Faded, and all was still,
And the wondering shepherds
    left their flocks,
  To feed upon the hill:
Towards the blessed city
  Quickly their course they held,
And in a lowly stable
  Virgin and Child beheld.

Beside a humble manger
  Was the Maiden Mother mild.
And in her arms her Son divine,
  A new-born Infant, smiled.
No shade of future sorrow
  From Calvary then was cast;
Only the glory was revealed,
  The suffering was not passed.

The Eastern kings before him
    knelt,
  And rarest offerings brought;
The shepherds worshipped and
    adored
  The wonders God had
    wrought:
They saw the crown for Israel's
    King,
  The future's glorious part:—
But all these things the Mother
    kept
  And pondered in her heart.

Now we that Maiden Mother
  The Queen of Heaven call;
And the Child we call our Jesus,
  Saviour and Judge of all.
But the star that shone in Beth-
    lehem
  Shines still, and shall not
    cease,
And we listen still to the tidings,
  Of Glory and of Peace.

OUR TITLES.

Are we not Nobles? we who
    trace
  Our pedigree so high
That God for us and for our race
  Created Earth and Sky,
And Light and Air and Time
    and Space,
  To serve us and then die.

Are we not Princes? we who
    stand
  As heirs beside the Throne;
We who can call the promised
    Land
  Our Heritage, our own;
And answer to no less command
  Than God's and His alone.

Are we not Kings? both night
    and day,
  From early until late,
About our bed, about our way,
  A guard of Angels wait;
And so we watch and work and
    pray
  In more than royal state.

Are we not holy? Do not start:
It is God's sacred will
To call us Temples set apart
His Holy Ghost may fill:
Our very food .... O hush, my
Heart,
Adore IT and be still!

Are we not more? our Life shall
be
Immortal and divine.
The nature Mary gave to Thee,
Dear Jesus, still is Thine;
Adoring in Thy Heart, I see
Such blood as beats in mine.

O God, that we can dare to fail,
And dare to say we must!
O God, that we can ever trail
Such banners in the dust,
Can let such starry honors pale,
And such a Blazon rust!

Shall we upon such Titles bring
The taint of sin and shame?
Shall we, the children of the
King
Who hold so grand a claim,
Tarnish by any meaner thing
The glory of our name?

MINISTERING ANGELS.

Angels of light, spread your
bright wings and keep
Near me at morn:
Nor in the starry eve, nor mid-
night deep,
Leave me forlorn.

From all dark spirits of unholy
power
Guard my weak heart,
Circle around me in each peril-
ous hour,
And take my part.

From all foreboding thoughts
and dangerous fears,
Keep me secure;
Teach me to hope, and through
the bitterest tears
Still to endure.

If lonely in the road so fair and
wide
My feet should stray,
Then through a rougher, safer
pathway guide
Me day by day.

Should my heart faint at its un-
equal strife,
O still be near!
Shadow the perilous sweetness
of this life
With holy fear.

Then leave me not alone in this
bleak world,
Where'er I roam,
And at the end, with your bright
wings unfurled,
O take me home!

THE SHRINES OF MARY.

There are many shrines of Our Lady,
In different lands and climes,
Where I can remember kneeling
In old and belovéd times.

They arise now like stars before me,
Through the long, long night of years;
Some are bright with a heavenly radiance,
And others shine out through tears.

They arise too like mystical flowers,
All different, and all the same,—
As they lie in my heart like a garland
That is wreathed round Mary's name.

Thus each shrine has two consecrations;
One all the faithful can trace,
But one is for me and me only,
Holding my soul with its grace.

I.

A shrine in a quaint old Chapel
Defaced and broken with years,
Where the pavement is worn with kneeling,
And the step with kisses and tears.

She is there in the dawn of morning,
When the day is blue and bright,
In the shadowy evening twlighti
And the silent, starry night.

Through the dim old painted window
The Hours look down, and shed
A different glory upon her,
Violet, purple, and red.

And there — in that quaint old Chapel
As I stood one day alone —
Came a royal message from Mary.
That claimed my life as her own.

II.

I remember a vast Cathedral
Which holds the struggle and strife
Of a grand and powerful city,
As the heart holds the throb of a life.

Where the ebb and the flow of passion,
And sin in its rushing tide,
Have dashed on that worn stone chapel,
Dashed, and broken, and died.

And above the voices of sorrow
And the tempter's clamorous din,

The voice of Mary has spoken
  And conquered the pain and
    the sin:

For long ages and generations
  Have come there to strive and
    to pray;
She watched and guided them
    living,
  And does not forget them to-
    day.

And once, in that strange, vast
    City
I stood in its great stone square,
Alone in the crowd and the turmoil
  Of the pitiless Southern glare;

And a grief was upon my spirit,
  Which I could not cast away,
It weighed on my heart all the
    night-time,
  And it fretted my life all day.

So then to that calm, cool refuge
  I turned from the noisy street,
And I carried my burden of sor-
    row —
  And left it at Mary's feet.

III.

I remember a lonely chapel
  With a tender claim upon me;
It was built for the sailors only,
  And they call it the Star of the
    Sea.

And the murmuring chant of the
    Vespers
  Seems caught up by the wail-
    ing breeze,
And the throb of the organ is
    echoed
  By the rush of the silver seas.

And the votive hearts and the
    anchors
  Tell of danger and peril past;
Of the hope deferred and the wait-
    ing,
  And the comfort that came at
    last.

I too had a perilous venture
  On a stormy and treacherous
    main,
And I too was pleading to Mary
  From the depths of a heart in
    pain.

It was not a life in peril, —
  O God, it was far, far more!
And the whirlpool of Hell's
    temptations
  Lay between the wreck and the
    shore.

Thick mists hid the light of the
    beacon,
  And the voices of warning
    were dumb;
So I knelt by the Altar of Mary,
  And told her Her hour was
    come.

For she waits till Earth's aid forsakes us,
  Till we know our own efforts are vain ;
And we wait, in our faithless blindness,
  Till no chance but her prayers remain.

And now in that seaside chapel
  By that humble village shrine
Hangs a heart of silver, that tells her
  Of the love and the gladness of mine.

IV.

There is one far shrine I remember
  In the years that are fled away,
Where the grand old mountains are guarding
  The glories of night and day.

Where the earth in her rich, glad beauty
  Seems made for our Lady's throne,
And the stars in their radiant clusters
  Seem fit for her crown alone.

Where the balmy breezes of summer
  On their odorous pinions bear
The fragrance of orange-blossoms,
  And the chimes of the Convent prayer.

There I used to ask for Her blessing
  As each summer twilight was gray ;
There I used to kneel at her Altar
  At each blue, calm dawn of day.

There in silence was Victory granted,
  And the terrible strife begun,
That only with Her protection
  Could be dared, or suffered, or won.

If I love the name of that Altar,
  And the thought of those days gone by,
It is only the Heart of Mary
  And my own that remember why.

V.

Where long ages of toil and of sorrow,
  And Poverty's weary doom,
Have clustered together so closely
  That life seems shadowed with gloom,

Where crime that lurks in the darkness
  And vice that glares at the day

Make the spirit of hope grow weary,
And the spirit of love decay,

Where the feet of the wretched and sinful
Have closest and oftenest trod,
Is a house, as humble as any,
Yet we call it the House of God.

It is one of our Lady's Chapels;
And though poorer than all the rest,
Just because of the sin and the sorrow,
I think she loves it the best.

There are no rich gifts on the Altar,
The shrine is humble and bare,
Yet the poor and the sick and the tempted
Think their home and their heaven is there.

And before that humble Altar
Where Our Lady of Sorrow stands,
I knelt with a weary longing,
And I laid a vow in her hands.

And I know, when I enter softly
And pause at that shrine to pray,
That the fret and the strife and the burden
Will be softened and laid away.

And the Prayer and the Vow that sealed it
Have bound my soul to that shrine,
For the Mother of Sorrows remembers
Her promise, and waits for mine.

It is one long chaplet of memories
Tender and true and sweet,
That gleam in the Past and the Distance
Like lamps that burn at her feet.

Like stars that will shine forever,
For time cannot touch or stir
The graces that Mary has given,
Or the trust that we give to her.

Past griefs are perished and over,
Past joys have vanished and died,
Past loves are fled and forgotten,
Past hopes have been laid aside.

Past fears have faded in daylight,
Past sins have melted in tears;—
One Love and Remembrance only
Seems alive in those dead old old years.

So wherever I look in the distance,
    And whenever I turn to the Past,
There is always a shrine of Mary
    Each brighter still than the last.

I will ask for one grace, O Mother!
    And will leave the rest to thy will:
From one shrine of thine to another,
    Let my Life be a Pilgrimage still!

At each one, O Mother of Mercy!
    Let still more of thy love be given,
Till I kneel at the last and brightest,—
    The Throne of the Queen of Heaven.

THE HOMELESS POOR.

CALM the city lay in midnight silence,
    Deep on streets and roofs the snow lay white;
Then I saw an Angel spread his pinions
    Rising up to Heaven to meet the night.

In his hands he bore two crowns of lilies,
    Sweet with sweetness not of earthly flowers,
But a coronal of prayers for Heaven
    He had gathered through the evening hours;—

He had gathered in that mighty city
    Through whose streets and pathways he had trod,
Till he wove into a winter garland
    Prayers that faithful hearts had sent to God.

Through the azure midnight he was rising;
    As I watched, I saw his upward flight
Checked by a mighty Angel, whose stern challenge,
    Like a silver blast, rang through the night.

Then strange words upon the silence broke,
And I listened as the Angels spoke.

THE ANGEL OF PRAYERS.

"I have come from wandering through the city,
    I have been to seek a garland meet

To be placed before His throne in Heaven,
To be laid at His dear Mother's feet.

"I have been to one of England's Havens, —
To a HOME for peace and honor planned,
Where the kindly lights of joy and duty
Meet and make the glory of the land.

"There I heard the ring of children's laughter
Hushed to eager silence; I could see
How the father stroked their golden tresses
As they clustered closer round his knee.

"And I heard him tell, with loving honor,
How the wanderers to Bethlehem came,
And I saw each head in reverence bowing
When he named the Holy Child's dear name.

"Then he told how houseless, homeless, friendless,
They had wandered wearily and long, —
Of the manger where our Lord was cradled,
Of the Shepherds listening to our song.

"As he spoke, I heard his accents falter,
And I saw each childish heart was stirred
With a loving throb of tender pity
At the sorrowful, sweet tale they heard.

"As the children sang their Christmas carol
I could see the mother's eyes grow dim,
And she held her baby closer, — feeling
Most for Mary through her love for him.

"So I gathered from that home, as flowers,
All the tender, loving words I heard
Given this night to Jesus and to Mary, —
Look at them, and say if I have erred."

THE ANGEL OF DEEDS.

"In that very street, at that same hour,
In the bitter air and drifting sleet,
Crouching in a doorway was a mother,
With her children shuddering at her feet.

"She was silent; — who would hear her pleading?
Men and beasts were housed; but she must stay
Houseless in the great and pitiless city,
Till the dawning of the winter day.

"Homeless — while her fellow-men are resting
Calm and blest: their very dogs are fed,
Warm and sheltered, and their sleeping children
Safely nestled in each little bed.

"She can only draw her poor rags closer
Round her wailing baby, — closer hold
One, the least and sickliest, — while the others
Creep together, tired, hungry, cold.

"What are these poor flowers thou hast gathered?
Cast such fragile, worthless tokens by:
Will He prize mere words of love and honor
While His Homeless Poor are left to die?

"He has said — His truths are all eternal —
What He said both has been and shall be, —

*What ye have not done to these my poor ones,
Lo! ye have not done it unto Me.*"

Then I saw the Angel with the flowers
Bow his head and answer, "It is well,"
As he cast a wreath of lilies earthward,
And I saw them wither as they fell.

Once again the Angel raised his head,
Smiled and showed the other wreath and said: —

THE ANGEL OF PRAYERS.

"I have been where, kneeling at the Altar,
Hushed in reverent awe, a faithful throng
Have this night adored the Holy Presence,
Worshipping with incense, prayer, and song.

"Every head was bowed in loving honor,
Every heart with loving awe was thrilled;
Earth and things of earth seemed all forgotten;
He was there — and meaner thoughts were stilled.

" There on many souls in strait
and peril
Did that gracious Benediction
fall,
With the strength or peace or
joy or warning
He could give, who loved and
knew them all.

" There was silence, but all
hearts were speaking :
When the deepest hush of
silence fell,
On the fragrant air and breathless longing
Came the echo of one silver bell.

" On each spirit such a flood of
sweetness
Broke — as we who dwell in
Heaven feel,
Then the *Adoremus in eternum,*
Jubilant and strong, rolled
peal on peal.

" They had given holy adoration,
Tender words of love and
praise ; all bright
With the dew of contrite tears —
such blossoms
I am bearing to His throne to-
night."

THE ANGEL OF DEEDS.

" Pause again : these flowers are
fair and lovely,
Radiant in their perfume and
their bloom ;

But not far from where you
plucked this garland
Is a squalid place in ghastly
gloom.

" There black waters in their
luring silence
Under loathsome arches crawl
and creep,
There the rats and vermin herd
together....
*There God's poor ones sometimes
come to sleep.*

" There the weary come, who
through the daylight
Pace the town, and crave for
work in vain ;
There they crouch in cold and
rain and hunger,
Waiting for another day of
pain.

" In slow darkness creeps the
dismal river ;
From its depths looks up a
sinful rest ;
Many a weary, baffled, hopeless
wanderer
Has it drawn into its treacherous breast.

" There is near *another River* flowing,
Black with guilt, and deep as
hell and sin ;
On its brink even sinners stand
and shudder, —
Cold and hunger goad the
homeless in.

"Yet these poor ones to His heart are dearer
For their grief and peril: dear indeed
Would have been the love that sought and fed them,
Gave them warmth and shelter in their need.

"For His sake those tears and prayers are offered
Which you bear as flowers to His throne;
Better still would be the food and shelter,
Given for Him and given to His own.

"Praise with loving deeds is dear and holy,
Words of praise will never serve instead:
Lo! you offer music, hymn, and incense —
When *He has not where to lay His head.*"

Then once more the Angel with the Flowers
Bowed his head, and answered, "It is well,"
As he cast a wreath of lilies earthwards,
And I saw them wither as they fell.

So the Vision faded, and the Angels
Melted far into the starry sky;
By the light upon the eastern Heaven
I could see another day was nigh.

Was it quite a dream? O God! we love Him;
All our love, though weak, is given to Him; —
Why is it our hearts have been so hardened?
Why is it our eyes have been so dim?

Still as for Himself the Infant Jesus
In His little ones asks food and rest, —
Still as for His Mother He is pleading
Just as when He lay upon her breast.

Jesus, then, and Mary still are with us, —
Night will find the Child and Mother near,
Waiting for the shelter we deny them,
While we tell them that we hold them dear.

Help us, Lord! not these Thy poor ones only,
They are with us always, and shall be: —
Help the blindness of our hearts, and teach us
In Thy homeless ones to succor Thee.

MILLY'S EXPIATION.

THE PRIEST'S STORY.

I.

There are times when all these terrors
Seem to fade, and fade away,
Like a nightmare's ghastly presence
In the truthful dawn of day.
There are times, too, when before me
They arise, and seem to hold
In their grasp my very being
With the deadly strength of old,
Till my spirit quails within me,
And my very heart grows cold.

II.

For I watched when Cold and Hunger,
Like wild beasts that sought for prey,
With a savage glare crept onward
Until men were turned at bay.
You have never seen those hunters,
Who have never known that fear,
When life costs a crust, and costing
Even that is still too dear:
But, you know, I lived in Ireland
In the fatal famine year.

III.

Yes, those days are now forgotten;
God be thanked! men can forget;
Time's great gift can heal the fevers
Called Remembrance and Regret.
Man despises such forgetting;
But I think the Angels know,
Since each hour brings new burdens,
We must let the old ones go, —
Very weak or very noble
Are the few who cling to woe.

IV.

As a child, I lived in Connaught,
And from dawn till set of sun
Played with all the peasant-children,
So I knew them every one.
There was not a cabin near us,
But I had my welcome there;
Though of money-help in those days
We had none ourselves to spare,
Yet the neighbors had no trouble
That I did not know and share.

V.

O that great estate! the Landlord
Was abroad, a good man too;

And the agent was not cruel,
  But he had hard things to do.
As a child I saw great suffering
  Which I could not understand,
So I went back as a man there
  With redress and helping planned;
But I found, on reaching Connaught,
  There was famine in the land.

VI.

Well, I worked, I toiled, I labored;
  So, thank God, did many more;
But I had a special pity
  For the place I knew before.
It was changed; the old were vanished;
  Those who had been workers there
Were grown old now; and the children,
  With their sunny eyes and hair,
Were a ragged army, fighting
  Hand to hand with black despair.

VII.

There were some I sought out, longing
  For the old familiar face,
For the hearty Irish welcome
  To the well-known corner place;
So I saw them, and I found it.
  But of all whom I had known,
I cared most to see the Connors.
  Their poor cabin stood alone
In the deep heart of the valley,
  By the old gray fairy stone.

VIII.

They were decent people, holding,
  Though no richer than the rest,
Still a place beyond their neighbors,
  With a tacit, unconfessed
Pride — it may have been — that held them
  From complaint when things went ill:
I might guess when work was slacker,
  But no shadow seemed to chill
The warm welcome which they offered;
  It was warm and cheerful still.

IX.

Yet their home was changed: the father
  And the mother were no more;
And the brothers, Phil and Patrick,
  Kept starvation from the door.
There were many little faces
  Gathered round the old hearthstone;

But the children I had played
　　with
　　Were the men and women
　　　grown;
Phil and Patrick, Kate and Milly,
　　Were the ones whom I had
　　　known.

x.

Kate was grown, but little al-
　　tered,
Just the sunburnt, rosy face,
With its merry smile, whose shin-
　　ing
　　Seemed to light the darkest
　　　place.
But all, young and old, held
　　Milly
As their dearest and their best,
From the baby orphan-sisters
　　Whom she hushed upon her
　　　breast, —
She it was who bore the burdens,
　　Love and sorrow, for the rest.

xi.

Yes, I knew the tall slight figure,
　　And the face so pale and fair,
Crowned with long, long plaited
　　tresses
　　Of her shining yellow hair;
She was very calm and tender,
　　Warm and brave, yet just and
　　　wise,
Meeting grief with tender pity,
　　Sin with sorrowful surprise:
I have fancied Angels watch us
　　With such sad and loving eyes.

xii.

Well, I questioned past and fut-
　　ure,
　　Heard of plans and hopes and
　　　fears;
How all prospects grew still
　　darker
　　With the shade of coming
　　　years.
Milly still deferred her marriage;
　　But the brothers urged of late
She would leave them and old
　　Ireland,
　　And at least secure her fate;
Michael pleaded too, — but vain-
　　ly;
Milly chose to wait and wait.

xiii.

Though all liked her cousin Mi-
　　chael, —
　　He was steady, a good son, —
Yet we wondered at the treasure
　　Which his careless heart had
　　　won.
Ah, he was not worth her! Milly
　　Must have guessed our thought
　　　in part,
For she feigned such special def-
　　erence
　　For his judgment and his
　　　heart:
The defiance and the answer
　　Of instinctive woman's art.

xiv.

But my duties would not let me
　　Stay in one place; I must go

Where the want and need were
  greatest ;
 So I travelled to and fro.
And I could not give the bounty
 Which was meant for all to
  share,
Save in scanty portions, counting
 What each hamlet had to
  bear ;
So my old home and old com-
  rades
 Had to struggle with despair.

XV.

I could note at every visit
 How all suffered more and
  more ;
How the rich were growing
  poorer,
 The poor, poorer than before.
And each time that I returned
  there,
 I could see the famine spread ;
Till I heard of each fresh horror,
 Each new tale of fear and dread,
With more pity for the living,
 More rejoicing for the dead.

XVI.

Yet through all the bitter trials
 Of that long and fearful time,
Still the suffering came untended
 By its hideous sister, Crime.
Earthly things seemed grown less
  potent,
 Fellow-sufferers grown more
  dear,
Murmurs even hushed in silence,
 Just as if, in listening fear,
While God spoke so loud in sor-
  row,
 They all felt He must be near.

XVII.

But one day — I well remember
 How the warm soft autumn
  breeze,
And the gladness of the sunshine,
 And the calmness of the seas,
Seemed in strange unnatural con-
  trast
 To the tale of woe and dread
Which I heard with painful won-
  der, —
 That the agent — I have said
That he was not harsh or cruel —
 Had been shot at, and was
  dead.

XVIII.

For I felt in that small hamlet
 More or less I knew them all,
And on some I cared for, surely,
 Must this bitter vengeance fall ;
But I little dreamed how bitter,
 And the grief how great and
  wide,
Till I heard that Michael Connor
 Was accused, and would be
  tried
For this base and bloody murder ;
 Then I cried out that they lied !

XIX.

He, who might be weak and reckless,
 Yet was gentle and humane ;

He who scarcely had the courage
  To inflict a needful pain, —
Why, it could not be! And
    Milly,
  With her honest, noble pride,
And her faith and love, God help
    her!
  It were better she had died.
So I thought, and thought, and
    pondered,
  Till I knew they must have
    lied.

XX.

There was want and death and
    hunger
  Near me then; but this great
    crime
Seemed to haunt me with its ter-
    ror,
  And grow worse and worse
    with time,
Till I could not bear it longer,
  And I turned my steps once
    more
To the hamlet; did not slacken
  Till I reached the cabin-door:
Then I paused; I never dreaded
  The kind welcome there be-
    fore.

XXI.

So I entered. Kate was sitting
  By the empty hearth; around
Were the children, ragged, hun-
    gry,
  Crouching silent on the
    ground.
But a wail of grief and sorrow
  Rose, and Katie hid her face,
Sobbing out she had no welcome,
  For a curse was on the place,
And their honest name was cov-
    ered
  With another's black disgrace.

XXII.

Then I soothed her; asked for
    Milly;
  And was told she was away;
Gone as witness to the trial,
  And the trial was that day.
But all knew, so Katie told me,
  Hope or comfort there was
    none;
They were sure to find him guilty,
  And before to-morrow's sun
He must die. I dared not loiter,
  For the trial had begun.

XXIII.

Yet I asked how Milly bore it;
  And Kate told me some strange
    gleam
Of wild hope seemed living in
    her,
  But all knew it was a dream.
Then I mounted; rode on faster,
  Faster still; the way was
    long;
Hope and anger, fear and pity,
  Each by turns were loud and
    strong,
And above all, infinite pity
  For the sorrow and the wrong.

XXIV.

So I rode and rode, and entered
  On the crowded market-place.
There was wonder, too, and pity
  Upon many a hungry face;
But I pushed on quicker, quicker,
  Every moment held a fate.
As the great town-clock struck mid-day,
  I alighted at the gate:
No, the trial was not over;
  I was not, thank God, too late.

XXV.

For I hoped — the chance was meagre —
  That my true and earnest word
Might avail him, if the question
  Of his former life was stirred;
So the crowd believed: they parted,
  Let me take a foremost place,
Till I saw a shaking figure
  And a terror-stricken face:
Was it guilt, or only terror?
  Fear of death, or of disgrace?

XXVI.

But a sudden breathless silence
  Hushed the lowest whisper there,
And I saw a slight young figure
  Crowned with yellow plaited hair,
Rise, and answer as they called her;
Rise before them all, and stand
With no quiver in her accent,
  And no trembling in her hand,
Just a flush upon her forehead
  Like a burning crimson brand.

XXVII.

Slowly, steadily, and calmly,
  Then the awful words were said,
Calling God in Heaven to witness
  To the truth of what she said.
As the oath in solemn order
  On the reverent silence broke,
Some strange terror and misgiving
  With a sudden start awoke:
What fear was it seized upon me
  As I heard the words she spoke?

XXVIII.

As she stood there, looking onward,
  Onward, neither left nor right,
Did she see some deadly purpose
  Buried, hidden out of sight?
Did she see a blighting shadow
  From the cloudy future cast?
Or reluctant fading from her
  Right and honor, — fading fast

All her youth's remembered lessons,
All the honest, noble past?

XXIX.

But her accents never faltered,
As she swore the day and
time,
At the hour of the murder,
At the moment of the crime,
She had spoken with the prison-
er . . . .
Then a gasping joyful sigh
Ran through all the court; they
knew it, —
Now the prisoner would not
die . . . . .
And I knew that God in Heaven
Had been witness to a lie!

XXX.

Then I turned and looked at
Michael;
Saw a rush of wonder stir
Through his soul; perplexed, be-
wildered,
He looked strangely up at her.
Would he speak? could he have
courage?
Where she fell, could he be
strong?
Where she sinned, and sinned to
save him,
Could he thrust away the
wrong?
That one moment's strange re-
vulsion
Seemed to me an hour long.

XXXI.

And I saw the sudden shrinking
In her brothers; wondering
scorn
In the glance they cast upon her
Showed they knew she was
forsworn.
They were stern, by want made
sterner;
But the spot where Milly
came
In their hearts was soft and ten-
der
For her dear and honored
name:
Now the very love was hardened,
And the honor turned to
shame.

XXXII.

So I left the place, nor lingered
To see Michael, or to feign
Joy where joy was mixed so
strangely
Both with pity and with pain.
Many weeks I toiled and labored
Far from there, but night and
day
One sad memory dwelt beside me,
On my heart one shadow
lay; —
Light was faded, glory tarnished,
And a soul was cast away.

* * * *

XXXIII.

It was evening; and the sunset
Glowed and glittered on the
seas,

When a great ship heaved its an-
    chor,
  Loosed its sails to meet the
    breeze,
Sailing, sailing to the westward.
  Eyes were wet and hearts
    were sore;
Many a heart that left its coun-
    try,
  Many a heart upon the shore,
Knew that parting was forever,
  Said farewell forevermore.

XXXIV.

In that sad and silent evening,
  On the sunny, quiet beach,
Lingered little groups of watch-
    ers,
  But with hearts too full for
    speech.
As I passed, I knew so many,
  That my heart ached too that
    night,
For the yearning love, that, gaz-
    ing,
  Strained to see the last faint
    sight
Of the great ship, sailing west-
    ward,
  Down the track of evening
    light.

XXXV.

None were lonely though, — one
    sorrow
  Drew that evening heart to
    heart;
Only far from all the others
  One lone woman stood apart.

There was something in the fig-
    ure,
  Tall and slender, standing
    there,
That I knew — yet no, I doubt-
    ed —
  That forlorn and helpless air;
When a gleam of sunset glory
  Showed her yellow braided
    hair.

XXXVI.

It was Milly: ere I sought her,
  One who knew her, standing
    by,
Said, "Her people sailed from
    Ireland,
  And she stayed, but none knew
    why.
They were strong; in that far
    country
  Work such men were sure to
    find;
They had offered to take Milly,
  Pressed her often, and been
    kind;
They had taken the young chil-
    dren,
  Only she was left behind.

XXXVII.

"Michael, too, was with them:
    doubly
  Had his fame been cleared by
    time;
For the murderer, lately dying,
  Had confessed and owned the
    crime:

And yet Milly, none knew where-
   fore,
   Broke her plighted troth to
     him;
   Parted, too, with all her loved
     ones
   For some strange and selfish
     whim." . . .
O, my heart was sore for Milly,
   And I felt my eyes grow dim.

XXXVIII.

She is still in Ireland; dwelling
   Near the old place, and alone;
Just the same kind, loving spirit,
   But the old light heart is flown.
When the humble toil is over
   For her scanty daily bread,
Then she turns to nurse the
    suffering,
   Or to pray beside the dead:
Many, many thankful blessings
   Fall each day upon her head.

XXXIX.

There is no distress or sorrow
   Milly does not try to cheer;
There is never fever raging
   But you always find her near;
And she knows — at least I think
    so —
That I guess her secret pain,
Why her Love and why her Sor-
    row
   Need be purified from stain,
Need in special consecration
   Be restored to God again.

A CASTLE IN THE AIR.

I BUILT myself a castle,
   So noble, grand, and fair;
I built myself a castle,
   A castle — in the air.

The fancies of my twilights
   That fade in sober truth,
The longing of my sorrow,
   And the vision of my youth;

The plans of joyful futures;
   So dear they used to seem;
The prayer that rose unbidden,
   Half prayer — and half a
    dream;

The hopes that died unuttered
   Within this heart of mine; —
For all these tender treasures
   My castle was the shrine.

I looked at all the castles
   That rise to grace the land,
But I never saw another
   So stately or so grand.

And now you see it shattered,
   My castle in the air;
It lies, a dreary ruin,
   All desolate and bare.

I cannot build another,
   I saw that one decay;
And strength and heart and
    courage
Died out the self-same day.

Yet still, beside that ruin,
  With hopes as deep and fond,
I waited with an infinite longing,
  Only — I look beyond.

PER PACEM AD LUCEM.

I DO not ask, O Lord, that life may be
  A pleasant road;
I do not ask that Thou wouldst take from me
  Aught of its load;

I do not ask that flowers should always spring
  Beneath my feet;
I know too well the poison and the sting
  Of things too sweet.

For one thing only, Lord, dear Lord, I plead,
  Lead me aright —
Though strength should falter, and though heart should bleed —
  Through Peace to Light.

I do not ask, O Lord, that thou shouldst shed
  Full radiance here;
Give but a ray of peace, that I may tread
  Without a fear.

I do not ask my cross to understand,
  My way to see;
Better in darkness just to feel Thy hand
  And follow Thee.

Joy is like restless day; but peace divine
  Like quiet night:
Lead me, O Lord, — till perfect Day shall shine,
  Through Peace to Light.

A LEGEND.

I.

THE Monk was preaching: strong his earnest word,
  From the abundance of his heart he spoke,
And the flame spread, — in every soul that heard
  Sorrow and love and good resolve awoke: —
The poor lay Brother, ignorant and old,
  Thanked God that he had heard such words of gold.

II.

"Still let the glory, Lord, be thine alone," —
  So prayed the Monk, his heart absorbed in praise:

"Thine be the glory: if my
  hands have sown
The harvest ripened in Thy
  mercy's rays,
It was Thy blessing, Lord, that
  made my word
Bring light and love to every soul
  that heard.

III.

"O Lord, I thank Thee that my
  feeble strength
Has been so blest; that sinful
  hearts and cold
Were melted at my pleading, —
  knew at length
How sweet Thy service and
  how safe Thy fold:
While souls that loved Thee saw
  before them rise
Still holier heights of loving
  sacrifice."

IV.

So prayed the Monk: when sud-
  denly he heard
An angel speaking thus:
  "Know, O my Son,
Thy words had all been vain,
  but hearts were stirred,
And saints were edified, and
  sinners won,
By his, the poor lay Brother's
  humble aid
Who sat upon the pulpit stair
  and prayed."

BIRTHDAY GIFTS.

FOR A CHILD.

WHY do you look sad, my Min-
  nie?
Tell me, darling, — for to-day
Is the birthday of Our Lady,
  And Her children should be
  gay.

What? — You say that all the
  others,
Alice, Cyril, Effie, Paul,
All had got a gift to give Her,
  Only you had none at all.

Well, dear, that does seem a pity:
  Tell me how it came about
That the others bring a present,
  And my Minnie comes with-
  out.

Alice has a lovely Banner,
  All embroidered blue and
  gold: —
Then you know that sister Alice
  Is so clever and so old.

Cyril has his two camellias;
  One deep red, and one pure
  white:
They will stand at Benediction
  On the Altar steps to-night.

Effie, steady little Effie,
  Stitching many an hour away,
She has clothed a little orphan
  All in honor of to-day.

With the skill the good Nuns
    taught her
Angela herself has made
Two tall stems of such real lilies,
    They do all but smell — and
    fade.

Then with look of grave im-
    portance
Comes our quiet little Paul,
With the myrtle from his gar-
    den : —
He himself is not as tall.

Even Baby Agnes, kneeling
    With half-shy, half-solemn air,
Held up one sweet rose to Mary,
    Lisping out her tiny prayer.

Well, my Minnie, say, how was
    it ?
    Shall I guess? I think I
    know
All the griefs. Well, I will
    count them : —
    First, your rose-tree would not
    blow:

Then the fines have been so many
    All the pennies melt away ;
Then for work — I know my
    Minnie
Cares so very much for play,

That these little clumsy fingers
    Scarcely yet have learnt to sew,
Still less all the skilful fancies
    Angela and Alice know.

Yet my Minnie can't be treated
    Quite as Baby was to-day,
When Mamma or Alice gave her
    Something just to give away.

Well, my darling, there are many
    Who have neither time nor
    skill,
Gold nor silver, yet they offer
    Gifts to Mary if they will.

There are ways — Our Lady
    knows them,
    And Her children all should
    know
How to find a flower for Mary
    Underneath the deepest snow ;

How to make a lovely garland,
    Winter though it be and cold ;
How to buy the rarest offering,
    Costing — something — but
    not gold ;

How to buy, and buy it dearly,
    Gifts that She will love to take;
Nor to grudge the cost, but give it
    Cheerfully for Mary's sake.

Does that seem so strange, my
    darling ?
    Nay, dear, it is nothing new ;
All can give Her noble pres-
    ents, —
    Shall I tell you of a few ?

What were those the Magi offered,
    Frankincense and gold and
    myrrh : —

Minnie thinks that Saints and
    Monarchs
Are quite different from her!

. . . Sometimes it is hard to listen
    To a word unkind or cold
And to smile a loving answer;
    Do it — and you give Her
    Gold.

Thoughts of Her in work or
    playtime,
    Those small grains of incense
    rare,
Cast upon a burning censer,
    Rise in perfumed clouds of
    prayer.

There are sometimes bitter fan-
    cies,
    Little murmurs that will stir
Even a loving heart; — but crush
    them
And you give Our Lady myrrh.

Give your little crosses to her,
    Which each day, each hour
    befall;
They remind Her of Her Jesus,
    So she loves them best of all.

Some seem very poor and worth-
    less,
    Yet however small and slight,
Given to her by one who loves
    her,
    They are precious in her sight.

One may be so hard to carry
    That your hands will bleed
    and smart: —
Go and take it to Her Altar,
    Go and place it in her heart;

Check your tears and try to love
    it,
    Love it as His sacred will:
So you set the cross with jewels,
    Make your gift more precious
    still.

There are souls — alas! too
    many —
    Who forget that Jesus died,
Who forget that sin forever
    Is the lance to pierce His side.

Hearts that turn away from Je-
    sus;
    Sins that scourge Him and be-
    tray;
Cold and cruel souls that even
    Crucify Him day by day.

Ah! poor sinners! Mary loves
    them,
    And she knows no royal gem
Half so noble or so precious
    As the prayer you say for
    them;

Or resign some little pleasure,
    Give it her instead, to win
Help for some poor soul in peril,
    Grace for some poor heart in
    sin,

Mercy for poor sinners, — pleading
For their souls as for your own; —
So you make a crown of jewels
Fit to lay before Her throne.

Flowers, — why I should never finish
If I tried to count them too, —
If I told you how to know them,
In what garden-plot they grew.

Yet I think my darling guesses
They are emblems, and we trace
In the rarest and the loveliest
Acts of love and gifts of grace.

Modest violets, meek snow-drops,
Holy lilies white and pure,
Faithful tendrils — herbs for healing —
If they only would endure!

And they will, — such flowers fade not;
They are not of mortal birth;
And such garlands given to Mary
Die not like the gifts of Earth.

Well, my Minnie, can you tell me
You have still no gift to lay
At the feet of your dear Mother,
Any hour, any day?

Give Her now — to-day — forever,
One great gift, — the first, the best, —
Give your heart to Her, and ask her
How to give her all the rest.

A BEGGAR.

I beg of you, I beg of you, my brothers,
For my need is very sore;
Not for gold and not for silver do I ask you,
But for something even more:
From the depths of your hearts pity let it be —
Pray for me.

I beg of you whose robes of radiant whiteness
Have been kept without a stain;
Of you who, stung to death by serpent Pleasure,
Found the healing Angel Pain:
Whether holy or forgiven you may be —
Pray for me.

I beg of you calm souls whose wondering pity
Looks at paths you never trod:

I beg of you who suffer — for all sorrow
Must be very near to God —
And the need is even greater than you see —
   Pray for me.

I beg of you, O children, for He loves you,
And He loves your prayers the best:
Fold your little hands together, and ask Jesus
That the weary may have rest,
That a bird caught in a net may be set free —
   Pray for me.

I beg of you who stand before the Altar,
Whose anointed hands upraise
All the sin and all the sorrow of the Ages,
All the love and all the praise,
And the glory which was always and shall be —
   Pray for me.

I beg of you — of you who through Life's battle
Our dear Lord has set apart,
That while we who love the peril are made captives,
Still the Church may have its Heart
Which is fettered that our souls may be set free —
   Pray for me.

I beg of you, I beg of you, my brothers,
For an alms this very day;
I am standing on your doorstep as a Beggar
Who will not be turned away,
And the Charity you give my soul shall be —
   Pray for me!

LINKS WITH HEAVEN.

Our God in Heaven, from that holy place,
   To each of us an Angel guide has given;
But Mothers of dead children have more grace, —
   For they give Angels to their God and Heaven.

How can a Mother's heart feel cold or weary
   Knowing her dearer self safe, happy, warm?
How can she feel her road too dark or dreary,
   Who knows her treasure sheltered from the storm?

How can she sin? Our hearts may be unheeding,
   Our God forgot, our holy Saints defied;

But can a mother hear her dead child pleading,
  And thrust those little angel hands aside?

Those little hands stretched down to draw her ever
  Nearer to God by mother love: — we all
Are blind and weak, yet surely she can never,
  With such a stake in Heaven, fail or fall.

She knows that when the mighty Angels raise
  Chorus in Heaven, one little silver tone
Is hers forever, that one little praise,
  One little happy voice, is all her own.

We may not see her sacred crown of honor,
  But all the Angels flitting to and fro
Pause smiling as they pass, — they look upon her
  As mother of an angel whom they know,

One whom they left nestled at Mary's feet, —
  The children's place in Heaven, — who softly sings
A little chant to please them, slow and sweet,
  Or smiling strokes their little folded wings;

Or gives them Her white lilies or Her beads
  To play with: — yet, in spite of flower or song,
They often lift a wistful look that pleads
  And asks Her why their mother stays so long.

Then our dear Queen makes answer she will call
  Her very soon: meanwhile they are beguiled
To wait and listen while She tells them all
  A story of Her Jesus as a child.

Ah, Saints in Heaven may pray with earnest will
  And pity for their weak and erring brothers:
Yet there is prayer in Heaven more tender still, —
  The little Children pleading for their Mothers.

HOMELESS.

It is cold, dark midnight, yet listen
  To that patter of tiny feet!

Is it one of your dogs, fair lady,
   Who whines in the bleak cold street?
Is it one of your silken spaniels
   Shut out in the snow and the sleet?

My dogs sleep warm in their baskets,
   Safe from the darkness and snow;
All the beasts in our Christian England,
   Find pity wherever they go —
(Those are only the homeless children
   Who are wandering to and fro).

Look out in the gusty darkness,—
   I have seen it again and again,
That shadow, that flits so slowly
   Up and down past the window-pane : —
It is surely some criminal lurking
   Out there in the frozen rain?

Nay, our criminals all are sheltered,
   They are pitied and taught and fed :
That is only a sister-woman
   Who has got neither food nor bed,—

And the Night cries, " Sin to be living,"
And the River cries, " Sin to be dead."

Look out at that farthest corner
   Where the wall stands blank and bare : —
Can that be a pack which a Pedler
   Has left and forgotten there?
His goods lying out unsheltered
   Will be spoilt by the damp night-air.

Nay; — goods in our thrifty England
   Are not left to lie and grow rotten,
For each man knows the market value
   Of silk or woollen or cotton...
But in counting the riches of England
   I think our Poor are forgotten.

Our Beasts and our Thieves and our Chattels
   Have weight for good or for ill;
But the Poor are only His image,
   His presence, His word, His will; —
And so Lazarus lies at our doorstep
   And Dives neglects him still.

www.ingramcontent.com/pod-product-compliance
Lightning Source LLC
Chambersburg PA
CBHW032138230426
43672CB00011B/2373